HAUNTING
MUSEUMS

John Schuster

HAUNTING MUSEUMS

*The Strange and Uncanny Stories
Behind the Most Mysterious Exhibits*

A Tom Doherty Associates Book

New York

HAUNTING MUSEUMS

Copyright © 2009 by The Literary Group International

A Forge Book
Published by Tom Doherty Associates, LLC
175 Fifth Avenue
New York, NY 10010

www.tor-forge.com

Forge® is a registered trademark of Tom Doherty Associates, LLC.

Library of Congress Cataloging-in-Publication Data

Schuster, John.
    Haunting museums / John Schuster.—1st trade pbk. ed.
      p. cm.
    "A Tom Doherty Associates Book."
    ISBN-13: 978-0-7653-2292-0
    ISBN-10: 0-7653-2292-7
    1. Museums—United States—Anecdotes. 2. Museum exhibits—
United States—Anecdotes. 3. Haunted places—United States—
Anecdotes. 4. Curiosities and wonders—United States—
Anecdotes. I. Title.
    AM11.S295 2009
    133.1'.29—dc22

                                                    2008050418

First Edition: May 2009

Printed in the United States of America

0 9 8 7 6 5 4 3 2 1

For Robert and Robbie Greenberger,

Fighters All

(and an inspiration as well)

———————

A Dedication from Frank Weimann, literary agent,
with The Literary Group International

I would like to dedicate this book to my good friend, Brian
Thomsen, who passed away suddenly and quite unexpectedly. It
was a terrible loss to the literary community and to all of us
who loved him dearly. Brian conceived the idea for this book
and many dozens of others in his life. I nicknamed him "the
Genius" because of his unparalleled knowledge of books. He
could quickly quote the classics or the latest obscure title with
unequivocal ease.

All of us who had the privilege of knowing Brian will be
forever grateful to him for his friendship, knowledge, sense of
humor, and dedication to his authors. Perhaps the most ad-
mirable trait that "the Genius" possessed was his unbound loyalty to his wife, Donna, his family, and his friends.

While we will all forever miss his presence, we're fortunate
that his legacy will live on in his books.

Contents

Introduction

Museums—and Why
Haunting Them Is a Good Thing

Museum.

You say the word and what comes to mind.

A dusty old compendium of stationary exhibits that pale next to their Disneyfied theme park brethren?

A stodgy old gallery of oils and marble that—to paraphrase Denis Leary's character in the remake of *The Thomas Crown Affair*—only really concern some very silly rich people?

A foreboding lair of the unknown where something long dead comes to life?

(Okay, maybe I've been watching too many straight-to-video releases late at night on the Sci-Fi Channel.)

Okay, but what does the dictionary say?

Museum: A building, place, or institution devoted to the acquisition, conservation, study, exhibition, and educational interpretation of objects having scientific, historical, or artistic value. From the Latin meaning a temple of the Muses, hence, a place of study.

Hmm . . . "a temple of the Muses"?

Muses: the heavenly source of inspiration.

What better word origin for museums!

Both an homage to the past and an inspiration for the future.

But enough about generalities and misconceptions—museums are places of learning, inspiration, and fun . . . but they are also places of mystery and wonder.

Indeed, some of the most famous museums themselves inspire questions about their origins that are worthy of Trivial Pursuit, such as:

- What famous museum owes its endowment to an "heirless legacy"?
- What famous museum owes its endowment to a department store?
- And, what the heck was Robin Williams doing playing Teddy Roosevelt in *Night at the Museum*?

Easy answers all.

The first: What famous museum owes its endowment to an "heirless legacy"?

The answer: The Smithsonian.

According to the official history of the institute:

In 1826, James Smithson, a British scientist, drew up his last will and testament, naming his nephew as beneficiary. Smithson stipulated that, should the nephew die without heirs (as he would in 1835), the estate should go "to the United States of America, to found at Washington, under the name of the Smithsonian Institution, an establishment for the increase and diffusion of knowledge among men."

The motives behind Smithson's bequest remain mysterious. He never traveled to the United States and seems to have had no correspondence with anyone here. Some have suggested that his bequest was motivated in part by revenge against the rigidities of British society, which had denied Smithson, who was illegitimate, the right to use his father's name. Others have suggested it reflected his interest in the Enlightenment ideals of democracy and universal education.

Smithson died in 1829, and six years later President Andrew Jackson announced the bequest to Congress. On July 1, 1836, Congress accepted the legacy bequeathed to the nation and pledged the faith of the United States to the charitable trust. In September 1838, Smithson's legacy, which amounted to more than 100,000 gold sovereigns, was delivered to the mint in Philadelphia. Recoined in U.S. currency, the gift amounted to more than $500,000.

After eight years of sometimes heated debate, an act of Congress signed by President James K. Polk on August 10, 1846, established the Smithsonian Institution as a trust to be administered by a Board of Regents and a Secretary of the Smithsonian.

The second: What famous museum owes its endowment to a department store?
The answer: The Chicago Field Museum.
From their official bio:

The Field Museum was incorporated in the State of Illinois on September 16, 1893, as the Columbian Museum of Chicago with its purpose the "accumulation and dissemination of knowledge, and the preservation and exhibition of objects illustrating art, archaeology, science and history." In 1905, the Museum's name was changed to Field Museum of Natural History to honor the Museum's first major benefactor, Marshall Field (whose department store chain also bears his name), and to better reflect its focus on the natural sciences. In 1921 the Museum moved from its original location in Jackson Park to its present site on Chicago Park District property near downtown, where it is part of a lakefront Museum Campus that includes the John G. Shedd Aquarium and the Adler Planetarium. These three institutions are regarded as among the finest of their kind in the world and together attract more visits annually than any comparable site in Chicago.

And the third: What the heck was Robin Williams doing playing Teddy Roosevelt in *Night at the Museum*?
The answer: As any visitor to New York's American Museum of Natural History knows, having a great old time.

But seriously, old Teddy was a great supporter of all things natural history as well as of the museum itself. Overlooked in terms of the film and memorial space within the museum itself, however, was Teddy's father (also named Theodore Roosevelt), who along with such New York bigwigs as Robert Colgate, J. Pierpont Morgan, Charles Dana, and numerous others were among the sponsoring founders of the museum back in 1869. (Though the museum itself was not officially opened until December 21, 1877, in the words of *The New York Times*: "The formal opening, by the President of the United States [Rutherford B. Hayes], of the new American Museum of Natural History, in Manhattan-square, at Seventy-seventh-street and Eighth-avenue, was the occasion yesterday afternoon of one of the most brilliant daylight assemblages that New York has ever seen.")
Museums such as these have been perfect settings for numerous big-budget films, even when meeting shooting schedules required changes of locale, such as in the film version of *Relic* (based on the thrilling novel by Preston and Child, who infuse their thrilling storytelling with insider info on the workings of the American Museum of Natural History in New York). New York was changed to Chicago, resulting in a trade of the American Museum of Natural History for Chicago's Field Museum.

But even in person one cannot help but be enticed by the ever-present miasma of mystery that surrounds them.

Sometimes it's a bit of thrilling history—like in New York, with the heist tale of Murph the Surf, who stole the Star of India, or perhaps the thrilling tales of Frank "Bring 'Em Back Alive" Buck, who captured a rare giant cobra that became part of the museum's holdings; or maybe even the mysterious secret entrance to the museum that was supposed to be located in Central Park proper, where visitors would be able to metaphorically ascend out of the caves of darkness and ignorance up to the halls of the Muses.

Other times it's an exhibit that tries to unlock a secret of the past, or perhaps a chimerical remnant of another time whose meaning has been lost and is waiting to be rediscovered.

Museums come in all shapes and sizes—ranging from the classic palaces of the Field and the Smithsonian to the storefront of the Voodoo Museum in New Orleans and the twentieth-century warship the *Hornet* moored on the West Coast—and there are no limits to the variety of exhibits that are bound to raise a question or two.

Maybe it's a secret mark on a famous flag.

A famous inventor's dying breath.

An exhibit of real, living people.

A famous plane or two.

Or any old artifact of the past whose origins or influence (dare I say curse?) is shrouded in mystery.

Haunting museums is a fun pastime for tourists, families, students, and professionals.

A pleasant outing that entertains and informs.

But haunting museums has another meaning as well.

For every exhibit, there is a story; for some of them the past refuses to die.

Sometimes it's a question of history.

Sometimes it's a mystery yet to be solved.

And sometimes it's just so uncanny that it is just a wonder to behold.

Sometimes things are noteworthy when they are
placed in context, whether it is set against the course
of history or the paradigms of the natural sciences.
(Which still doesn't rule out a mystery
or two or three.)

HISTORY AND
NATURAL HISTORY

Sometimes mythology begets science. Dragons lead unto dinosaurs . . . and sometimes you add a little improvisation and try to get the details right later on.

The Carnegie Sauropods,
or
Bring Me the Head of
Apatosaurus Louisae

For almost a hundred years, the heart of the Carnegie Museum in Pittsburgh, Pennsylvania, was its Dinosaur Hall. This huge, darkened, two-story chamber was filled with varnished fossilized bones from varied eras, all gathered together by size. It was dominated by two huge sauropod skeletons of the Jurassic period—one skeleton of the towering *Diplodocus carnegii* and the other of the *Apatosaurus louisae*.

These sauropods are the dinosaurs of our youth, the creatures whose image was conjured up when we said "dinosaur." They are the great bronto-beasts of *Lost World* movies and Fred Flintstone cartoons. They have adorned gas station signs and filled toy boxes with brightly colored replicas. They are very narrow at the ends and very large in the middle.

But these two fossilized titans have their own stories, involving rivalries, controversy with other museums, a gift to the king of England, and, most of all, the fact that the *Apatosaurus*, the foundation of the brontosaurus name, bore not only the wrong name but the wrong head for decades.

Let's start, as one must start with such ancient beasts, with history, in particular with the dinosaur explosion of the late nineteenth century. This is when American dinosaurs came to the fore, recognized as creatures of an earlier age. In the American West, two great early paleontologists and fossil hunters— Edward Drinker Cope and Othniel C. Marsh—competed for new discoveries. Each man sought to outdo the other, and this period of discovery was known as the "Bone Wars." Speed and dramatics in their discoveries were more important than complete accuracy, and over the course of discovery, identification, and mounting, errors cropped up in their work.

Indeed, taking a fossil from its original location to its final display is a long, frustrating process. The bones themselves, their organic bits replaced by rock, are located in situ, buried within a stone matrix. They are usually not in any particular order, and extremely rich bone fields may have the remains of dozens or hundreds of creatures. It is not just like putting together a jigsaw puzzle—it is dealing with the pieces of a dozen puzzles dipped in concrete.

As a result of this a long time may pass between when a fossil is discovered and unearthed and when it is described scientifically, and longer still before it is mounted for display. And even then the accuracy of its description may be questionable. Complete skeletons are extremely rare, and often the displayed version is made up of several similar skeletons, its story filled in with guesswork and conventional wisdom.

An excellent example is the *Apatosaurus*, which was discovered and named twice, with its later name being the one grounded in most people's minds—*Brontosaurus*. The first *Apatosaurus* was discovered in 1877 by Marsh, who named it "deceptive lizard"—a reference to the fact that its first bones resembled those of a marine lizard, the *Mosasaurus*, instead of a dinosaur. Marsh discovered the dinosaur again in the form of a larger and more complete skeleton in 1879, and named it *Bron-tosaurus* this time—the "thunder lizard" we are comfortable with. Through the rules of naming priority, the first is the official one," but it was the second, more evocative name that stuck in people's minds. Brontosaurus became the popular name of the creature, even though it was discovered to be the same as the earlier *Apatosaurus,* even before the creature was first displayed in a museum. Among paleontologists and experts there remained debate about which was more appropriate, with the result that both tended to be used: *Apatosaurus* would be given most fully, with *Brontosaurus* as the aka for this sauropod's rap sheet.

Marsh's *Apatosaurus* was fully named *Apatosaur ajax,* and considered the holotype for the creature (his second version of the creature was named *Brontosaurus excelsus,* which was changed to *Apatosaurus excelsus*). A holotype is the model against which other fossils would be compared to determine if they were truly apatosaurs or not. The trouble was, this second *Apatosaurus* skeleton lacked a clear head. (At the end of a long neck, the heads of the sauriels would often be lost in the process of becoming fossils.) Marsh used a likely looking head from nearby (another quarry five miles away) to finish the creature.

The choice of this distantly located head was based on guesswork, and often Marsh guessed very well. The excavations of the other quarry were of a similar age, and the chosen skull seemed to fit the image of the imagined living beast—large, high-domed, with heavy teeth capable of ripping foliage from the trees. It was similar to that of the *Camarasaurus* ("vaulted-chamber lizard," a reference to the shape of the skull), which was a common dinosaur in the formations.

Marsh described his *Apatosaurus/Brontosaurus* with the heavy skull, and the creature made its public appearance in 1905 at the Peabody Museum at Yale, which was funded by George Peabody, who was both a philanthropist and Marsh's uncle. Its heavy-faced appearance was cemented, with its name, in the public's mind.

The *Apatosaurus* entered the world of industrialist Andrew Carnegie in 1898, with the announced discovery of a tremendous dinosaur, larger than any previously found. Dinosaurs were still popular in the public mind, and pictures of the imagined beast lounging alongside the new metal-framed skyscrapers ran in the papers. Andrew Carnegie, who had already begun building the public libraries and small museum in the Pittsburgh area that bear his name, sent the museum's director, William J. Holland, west with a check to buy the dinosaur.

Holland and his group were sorely disappointed upon reaching the discovery, because the great beast consisted of one bone, an *Apatosaurus* thigh, from which the rest of the creature was spun. (They did purchase the bone, which later was displayed as part of a *Brontosaurus*. But since they were out in the West on Mr. Carnegie's dime, they decided to hunt for dinosaurs themselves.)

What they found was a nearly complete skeleton of an equally large beast, the *Diplodocus*. This first *Diplodocus* was another creature first uncovered and named by Marsh, in 1878 (the name meant "double beam," a reference to the bones on the underside of the tail). But Holland's team's new discovery was a nearly complete specimen, which they named *Diplodocus carnegii*, after their sponsor. While this creature was not the holotype for the line, it would become one of the best-known dinosaurs in the world, and catapult the Carnegie Museum into the forefront of the dinosaur museums.

Mr. Carnegie's dinosaur was a sensation—so huge that it could not be mounted in any of his libraries, nor in his infant museum. Carnegie agreed to build a new hall for the great creature, and in the process began the expansion of the Carnegie Museum in Pittsburgh, east of the city proper, overlooking the deep ravine of Panther Hollow and situated between the modern

University of Pittsburgh and what would become the Carnegie Institute of Technology (now known as Carnegie Mellon University).

But the Carnegie's completed *Diplodocus* did not make its first appearance in Carnegie's museum, but rather in England, and when it did appear it was not the real fossil. When staying at Skibo Castle, his property in Scotland, Carnegie hosted King Edward VII, monarch of the British Empire. His majesty admired a drawing of Mr. Carnegie's as-yet-unassembled dinosaur, which was still in the process of being readied for display. Mr. Carnegie, being magnanimous toward royalty, offered to get the king one of his own. Edward agreed, and Carnegie contacted Holland and ordered up another *Apatosaurus*.

Holland and his paleontologists were concerned by this demand, for while the American West was producing a prodigious amount of fossils, it was unlikely they could whistle one up at the spur of the moment, even for a king. Instead, they made a duplicate of the bones in plaster and wire frame and sent *that* to King Edward. In the end, Holland, accompanied by preparer Arthur Coggeshall, late of the American Museum of Natural History, arrived with thirty-three boxes of plaster-cast bones, ready to assemble the beast.

His majesty was delighted, and unlike Carnegie he *did* have the space to display it immediately. So the first time *Diplodocus carnegii* met the public was in the gallery of reptiles in the British Museum, and that was a copy of the original. While not the most massive dinosaur to date (that would be the *Apatosaurus*), it was the longest, and for many it was the first, and it was popular instantly.

So great was the sudden demand for *Diplodoci* that Carnegie had the team generate more, to be presented as gifts to various heads of state and other museums. Nine replicas were created, each costing around $30,000 in that day, and were sent to cities including Vienna, Paris, Madrid, Berlin, St. Petersburg, Mexico City, and La Plata, in Argentina. They were princely gifts for the time, and cemented Pittsburgh, and Carnegie, as a leader in dinosaurs.

The teams assembling the great specimens had their own adventures in international diplomacy as well as in science. Coggeshall was in Berlin shortly before World War I assembling the *Diplodocus* given to the kaiser, when he changed hotels. The change suggested suspicious activity to the local police, and he was picked up as a suspected British spy. He made little headway with the police until he invoked the kaiser's name and produced a letter from the kaiser to Carnegie. At that point the police became very polite, the investigation was dropped, and the preparer was allowed to return to his dinosaur.

The Germans created a scholarly scandal as well. When Marsh first mounted his sauropods, he was guessing. Some guesses have since been proved to be correct; others, such as that the beasts dragged their tails behind them, have been disproved. One correct choice was to mount the legs of the great dinosaurs like those of an elephant. Several European experts disagreed—were not the dinosaurs cold-blooded, like alligators? Therefore, would it not be more correct to mount them with legs splayed out to the sides?

Curator Holland's response was swift and caustic. In a published paper he pointed out to the learned heads of the rival museums that were the *Diplodoci* slung as low as they suggested, their rib cages would be lower than their feet! And, therefore, the only way they could have moved through the Jurassic landscape was along great trenches. Holland mocked the Germans kindly for their position, pointing out sarcastically, "This might perhaps account for their early extinction. It is physically and mentally bad to 'get into a rut.'" The Germans corrected their mounting accordingly.

The *Diplodocus* of Carnegie's Dinosaur Hall had a long, varied, and sometimes controversial career in the modern world, but its companion skeleton, that of *Apatosaurus louisae,* put it to shame. It was this creature that was headless for its first twenty years on display, then had the wrong head mounted on it for the next forty-five, until finally it was corrected by Drs. John S. ("Jack") McIntosh and David S. Berman.

Apatosaurus, as noted earlier, was discovered by Marsh in 1877 (and again in 1879), but the one that resides in the Carnegie was not found until 1909, in what was then called Carnegie Quarry and is now known as Dinosaur National Monument. The creature was named *Apatosaurus louisae*, after Carnegie's wife, Louise. The almost-complete specimen was found in a rich fossil deposit consisting of *Apatosaurus* and *Diplodocus* skeletons, along with those of the *Camarasaurus*. Again, the question was which bones belonged to which creature? As Dr. Berman noted, "They had three types of skeletons and two types of skulls."

The *Diplodocus*-style skull was a slender specimen, with a narrowed face and splaying, pencillike teeth, mounted atop a more delicate neck. The *Camarasaurus*-style ones, in comparison, had a blunted profile with peglike teeth. Marsh, in mounting the original *Apatosaur ajax*, had selected a *Camarasaurus*-type head from another quarry as the likely one. This approach had stuck, and indeed there were *Camarasauri* bones among the apatosaurs. Holland, though, was unsure if the snub-nosed skull belonged to the rest of the beast, and based on the locations of the skulls in the matrix suggested that the slenderer *Diplodocus*-style one would be more appropriate.

Henry Fairfield Osborn, director at the prestigious American Museum of Natural History, disagreed strongly with Holland's theory. Osborn was a paleontologist and bone hunter himself, as well as being a follower of E. D. Cope, Marsh's rival. Despite this rivalry, Osborn believed Marsh's original mounting of the *Camarasaurus*-style head was correct. Osborn was known for both his strong opinions and his pull in the scientific community, and, when Holland theorized that the *Diplodocus*-style head was correct, dared the Pittsburgh curator to publicly mount the "alternative" skull atop the *Apatosaurus* skeleton.

Holland, who thought nothing of taunting the "broom closet naturalists" of the European museums, refrained from taking up the challenge in this case. But neither did he agree with Osborn's conclusion, and for the first twenty-some years of the *Apatosaurus*'s public display its skeleton remained headless in the Dinosaur Hall, while other museums followed Osborn's lead.

In 1934, *Apatosaurus louisae* finally got its head, and it was the *Camarasaurus* head, fitting with Marsh/Osborn's view of the creature. Part of it might have been the inertia of conventional wisdom coming to the fore, but the Pittsburgh curator at the time, J. Leroy "Pop" Kay was no expert in dinosaurs, and his chief dinosaur curator, C. W. Gilmore, had received his training from Osborn at the AMNH. In addition, there was a *Camarasaurus* skull from the original expedition that looked like it belonged to the *Apatosaurus,* and was just one number off from the head Holland believed to belong to the beast, and it might be assumed that they were correcting a labeling error from the field. Regardless of the reason, the *Camarasaurus*-style head was installed, and for the next forty-five years the *Apatosaurus louisae* stood in the museum as a chimera, a fictional creature made up of different species—the fossil equivalent of a jackalope.

This changed in the seventies, which was a time of academic revolution in paleontology. At this time we saw the first theories of the hot-blooded dinosaurs and the extinction event at the K-T boundary. At this time Dr. Jack McIntosh arrived at the Carnegie to study a *Diplodocus* skull still locked in the matrix, with an eye to reconstructing the creature's palate bone. Dr. Berman's own specialty was in Permian fossils, but he had valid contributions to offer the reconstruction. The two men hit it off, so much so that after the publication of the paper, they continued to work together. Among the projects they took on was the matter of the head of *Apatosaurus louisae.*

It had been known in paleontological circles for some time that the *Apatosaurus* was a bit "off," but no one had thought to reopen the debate—it was a scholarly cold case. McIntosh and Berman began to reexamine not only the fossils themselves, but the paper trail that had brought the skeletons together, both in Marsh's originals and Holland's later discovery. They confirmed that the head combined with Marsh's original *Apatosaurus* had been found far from the rest of the skeletons, while Holland's was sufficiently close to the body such that, as Holland said in his 1915 paper on the subject, "Had nothing in the past been written in reference to the structure of the skull of *Brontosaurus*, the conclusion would naturally and almost inevitably have been reached that this skull belongs to the skeleton the remainder of which has been recovered."

More important, Berman and McIntosh also uncovered in their studies the fact that a partial *Diplodocus*-style skull had been found near Marsh's original 1877 *Apatosaurus*, but over the course of moving the fossils, this more delicately shaped one had been placed with those of another dinosaur entirely. Marsh had kept copious and detailed notes, but this misfiling got past him when he was putting together his *Brontosaurus*. It turned out that there was a clerical error, but it was one that gave the specimen the wrong head in the first place.

McIntosh and Berman had better tools than Marsh and Holland had had almost a hundred years previously, and they could offer cogent and decisive proof that the *Diplodocus*-style head found near Holland's *Apatosaurus* from the Carnegie quarry was more appropriate than the *Camarasaurus* one, in particular in the joining of the neck to the skull itself. The fact that Marsh himself had found a *Diplodocus*-style skull near his initial, incomplete discovery of the creature was icing on the cake.

Berman and McIntosh published their results fully in 1978, and far from an outcry among the scientific community, their results were greeted with support and agreement. The head of the *Apatosaurus louisae* at the Carnegie Museum of Natural History was replaced in 1979, to much fanfare. Since then, the heads of other *Apatosauri* have been updated, including the ones at the Peabody Museum at Yale and the American Museum of Natural History in New York.

The Carnegie Museum's ancient Dinosaur Hall has been replaced and expanded into a larger, more well-lit exhibit broken up by geological age as opposed to by available space. The heavy varnish of the original displays has been carefully removed and replaced with new preservatives. The two great sauropods have been remounted in the Jurassic Era exhibit in more natural positions, their long tails held up, their massive necks curved and animated.

At the feet of the huge specimens one can find the original *Apatosaurus* bone that Andrew Carnegie purchased all those years before, and the *Diplodocus* fossil skull, still half mired in the rock that brought together Drs. Berman and McIntosh.

And after several million years, the last hundred or so in public, *Apatosaurus louisae* has regained its original and rightful head.

———

Carnegie Museum of Natural History
4400 Forbes Avenue
Pittsburgh, PA 15213

———

Jeff Grubb

Dinosaurs had their tarpits . . . and sometimes our ancestors seemed to follow suit.

Bog Bodies

In the British Museum of London, England, a dried husk of a body lies curled on its back, waiting for hundreds of visitors to walk by each day. He appears to be lifting his arms, which are more bones than skin, toward his upper body, and looking down at what might be an absent child. It is almost shocking that he has no lower body, and indeed the rest of his torso and legs were never found, only pieces of his right foot, right thigh, and buttocks. His face is amazingly detailed and, if you are inclined to set aside the macabre notion of seeing the dead in the light, a closer inspection reveals that he is naked except for an armband and a rope around his neck. He used to be displayed more prominently, in the middle of the second floor, but natural light and photo flashes were causing him to dry out more quickly, so he is now located in an out-of-the-way dark corner in Gallery 50.

Lindow Man, named because of where he was discovered—in the peat bogs of northwest England in 1984—was found by peat cutters. Carbon dating revealed that he lived during the Iron Age, about two thousand years ago. He was not alone in the bogs, as some two hundred bodies have been located in similar areas all over the world, preserved in the oxygen-deprived vaults of vegetation, earth, and water, their bodies tanned to leather, their organs preserved by the absence of bacteria.

Lindow Man is typical of the bodies found in Great Britain, as he did not die from old age, illness, or accident, but was murdered and deliberately buried in the bogs. A forensic examination by scientists determined that he had been struck on the head three times with an ax and strangled, and that his throat had been cut. An examination of the contents of his stomach, remarkably well preserved by the cold and wet of the bog, revealed that he had eaten a small meal of burnt cereal grains and mistletoe pollen. This means that while he may have been killed in the spring perhaps the pollen had been saved in another season and added to the meal. Mistletoe figured prominently in the lore of the Druids, but the plant itself is poisonous, so it is not certain what the pollen could mean; the only thing that is sure is that he ate it shortly before he died.

Much speculation has been made on why a man would be killed three different ways, then drowned in the bogs to be enveloped by peat, but the favorite theory draws on what is known about other bog bodies and the Celts of the Iron Age. On May 1 of each year the Beltane season was celebrated and a sacrifice made to ensure that the crops were bountiful over the summer. No one knows exactly what the ritual was, but anthropologists speculate that it was done by roasting a bannock, or oatcake, in a fire and charring a tiny bit of it. The bannock was then broken up and placed in a bag for each person to take a piece. The one who chose the charred piece was then burned in the fire to the goddess of spring. A variation of this sacrifice was documented by the invading Romans and involved three gods: Taranis, the god of thunder, who demanded prisoners of war be burned alive in a wicker cage or killed with a weapon; Esus, the god of the underworld, whose victims were hung from sacred trees or stabbed to death, or both; and Teutates, the god of the tribe, whose sacrifices are associated with watery graves such as sacred wells and pools. Due to the findings of the contents of Lindow Man's stomach, which had him possibly die in the spring, his ax wounds, the hanging, the knife to the throat, and the burial in the bog, it has been surmised that he was a sacrifice and not an executed criminal. The lack of legs could be explained by the burning of his lower half while the top half was buried. There is no real proof that either theory is correct, or that he was a sacrifice at all.

Tollund Man is a sharp contrast to the half-dried husk of Lindow Man. Tollund lies serenely on display in the Silkeborg Museum in Denmark, and also appears to be a sacrifice, but in this case specifically by the Druids. Tollund lies on his side with his legs drawn up and his arms folded in a manner reminiscent of a sleeping child, and has an eerily serene look on his face. He has a leather cap on his head and a belt around his waist, so it is assumed that he wore clothes to his grave, but time has withered the cloth away. He also has a three-foot length of leather rope around his neck, so the effect of sleep is jolted sharply from the viewer's mind.

The Druidic connection comes into play because of where he was found, and because his stomach contents revealed that barley covered with the hallucinogenic ergot fungus was his last meal. The theory is that he was chosen carefully for sacrifice and given a mind-altering meal to ease his transition into death, then was hanged, cut down from the tree, and buried carefully in the bog with the noose still around his neck. Much has been written about Druids and the "otherworld," and burial in places that were considered to be sacred, so it isn't a far cry to assume that the man went willingly and felt honored. He has a companion in death while on display. The bog body known as Elling Woman was discovered about fifty meters from Tollund Man, and she, too, had been hanged and then buried carefully. Testing also shows that she died around the same time and was hanged similarly.

For a less peaceful view of bog deaths we can turn to the National Museum of Ireland, where three bodies from their extensive collection of bog bodies are on display. They are named Old Croghan Man, Clonycavan Man, and Gallagh Man. Gallagh Man was found in 1823, and is unique because it is an entire body. It seems he was strangled with willow rods, but because he was found so long ago and is not well preserved his body has not yielded much by way of forensics. In fact, he does look more like a dehydrated piece of leather in the rough shape of a human rather than a body. The most interesting thing about Gallagh Man is that when farmers first found him in the 1800s, he was left in the bog and was unearthed and reburied repeatedly as a local curiosity before finally being turned over to the museum. Truly, unexplained death and morbid curiosity are no modern thing. Ironically, if he had been left in the bogs for another hundred years, more would be known about his demise, but preservation of such bodies is definitely a trial-and-error type of science.

His less dehydrated companions, Old Croghan Man and Clonycavan Man, were discovered in 2003 and consequently were better preserved. Clonycavan was a short man of about five feet tall who pomaded his hair into a Mohawk style with a rare tree resin that suggests he was a traveler from Spain or France rather than a local citizen. He might have been a young traveling merchant from a wealthy family. What is known from modern forensic examination is that at about the age of twenty he was bashed in the head and face with an ax, and then buried in the bog: hardly a well-thought-out and ritualistic sacrifice, and more likely a brutal murder of chance. When he was found it was first thought that his death had been more recent, and the police conducted an investigation before turning him over to archaeologists.

Old Croghan Man is also in his twenties, but was a tall six feet six inches. His death was also quite violent but perhaps more intriguing, as he had defensive wounds and bore signs of torture. The body consists of little more than the upper torso and arms, but is without a head or belly; his nipples had been cut off and his arms run through with a rope before being staked down into a bog. Surprisingly, this mutilation tells more about Old Croghan Man than his stomach contents or a noose possibly could. During the Iron Age the kings of Ireland demonstrated their God-given fertility and right to rule by demanding their followers symbolically suckle at their nipples. In essence this meant that without nipples a man could not be king. Many bodies found in the bogs and written of in the history of this area of Ireland were similarly mutilated, cut up, and buried on the borders of kingdoms. Much speculation has been made that these bodies were men who lost a fight to be king, or offended the existing king, or were perhaps sacrifices for the fertility of their king. When defensive wounds are present, the last theory is the least likely.

Speaking of mutilation in the name of gods, in the Drents Museum of Assen, Netherlands, lie two men who died together. They are called the Weerdinge Men, and are semidried husks. They were found faceup in semiembrace, but missing their heads and genitalia. One had his stomach slit, and his entrails, in remarkable detail, are spilled out across him. In their time it was speculated that they had been killed through the art of divination, specifically, through a sacred skill called "anthropomancy": cutting open a sacrificed enemy's abdomen and reading the flailing motions of the limbs and how the intestines spilled out to foretell the future or learn the wishes of the gods. A disturbingly wide range of methods and history exist on this subject, so the theory that these two men were prisoners of war and sacrificed, and then split open to determine divine information, is quite viable. They probably fought together before their deaths, given their young age, and most likely died together. Their true relation is unknown, and because of the missing pieces it was originally thought that this was a man and a woman due to the semi-embraced pose. Once sex could be determined it was thought that they might be father and son, because one was about twenty years old and the other in his forties. They might have been just soldiers or local farmers defending their fields. Their true relationship cannot yet be determined, as the chemical process of mummification within a bog hampers current methods of DNA testing.

In this same museum is a young female of about sixteen called Yde Girl, who was discovered in the peat of the Netherlands in 1897. She is remarkable for her deformities: Before her death she had a marked scoliosis, or curvature of the spine, that left her only four and a half feet tall, with a rather large forehead. She is thought to have been strangled around the year A.D. 1 with a woolen belt looped around her neck three times. A stab wound was also found at the base of her collarbone. The sight of her twisted face, deformed body, and long red hair made the peat farmers who discovered her run in fear, thinking she was some kind of devil. Strangely, the left side of her head was missing all hair, and she was wrapped in a cloak. The local mayor contacted the Drents Museum to pick up the body for the sake of science, but before they arrived the villagers snatched most of the remainder of her hair, dug out her teeth, and took a few bones. It is thought they did this more from morbid curiosity rather than for superstitious reasons. Fortunately, most of the girl remained, and using the notes of the mayor, a reconstruction of her head was done in 1993. The realistic bust is on display next to her remains, and is now more famous than the body itself, if only for the forensic challenge it represented.

Another youth who died around A.D. 1 and had a half-shaven head lies in Landesmuseum in Schleswig, Germany, along with three other bog bodies. She was named the Windeby Girl, but later testing revealed she needed to be renamed Windeby Boy. His body was discovered in 1952, with what was thought to be a blindfold on. Later examination proved that, like many other bog bodies with half a head of hair, he had not been shaved but that the oxygenation process had had more of a chance to work on the side facing upward, and that the blindfold was actually a headband that had moved downward during decay. This boy had been drowned in the bog, and then heavy logs and stones were placed on top to keep him down. Another body, which became known as Windeby 2, was found a short time later about sixteen feet away from the first. This one was clearly a man, but he had been strangled first and then staked into the bog like many others.

As usual, there are those who believe that all the bodies are sacrifices, but there are many alternative theories. Perhaps the most interesting of them is the one that surrounds another body in the Landesmuseum. He is officially called Dätgen Man, but is also known as the *Wiederganger*, or Zombie Man. He was discovered beaten, stabbed, decapitated, and spiked into the bog, his head some ten feet from his body. Many of the wounds were considered to have been made after death, with the mutilation done to prevent his undead body from walking the earth; thus the term *Wiederganger*.

So many bodies have been found that the romantic notion of all of them resulting from noble sacrifices for the greater good or to please the gods becomes questionable. Why aren't there more bodies? Were they chopped into peat fuel by accident or were these random killings that were few and far between? The most likely answer is that time and decay took care of most organic matter, and only rarely does a body survive the bog process and father time to be eternally preserved. What we found was perhaps a collection of random killings, executions, and the occasional sacrifice. At any rate many of the results can be seen on full display at a variety of museums around the world and are available for anyone's speculation.

————

British Museum
Great Russell Street
London
WC1B 3DG

National Museum of Ireland
Kildare Street
Dublin 2
Ireland

————

Kerrie Hughes

The flag has an honored place in our American history . . . but are we really expected to believe that one of our most famous flags was monogrammed?

What's on That Broad Stripe with Those Bright Stars?

One of the prized holdings of the Smithsonian Institution's Museum of American History is the original flag that was christened the "Star-Spangled Banner."

First, a few misconceptions need to be cleared up.

This flag was not made by Betsy Ross for George Washington. That flag was designed during the American Revolution and features thirteen stars to represent the original thirteen colonies. The distinctive feature of the Ross flag is the arrangement of the five-point stars in a circle. Betsy's signature contribution to the design was the use of stars with five points instead of six.

This flag is also not known as the original Old Glory. That flag was made in 1824 for Captain William Driver, who flew it on his ship twice around the world and displayed it regularly on patriotic occasions and holidays. Originally bearing twenty-four stars, this worn and tattered flag was remade in 1861 with thirty-four stars; a white anchor was added to signify Driver's years at sea. When the Civil War began and Tennessee, where Driver had moved, seceded from the Union, the flag survived, sewn inside a quilt. It was unfurled when Union troops occupied Nashville in 1862. It never flew again but passed into legend and bequeathed its name to all American flags, and it is also on display in the Smithsonian Armed Forces history section.

The Star-Spangled Banner was the garrison flag that flew over Fort McHenry during the Battle of Baltimore in the War of 1812 and provided Francis Scott Key with the inspiration for the lyrics that became the United States, national anthem:

Oh say can you see, by the dawn's early light,
What so proudly we hail'd at the twilight's last gleaming,
Whose broad stripes and bright stars, through the perilous
 fight
O'er the ramparts we watch'd were so gallantly streaming?
And the rockets' red glare, the bombs bursting in air,
Gave proof through the night that our flag was still there,
O say, does that star-spangled banner yet wave
*O'er the land of the free and the home of the brave?**

This flag was made under government contract in the summer of 1813 by a professional Baltimore flag maker, Mary Pickersgill, under contract to the garrison commander, George Armistead, who had requested "a flag so large that the British would have no trouble seeing from a distance." Mary was assisted by her thirteen-year-old daughter, Caroline, and by two of her nieces, Eliza and Margaret Young, and may also have received help from her mother, Rebecca Young, who was a flag maker as well. She used English woolen bunting for the stripes and the union and cotton for the stars.

The final flag measured 30 by 42 feet (about one-quarter the size of a basketball court), and each star was about two feet

*The United States Congress officially proclaimed it as the national anthem on March 3, 1931, 116 years after the song was first written.

across. To assemble the unusually large flag, Pickersgill laid it out on the floor of a neighboring brewery.

Mary was paid the princely sum of $405.90 (the receipt is also available as part of the Smithsonian exhibit).

According to the exhibit:

On Lieutenant Colonel Armistead's death in 1818, the Star-Spangled Banner passed to his widow, Louisa Hughes Armistead. For nearly forty years, Louisa Armistead kept it in her Baltimore home. She made several alterations to the flag. Occasionally she allowed it to be displayed for patriotic events. She lent both the flag and her late husband's silver service for display at a reception for Revolutionary hero General Lafayette at Fort McHenry in 1824. She also lent the flag for a celebration by the Old Defenders of the Battle of Fort McHenry's 25th anniversary in 1839.

As related in these excerpts from a letter written by Colonel Armistead's daughter, Georgiana Armistead Appleton, on June 17, 1873:

I like to think of my treasure in such appreciative hand as yours, and am obliged for the safety you ensure it, until I decide on its final destination. Pieces of the flag have occasionally been given to those who deemed to have a right to such a memento—indeed had we have given all that we have been importuned for little would be left to show. My impression is that the star was cut out for some official person. The red A was I presume sewn on by my mother. My father's name is in his own handwriting. The bag is the same in which I always remember it, I therefore feel sure that it is the identical one in which it was placed after the bombardment & which I gave official orders should be sent to you as the old casket in which was contained the jewel. It is my wish to visit the Historical Society when the flag is on exhibition, will you kindly let me know the days on which it will be shown. I do hope you will succeed in obtaining a good photograph and must be[g] you to remember to give me a negative of the Banner. Should I not see you again before the Banner is stored my [sic] I beg you to take for your own private collection such a portion as you think right, which will too I hope remind you of yours most truly respectfully, Georgiana Armistead Appleton. Pray do not think I wish to appear before the public but in any future notice of the Flag will you kindly say that the Banner continues to be my property. Of course I have a special reason for this request. G.A.A.

The Appletons eventually turned it over to the Smithsonian, and it has become one of its most treasured holdings.

When it arrived at the Smithsonian in July 1907, the Star-Spangled Banner was hung on the exterior wall of the Smithsonian Institution Building (also called the "Castle") to be photographed. The assistant secretary of the Smithsonian wrote to Eben Appleton saying, "The newspaper men are after me, and they all want a photograph of it to publish in the various local papers. . . . Its presence in the Museum has caused a wave of patriotism, which is very good to see." But needless to say, concern for the preservation of this seminal relic of American history required that its permanent placement be indoors.

Eventually, the forces of gravity and general wear and tear required that the remaining vestiges of the flag no longer be hung as a banner but instead be mounted on an incline. A recent mammoth upgrading of the exhibit also added additional precautions to preserve its survival, including a careful removing of dust particles from its fabric and the construction of a viewing chamber that would minimize further dust contamination or light damage to the fabric, while also making it available for exhibit to the public on an ongoing basis.

Now concerning the red A alluded to in the Appleton letter. What the flag's owner is obviously referring to is an embroidered inverted red V in the white stripe that is fifth from the top of the flag, which the Smithsonian staff refer to as a "chevron."

The current explanation, according to Museum of American History historian Lonn Taylor, is based on the collected pieces of Appleton correspondence: "In addition to explaining that the fly edge and star were cut away to give as mementos to deserving people, she also refers to the red chevron on the white stripe. In her words, 'the red A was presumably sewn on by my mother.' This was a very exciting find because we have never been sure of the significance of that chevron. I suspect it is simply an A for Armistead."

The problems with this explanation are manifold. First, the flag itself is rather distinctive in size and singular in appearance, given its scars of battle. Moreover, the fact remains that the "chevron" really doesn't look like an A, and indeed lacks a crossbar as such. The conclusion in the correspondence is guesswork at best; in Appleton's words, "the red A was presumably sewn on by my mother." Indeed, less than resembling an A, a case can be made that it is in reality an inverted V, which actually plays into another mysterious element of the founding of this nation, because the V and its inversion are also representative of the compass and the square that make up one of the key symbols of Masonic symbology.

Consider the following.

Nine of the original fifty-six signers of the Declaration of Independence were high-level Masons (William Ellery, Ben Franklin, John Hancock, Joseph Hewes, William Hooper, Robert Treat Paine, Richard Stockton, George Walton, and William Whipple).

Thirteen of the original forty signers of the Constitution were high-level Masons (Gunning Bedford Jr., John Blair, David Breartley, Jacob Broom, Daniel Carroll, Jonathan Dayton, John Dickinson, Benjamin Franklin, Nicholas Gilman, Rufus King, James McHenry, William Paterson, and George Washington).

Also consider that the architect Pierre Charles L'Enfant, while designing the city of Washington, D.C., built the most famous

Masonic symbol (the compass and the square) and the five-pointed pentagram into the city grid ... For over two hundred years those symbols have been hidden in plain sight. (Note: The top point of the pentagram—which is formed by the intersection of Massachusetts Avenue, Rhode Island Avenue, Connecticut Avenue, Vermont Avenue, and K Street NW—lies at the White House, while the hinge of the compass in the street grid lies at the Capitol, with its vectors extending down Pennsylvania and Maryland avenues.)

But who are the Masons, and what do they believe?

Well, according to a press release from one of their current chapters:

> Freemasonry is the world's first and largest fraternal organization. It is based on the belief that each man can make a difference in the world. There are approximately 5 million Masons worldwide, including 2 million in the United States. The organization dates back to the guilds of European stonemasons, who built castles and cathedrals during the Middle Ages. Temporary buildings called lodges were built next to the cathedrals, and the Masons used them to meet, receive their pay, plan their work, train new apprentices, and socialize. The first Grand Lodge was established in England in 1717; by 1731, Masonry had spread to the American colonies. Benjamin Franklin, George Washington, Paul Revere, and other founding fathers were among the first Masons in the United States.

And it is obvious that from the architectural design of the Washington Mall to the graphic symbology featured on our currency (which includes a Masonic pyramid and a representation of the arcane "all-seeing eye"), Masonic symbols have been carefully inserted throughout the manifestations of the Founding Fathers' plans for the United States, and in most cases they are literally hidden in plain sight.

According to best-selling author Brad Meltzer, who did some

research on the subject in conjunction with his novel *The Book of Fate*:

> [O]n October 13, 1792, Maryland's Masonic Lodge Number 9 did lay the cornerstone of the White House in a Freemason ceremony. The same was true during the laying of the cornerstone of the U.S. Capitol Building, where George Washington himself presided over the Masonic ceremony. Washington's Masonic trowel was also used at the cornerstone laying of the Washington Monument, the U.S. Supreme Court, the Library of Congress, the National Cathedral *and the Smithsonian*. [Italics added]

Indeed, there is even a Masonic legend that involves a vision prophecy that George Washington witnessed that involved him being symbolically crowned king of America.

What all of this Masonic symbolism means is anyone's guess, but there is little doubt that the overt evidence in place relates to some mystical intent.

So the inclusion of a Masonic symbol on the most famous flag of the United States, war against Great Britain, which currently resides in an institution that has at least a tangential Masonic legacy, is a lot more likely than the incorporation of a family monogram on the most archetypal flag of the Founding Fathers' efforts.

National Museum of American History
Smithsonian Institution
On the National Mall
14th Street and Constitution Avenue NW
Washington, DC 20560

A few broken statues are some of the most famous works of art of the classical world, and their acquisition still seems to have a few strings attached.

The Elgin Marbles and the Curse of Minerva

For many a visitor to the British Museum, the remains of the statues and sculptures of the Parthenon are must-see viewing . . . even despite the fact that these irreplaceable artifacts of the glory of Greece are far from their native land.

According to materials made available by the British Museum,

the "Elgin Marbles" is a popular term that in its widest use may refer to the collection of stone objects—sculptures, inscriptions, and architectural features—acquired by Lord Elgin during his time as ambassador to the Ottoman court of the Sultan in Istanbul. More specifically, and more usually, it is used to refer to those sculptures, inscriptions, and architectural features that he acquired in Athens between 1801 and 1805. These objects were purchased by the British Parliament from Lord Elgin in 1816 and presented by Parliament to the

British Museum. The collection includes sculptures from the Parthenon, roughly half of what now survives: 247 feet of the original 524 feet of frieze; 15 of 92 metopes; 17 figures from the pediments, and various other pieces of architecture. It also includes objects from other buildings on the Acropolis: the Erechtheion, the Propylaia, and the Temple of Athena Nike.

How these works of art became available is still another story, about which the museum has carefully constructed a party-line account:

> Wishing to improve the arts of Great Britain, Elgin assembled a group of architects, painters, draughtsmen and moulders to make casts and drawings of Greek monuments. They began work in Athens in 1800. The following year, Elgin was granted a *firman* (letter of instruction) that required the authorities in Athens not to hinder his employees in this work, and in addition allow them to "take away any pieces of stone with inscriptions or figures." A further *firman* was secured by Sir Robert Adair in February 1810 which instructed the authorities in Athens to allow the embarkation of all the remaining antiquities collected by Elgin. It is a popular misconception that Elgin purchased the antiquities. In fact the *firman* was granted to him as a personal gesture after he encouraged the British forces in their fight to drive the French out of Egypt, which was then an Ottoman possession. The continuing destruction of classical sculpture in Athens prompted Elgin to rescue for posterity what sculptures he could. The Parthenon had been reduced to a ruin over a hundred years previously, in 1687, during the Venetian siege of the Acropolis. The defending Ottoman Turks were using the Parthenon as a gunpowder store, which was ignited by the Venetian bombardment. The explosion destroyed the roof and parts of the walls and the colonnade.

Moreover, the nineteenth-century public at large seemed to bend over backward in praise of the acquisition of these classic masterpieces, as evidenced by the following representative passages from *The Elgin and Phigaleian Marbles* by Sir Henry Ellis, which was published in 1846.

> It is but just that those who feel the value of this collection should pay a tribute of thanks to the nobleman to whose exertions the nation is indebted for it; and the more so as he was made the object of vulgar abuse by many pretended admirers of ancient learning. If Lord Elgin had not removed these marbles, there is no doubt that many of them would long since have been totally destroyed; and it was only after great hesitation, and a certain knowledge that they were daily suffering more and more from brutal ignorance and barbarism, that he could prevail on himself to employ the power he had obtained to remove them to England.

One might believe that Elgin was universally adored for his deed, but such was not the case.

Some believed that what he did was no better than pillaging and piracy.

Others ascribed his deeds to racial and national arrogance and prejudice.

And some felt there should be consequences.

In his poem "The Curse of Minerva," written in 1811, the master poet Lord Byron railed against Elgin and implied that England would suffer due to his deeds.

> *For Elgin's fame thus grateful Pallas pleads,*
> *Below, his name—above, behold his deeds!*
> *Be ever hailed with equal honour here*
> *The Gothic monarch and the Pictish peer:*
> *Arms gave the first his right, the last had none,*
> *But basely stole what less barbarians won.*

So when the lion quits his fell repast,
Next prowls the wolf, the filthy jackal last:
Flesh, limbs, and blood the former make their own,
The last poor brute securely gnaws the bone.
Yet still the gods are just, and crimes are cross'd:
See here what Elgin won, and what he lost!
Another name with his pollutes my shrine:
Behold where Dian's beams disdain to shine!
Some retribution still might Pallas claim,
When Venus half avenged Minerva's shame."

She ceased awhile, and thus I dared reply,
To soothe the vengeance kindling in her eye:
"Daughter of Jove! in Britain's injured name,
A true-born Briton may the deed disclaim.
Frown not on England; England owns him not:
Athena, no! thy plunderer was a Scot.
Ask'st thou the difference? From fair Phyles' towers
Survey Bœotia;—Caledonia's ours.
And well I know within that bastard land
Hath Wisdom's goddess never held command;
A barren soil, where Nature's germs, confined
To stern sterility, can stint the mind;
Whose thistle well betrays the niggard earth,
Emblem of all to whom the land gives birth;
Each genial influence nurtured to resist;
A land of meanness, sophistry, and mist.
Each breeze from foggy mount and marshy plain
Dilutes with drivel every drizzly brain,
Till, burst at length, each wat'ry head o'er-flows,
Foul as their soil, and frigid as their snows.
Then thousand schemes of petulance and pride
Despatch her scheming children far and wide:
Some east, some west, some everywhere but north,
In quest of lawless gain, they issue forth.

And thus—accursed be the day and year!
She sent a Pict to play the felon here.
Yet Caledonia claims some native worth,
As dull Bœotia gave a Pindar birth;
So may her few, the letter'd and the brave,
Bound to no clime, and victors of the grave,
Shake off the sordid dust of such a land,
And shine like children of a happier strand;
As once, of yore, in some obnoxious place,
Ten names (if found) had saved a wretched race."

"Mortal!" the blue-eyed maid resumed, "once more
Bear back my mandate to thy native shore.
Though fallen, alas! this vengeance yet is mine,
to turn my counsels far from lands like thine.
Hear then in silence Pallas' stern behest;
Hear and believe, for time will tell the rest.

"First on the head of him who did this deed
My curse shall light,—on him and all his seed:
Without one spark of intellectual fire,
Be all the sons as senseless as the sire:
If one with wit the parent brood disgrace,
Believe him bastard of a brighter race;
Still with his hireling artists let him prate,
and Folly's praise repay for Wisdom's hate;
Long of their patron's gusto let them tell,
Whose noblest, native gusto is—to sell;
To sell and make—may shame record the day!—
The state receiver of his pilfer'd prey.
Meantime, the flattering, feeble dotard, West,
Europe's worst dauber, and poor Britain's best,
With palsied hand shall turn each model o'er
And own himself an infant of fourscore.

Be all the bruisers cull'd from all St. Giles',
That art and nature may compare their styles;
While brawny brutes in stupid wonder stare,
And marvel at his lordship's stone shop there.
Round the throng'd gate shall sauntering coxcombs creep,
To lounge and lucubrate, to prate and peep;
While many a languid maid, with longing sigh,
On giant statues casts the curious eye;
The room with transient glance appears to skim
Yet marks the mighty back and length of limb;
Mourns o'er the difference of now and then;
Exclaims 'These Greeks indeed were proper men!'
Draws slight comparisons of these with those,
And envies Laïs all her Attic beaux.
When shall a modern maid have swains like these!
Alas! Sir Harry is no Hercules!
And last of all, amidst the gaping crew,
Some calm spectator, as he takes his view,
In silent indignation mix'd with grief,
Admires the plunder, but abhors the thief.
Oh, loath'd in life, nor pardon'd in the dust,
May hate pursue his sacrilegious lust!
Link'd with the fool that fired the Ephesian dome,
Shall vengeance follow far beyond the tomb,
And Eratostratus and Elgin shine
In many a branding page and burning line;
Alike reserved for aye to stand accursed,
Perchance the second blacker than the first.

"So let him stand, through ages yet unborn,
Fix'd statue on the pedestal of Scorn;
Though not for him alone revenge shall wait,
But fits thy country for her coming fate:
Hers were the deeds that taught her lawless son

To do what oft Britannia's self had done.
Look to the Baltic—blazing from afar,
Your old ally yet mourns perfidious war.
Not to such deed did Pallas lend her aid,
Or break the compact which herself had made;
Far from such councils, from the faithless field
She fled—but left behind her Gorgon shield;
A fatal gift that turn'd your friends to stone,
And left lost Albion hated and alone.

"Look to the East, where Ganges' swarthy race
Shall shake your tyrant empire to its base;
Lo! there Rebellion rears her ghastly head
And glares the Nemesis of native dead;
Till Indus rolls a deep purpureal flood
And claims his long arrear of northern blood.
So may ye perish! Pallas, when she gave
Your free-born rights, forbade ye to enslave.

"Look on your Spain!—she clasps the hand she hates,
But boldly clasps, and thrusts you from her gates.
Bear witness, bright Barossa! thou canst tell
Whose were the sons that bravely fought and fell.
But Lusitania, kind and dear ally,
Can spare a few to fight, and sometimes fly,
Oh glorious field! by Famine fiercely won,
The Gaul retires for once, and all is done!
But when did Pallas teach, that one retreat
Retrieved three long olympiads of defeat?

"Look last at home—ye love not to look there;
On the grim smile of comfortless despair:
Your city saddens: loud though Revel howls,
Here Famine faints, and yonder Rapine prowls.

See all alike of more or less bereft;
No misers tremble when there's nothing left.
'Blest paper credit;' who shall dare to sing?
It clogs like lead Corruption's weary wing.
Yet Pallas pluck'd each premier by the ear,
Who gods and men alike disdain'd to hear;
But one, repentant o'er a bankrupt state,
On Pallas calls,—but calls, alas! too late:
Then raves for . . . ; to that Mentor bends,
Though he and Pallas never yet were friends.
Him senates hear, whom never yet they heard,
Contemptuous once, and now no less absurd.
So, once of yore, each reasonable frog
Swore faith and fealty to his sovereign 'log.'
Thus hailed your rulers their patrician clod,
As Egypt chose an onion for a god.

"Now fare ye well! enjoy your little hour;
Go, grasp the shadow of your vanish'd power;
Gloss o'er the failure of each fondest scheme;
Your strength a name, your bloated wealth a dream.
Gone is that gold, the marvel of mankind,
And pirates barter all that's left behind.
No more the hirelings, purchased near and far,
Crowd to the ranks of mercenary war.
The idle merchant on the useless quay
Droops o'er the bales no bark may bear away;
Or back returning, sees rejected stores
Rot piecemeal on his own encumber'd shores:
The starved mechanic breaks his rusting loom,
And desperate mans him 'gainst the coming doom.
Then in the senate of your sinking state
Show me the man whose counsels may have weight.
Vain is each voice where tones could once command;

E'en factions cease to charm a factious land:
Yet jarring sects convulse a sister isle,
And light with maddening hands the mutual pile.

" 'Tis done, 'tis past, since Pallas warns in vain;
The Furies seize her abdicated reign:
Wide o'er the realm they wave their kindling brands,
And wring her vitals with their fiery hands.
But one convulsive struggle still remains,
And Gaul shall weep ere Albion wear her chains.
The banner'd pomp of war, the glittering files,
O'er whose gay trappings stern Bellona smiles;
The brazen trump, the spirit-stirring drum,
That bid the foe defiance ere they come;
The hero bounding at his country's call,
The glorious death that consecrates his fall,
Swell the young heart with visionary charms,
And bid it antedate the joys of arms.
But know, a lesson you may yet be taught,
With death alone are laurels cheaply bought:
Not in the conflict Havoc seeks delight,
His day of mercy is the day of fight.
But when the field is fought, the battle won,
Though drench'd with gore, his woes are but begun:
His deeper deeds as yet ye know by name;
The slaughter'd peasant and the ravish'd dame,
The rifled mansion and the foe-reap'd field,
Ill suit with souls at home, untaught to yield. "

For some this so-called curse was indeed brought to bear on
Britain as it slowly lost its mastery of the world to its upstart former colony across the Atlantic, and not to mention England's
own deaths of a thousand cuts, as its world empire fell to the
wayside one colony at a time.

England indeed almost lost its own sovereignty in the twentieth century, but it would appear that the Greek gods concluded that the British Empire had suffered enough, and handing it over to the even more barbarous thieves of the Third Reich would never have been acceptable.

To say that the debate over who should have possession of the marbles is still going on is an understatement. An article in *The Scotsman* on March 28, 2008, heralded the headline RETURN ELGIN MARBLES AND LAY 'CURSE OF MINERVA' TO REST.

And the debate rages on.

———

British Museum
Great Russell Street
London
WC1B 3DG

———

American history is filled with miraculous events . . .
and some of them even involve religion.

An Illinois Revelation:
The Mormon Sunstone Capital

In the permanent collection of the Smithsonian Institution's National Museum of American History stands one of the most historically layered and mystifying artifacts of modern Western religious history: the 1844 Mormon Sunstone Capital. According to Mormon faith, this object, a two-and-a-half-ton limestone block engraved with the face of a beaming sun that towers over onlookers atop a pedestal, was designed by divine guidance as revealed through a Mormon patriarch shortly before his assassination. For years it held a sacred duty, bearing the weight of the grand Mormon temple in Nauvoo, Illinois. Amazingly, it also remained as one of only two quarried stones to survive three disasters of near biblical proportions.

Both the block's sun-carved face and the temple it adorned first took shape in the thoughts of pioneer and prophet Joseph Smith in a series of lifelong described revelations. Born in 1805 to farmer parents, Joseph Smith Jr. grew to adulthood at a curious time in the "Burned-Over District" of upstate New York.

While most of his neighbors and family members gravitated to the increasingly popular denominations that prospered during the Second Great Awakening, Smith forswore organized religion in favor of interpreting the Bible himself, with his rudimentary homeschool education. According to believers, while walking in the woods in the spring of 1820, he was visited by two divine aspects of Christian ethos, God the Father and Jesus Christ, who commanded Smith to restore the original intent of the Christian gospel to the world.

In 1823, an angel called Moroni, robed in white and with a "countenance truly like lightning,"[1] also appeared before Smith. Like the previous visitations, this one directed the farmer's son to unearth an ancient set of records (etched into gold plates) and translate them for all to read so they could know the hidden history of Christianity.

"My son Joseph has had revelations from God since he was a boy," his mother later recalled,

> and he is indeed a true prophet of Jehova. The angel of the Lord appeared to him fifteen years since, and showed him the cave where the original golden plates of the book of Mormon were deposited. . . . I have myself seen and handled the golden plates; they are about eight inches long, and six wide; some of them are sealed together and are not to be opened, and some of them are loose. They are all connected by a ring which passes through a hole at the end of each plate, and are covered with letters beautifying engraved.[2]

Over time Smith collected his early revelations and divinations into a single volume. In March 1830, Smith published this work as *The Book of Mormon: An Account Written by the Hand of Mormon upon Plates Taken from the Plates of Nephi,* and in the following month he founded the Church of Jesus Christ of Latter-Day Saints (LDS). By 1831, Joseph Smith had gathered an astonishingly large following in such a small amount of time;

he then created a headquarters in Kirtland, Ohio, to coordinate the activities of his followers. While missionary work remained at the forefront of the organization's priorities, a number of Mormons found great reward in building new communities, first, in Missouri (where revelations, Smith claimed, had shown him that Independence had been the original site of the Garden of Eden), and, second, in Illinois. The settlers in Illinois turned their city of Nauvoo (which was derived from a fictitious Hebrew word for "beauty")[3] into a thriving urban center through rigorous land acquisition, militarism, political control, and prophetic revelation; Mormon prosperity then fostered bitter enmity between the newcomers and the Independence residents. Discrimination, militarism, and mob violence rapidly poisoned the Mormons' paradise. When they were finally expelled from Missouri, many of the LDS members looked to Joseph Smith's Nauvoo for hope.

"The colonists changed the desert to an abode of plenty and richness," reported one observer.[4] There were broad streets, stores, houses, centers of industry, a trained militia (called the Nauvoo Legion), and gardens filled with flowers from across the country and around the world. Steamboats made regular passage through the area, discharging steady streams of passengers, supplies, and refined goods destined to become a part of this burgeoning community—underneath a towering, partially constructed limestone temple.

Claiming new revelations, Joseph Smith declared that the LDS would build temples, where they would await the arrival of the divine, in fulfillment of the biblical prophecy of Malachi 3:1. In the meantime the Mormons, Smith directed, would also restore the ancient practice of temple worship to his Christian sect by erecting formal houses of worship that would be the center of Mormon communal life. There the faithful would gather under the guidance of the Melchizedek priesthood to fast, pray, teach, learn, baptize new members (living and dead), and anoint and seal couples in celestial marriages.[5] The LDS church previously had erected a meager temple in Kirtland, Ohio. The one being raised in Nauvoo, Smith asserted, which was being paid for by a membership tithe, would be a far grander, divinely inspired work of Greek Revival architecture managed by Gentile (non-Mormon) architect William Weeks.

"I wish you to carry out my designs," said Smith to his workers. "I have seen in vision the splendid appearance of that building illuminated and will have it built according to the pattern shown me."[6]

On April 6, 1841, the cornerstone for the revealed temple was laid in place at Nauvoo. The new temple, improving upon the Kirtland edifice at 128 feet long and 88 feet wide, was designed to house a baptismal font 16-feet long by 12-feet wide by 4-feet deep and built out of tongue. Grooved white pine adorned with twelve sculpted oxen, it was set two steps above a sloped basement floor to improve drainage. The temple surrounding this centerpiece of Mormon worship was even more elaborate. Made of wood, plaster, and limestone that was quarried from an old streambed northwest of the city and another site farther downriver, two assembly halls were housed on the first floor. Another hall was laid out on the second floor (they were referred to as the lower and upper courts, respectively) for communal meetings. Spiral staircases joined the two levels unobtrusively in the corners of the structure.

More significant, the temple ornamentation contained symbolic reminders of different facets of their faith: The floors, of red brick laid out in a herringbone pattern, the white walls, and the thirty pilasters were each engraved with images of the Three Degrees of Glory, sun, the moon, and the stars.[7] The roof was set under a 165-foot-tall bell tower that was topped by a golden weather vane in the shape of the angel Moroni blowing a horn, through which flowed emanations to the faithful symbolic of the Three Degrees of Glory.[8]

Drawing from the Gospel of John's reference concerning the afterlife—"In my Father's house are many mansions" (John

14:2)—and Paul of Tarsus's Corinthian epistle—"There are also celestial bodies, and bodies terrestrial; but the glory of the celestial is one, and the glory of the terrestrial is another. There is one glory of the sun, and another glory of the moon and another glory of the stars: for one star different from another star in glory (1 Corinthians 15:40–41)[9]—Mormon theology describes three different levels of luminescence, or degrees of heaven.

They are:

1. The Celestial Kingdom: the most elevated degree of glory, symbolically represented by the sun (Sunstone), where the divine is surrounded by deceased Mormons who have been married and sealed in the temple and children who die before the age of eight.
2. The Terrestrial Kingdom: the second-most elevated degree, symbolically represented by the moon (Moonstone), where individuals reside who have died without law; who have received a testimony of Christ after death but had rejected it in life; and who are honorable individuals blinded by the wickedness of the material world.
3. The Telestial Kingdom: the lowest level of glorification, symbolically represented by groups of stars (Starstone), where the last to be resurrected live, having in life rejected the gospel, the testimony of Jesus, the prophets, and the everlasting covenant; as well as liars, adulterers, murderers, thieves, and those individuals who disregarded the divine's commandments.

Visiting the temple construction site with Joseph Smith on May 15, 1844, Josiah Quincy remembered, "Near the entrance to the temple we passed a workman who was laboring upon a huge sun, which he had chiseled from the solid rock. The countenance was of the Negroid type, and it was surrounded by the conventional rays.

" 'General Smith,' said the man, looking up from his task, 'is this like the face you saw in vision?'

"'Very near it,' answered the Prophet, 'except' (this was added with an air of careful connoisseurship that was quite overpowering) 'except that the nose is just a thought too broad.'"[10]

The first of thirty carved Sunstone Capitals, measuring four feet high, six feet wide, nineteen inches thick, and costing about three hundred dollars at the time, was placed on a pilaster circling the temple's limestone facade on September 23, 1844.[11] Each weighing two and a half tons and hoisted into place by a rudimentary wooden crane, these revelations-made-stone were chiseled out of quarried Illinois rock in five pieces (the abacus, the trumpet stone, the main body, the base stone, and the pilaster, respectively) and tailored to meet Smith's specifications.[12] The two handheld horns paralleled the actions of the representation of Moroni fixed atop the temple, reflecting the divine eminence in Smith's otherworldly visitations. Finally, the radiant sun face, depicted as emerging from the clouds of mortal life, signified the elevation of an individual's growth in divine awareness of the Celestial Kingdom and Joseph Smith's prophetic visions.

By 1840, Nauvoo had become the largest and most powerful town in Illinois, holding approximately fifteen thousand inhabitants.[13] Now thrown out of the paradise in Missouri, the Mormons attempted to create a new Zion in this celestially inspired and sacred Illinois city by revelation and mortal vigilance. On November 21, 1841, the Mormons held the first baptisms for the dead in the unfinished temple, but Smith quickly suspended the practice until the site could be completed. Once the building was finished, their prophet declared, he would reveal to the membership secrets hidden from the world before the founding of the world. Still, conditions were far from utopian, and the weight of the temple bore heavy on the Sunstone and the surrounding community. Cracks were beginning to appear everywhere, first metaphorically, then metaphysically, and then, before long, literally.

First, the city's rapid growth had drawn more than just Mormon pilgrims. Waves of described "housebreakers," thieves, and speculators arrived with each new ferry. While Smith was able to neutralize the underworld threat to the Mormons by encouraging many of them to join his local militia, the speculators, in competition for Mormon land, were less than enthusiastic to join in a communal/quasi-communistic society. As a result, Smith set in motion an organized system of intimidation to oust the problematic individuals.

"A proper sum would be offered for their improvements and land and if not accepted, then petty annoyances were resorted to," described one nineteenth-century historian. "One of these was called 'whittling off.' Three men would be deputed and paid for their time to take their jack-knives and sticks—down-east Yankees, of course—and sitting down before the obnoxious man's door, begin their whittling. When the man came out they would stare at him, but say nothing. If he went to market, they followed and whittled."[14]

When intimidation did not remove the potential threat, the Mormons resorted to taunts and curses: "Three days are said to have been the utmost that human nature could endure of this silent annoyance; the man came to terms, sold his possessions for what he could get, or emigrated to parts unknown."[15]

Next, Smith played the size of "his" city in the great game of Illinois politics. As the city and his followers grew, he endorsed certain state candidates for political office, gently advising his followers in the city and across the state to vote for this person, who had been revealed to Smith through more revelations.

When the city was serving as a minor Mississippi and Des Moine rivers outpost, the state authorities of Illinois had been content to let Joseph Smith run his little section of the state as independently as every other frontier urban center. Now able to influence state politics radically, Smith's new political revelations were seen as a clear and present geopolitical threat to the state.

"From this time forth," said later Illinois governor Thomas Ford, "the Whigs generally, and a part of the democrats, determined upon driving the Mormons out of the State; and everything connected with the Mormons too became political and was considered almost entirely with reference to party."[16]

Indeed, in February 1844, Joseph Smith Jr. announced his candidacy for the presidency of the United States. Political tensions rose markedly in Illinois after the Mormon expulsion from Missouri. Yet, the Illinois leadership's hands were plagued by their own morality. The state authority felt bound to uphold the law, and could only act against this perceived heretical Christian usurper if he violated the law. Bound by the written law of the land, the Illinois leadership was relegated to sitting, watching, and waiting for Smith to make a strategic error.

They did not have long to wait.

Stirred up by the Nauvoo Mormon intimidation tactics, as well as by Smith's recent foray into the political world, an organized anti-Mormon press rose to counter Smith's emergent geopolitical, economic, and religious designs. "Mormonism," wrote one detractor earlier, in June 1842, "needs but to be seen in its true light to be hated; and if the following pages, consisting almost exclusively of the personal testimony of the Author, should assist in awakening public indignation against a cruel delusion and a preposterous heresy, he will consider himself amply rewarded."[17]

Unlike previous circumstances, however, Smith's efforts at intimidation and even menacing of the anti-Mormons only served to encourage the opposition's efforts. Mobs formed on both sides. Stores were looted. Fires were set and, inevitably, once again, shots were exchanged between the two polarizing factions. As a result, in 1844 Joseph Smith was finally forced to resort to overt action to retain his unchecked power and the integrity of his Mormon domain. He declared martial law in Nauvoo, and called in the militia, *his* Nauvoo Legion, to suppress the dissonance.

While the militia was successful in expelling the opposition and protecting the Mormon Nauvoo infrastructure, the act of declaring martial law and resorting to militarized violence to evict his opponents played right into the Illinois state authorities' hands.

"When these ordinances were published," remembered one Illinois politician, "they created general astonishment. Many people began to believe in good earnest that the Mormons were about to set up a separate government for themselves in defiance of the laws of the state. Owners of property stolen in other counties, made pursuit into Nauvoo, and were fined by the Mormon courts for daring to seek their property in the holy country."[18]

Under the direction of the governor, on June 24, 1844, Joseph and his brother, Hyrum Smith, were promptly arrested. Three days later, however, before they could be brought to trial a lynch mob arrived at the site of the brothers' incarceration, broke into the jail, and riddled the bodies of both men with bullets.

In response to the murders, the citizenry of Nauvoo rose up almost as one. They desired retaliation tenfold for the taking away of their prophet, his visions, and their political leaders in one cruel act. Yet, while the surviving Mormon elders were confused about the order of succession to head the church, they were certain of at least one thing: An insurgency against the region's Gentiles would provoke an overwhelming armed reprisal from the surrounding countryside that would finish off the Mormon Church. Instead of calling for a wholesale slaughter of the Gentiles, Brigham Young, the eventual successor to Smith, and the other church elders, persuaded the roused populace toward a more temperate object, promising "the vengeance of heaven upon their enemies, but that they were not quite ripe enough for the vials of wrath to empty their torments upon them. Shortly, the pestilence, the fire, and the sword, would do their work."[19]

While Joseph Smith's divine revelations had apparently been transferred to Brigham Young, the long-promised revelations of Nauvoo did not unfold as the faithful expected. Before the temple could be completed, in September 1844, rumors reached the church elders claiming that individuals in the surrounding countryside were plotting to burn the wood needed to finish it. In response, night watchmen were posted at the site. Over the next several years a series of violent incidents erupted on temple grounds between the anxious guards and those who were passing by (including the shooting of someone mistaken for a trespasser). A late arrival of winter allowed the last Sunstone Capital to be affixed to the temple wall. Before work could continue, construction was halted until spring by the sudden fall of four inches of snow.

On February 8, 1846, Young and the church leadership dedicated the temple and sealed 2,420 Mormon couples in Celestial Marriage. Yet the cracks already forming in the temple walls were spreading. Worse, in an almost symbolic act, several of the temple doorways were warping under the weight of the heavy floors, hampering members' ingress.[20] The morning after the dedication a section of the roof accidentally caught fire when a hot stovepipe ignited a misplaced cloth. Later, during a Sunday meeting, the main floor of the church dropped suddenly and settled into place, causing a commotion and several injuries among service attendees. Although workers would continue to labor on their dead prophet's revelations at the site, with the temple now in use three months Brigham Young said that he had effectively completed the building Smith prophesied.

As tensions rose and the surrounding region increasingly grew populated with non-Mormons, Young acted on the best chance for the survival of the church, a westward move away from the Gentiles and into the disorganized desertlike territory of modern-day Utah. On April 30, 1846, he ordered all work on the temple to end. As the Mormons began their new exodus, several anti-Mormon mobs descended upon Nauvoo, occupied the city, removed most of the area's remaining Mormons forcibly, and desecrated the temple. One member of the mob reportedly shouted, "Peace! Peace! Peace! To the inhabitants of the earth, now the Mormons are driven!"[21]

Yet, the violence over Nauvoo and its grand temple was not yet at an end. One might say that, in the years that followed, the Nauvoo temple became a nexus for divine retribution.

While settling into his new home, Brigham Young and the church courted buyers, from private individuals to the Roman Catholic Church, but no one was willing pay a reasonable rate for the opulent edifice. In September 1848, lightning struck the temple, leaving a visible scar on the abandoned structure. Two months later a mysterious fire, which many locals speculated to be the work of arsonists, engulfed it.

"Although the morning was tolerably dark," reported one witness, "still, when the flames shot upwards, the spire, the streets and houses for nearly a mile distant were lighted up, so as to render even the smallest objects discernible. The glare of the vast torch, pointing skyward, indescribably contrasted with the universal gloom and darkness around it; and men looked on with faces sad as if the crumbling ruins below were consuming all their hopes."[22]

Only the four outer walls of the structure survived the blaze. Yet, they, too, served as testament to the brevity of Mormon physical temporality, and celestial vengeance. For, on May 27, 1850, a twister blew into Nauvoo and tore the structure to pieces. Upon hearing about the series of man-made and natural disasters, Brigham Young was reported to have remarked, "I hoped to see it burned before I left, but I did not. I was glad when I heard of its being destroyed by fire, and of the walls having fallen in, and said, 'Hell, you cannot now occupy it.'"[23]

In 1865 the ruins of the near-decade-long product of perceived divine revelation and labor was ordered demolished by the government. Before it could be truly razed to the ground, however, this surviving Sunstone Capital was loaded onto a barge and sailed downriver to Quincy, Illinois, where, in 1913, the stone became the property of the Historical Society of Quincy and Adams Counties. In 1989, the object inspired by Joseph Smith's visions and survivor of the most mysterious series of man-made and elemental events came into the possession of the

Smithsonian Institution for $100,000.[24] Safe from violence and the elements, this historic artifact of westward expansion remains a symbol of Mormon theology, a relic of religious faith made flesh, and a perceived mystical testament to the durability of Joseph Smith's vision.

National Museum of American History
Smithsonian Institution
On the National Mall
14th Street and Constitution Avenue NW
Washington, DC 20560

Paul Thomsen

Notes

1. Book of Mormon JS-H 1:32–33 scriptures.lds.org/en/bm/jstestimony
2. Henry Caswall, *The City of the Mormons; or, Three Days at Nauvoo, in 1842* (London: J. G. F. and J. Rivington, 1842), 27.
3. J. W. Gunnison, Lieutenant, *The Mormons, or Latter-Day Saints, in the Valley of the Great Salt Lake: A History of Their Rise and Progress, Peculiar Doctrines, Present Condition, and Prospects Derived from Personal Observation, During a Residence Among Them* (Philadelphia: J. B. Lippincott and Co., 1860), 115.
4. Ibid.
5. Ibid.
6. Lisle Brown, *Chronology of the Construction, Destruction and Reconstruction of the Nauvoo Temple.* Revised, February 2000. users.marshall.edu/~brown/nauvoo/nt-parent.html
7. historywired.si.edu/detail.cfm?ID=125
8. Brown, *Chronology.* users.marshall.edu/~brown/nauvoo/nt-parent.html
9. 1 Corinthians 15:40–41 and John 14:2, Bible, King James Version, Old and New Testaments, Apocrypha, Electronic Text Center, University of Virginia, etext.virginia.edu/kjv.browse.html

10. Benson Whittle, "The Sunstones of Nauvoo: An Interpretive Account of the Temple Capitals," *Sunstone: Mormon Experience, Scholarship, Issues, and Art* 123 (July 2002): 24.

11. historywired.si.edu/object.cfm?ID=125 and Brown, *Chronology*. users .marshall.edu/~brown/nauvoo/nt-parent.html

12. Whittle, "The Sunstones of Nauvoo," 19.

13. Alexander Campbell, *Delusions: An Analysis of the Book of Mormon; with an Examination of Its Internal and External Evidences, and a Refutation of Its Pretences to Divine Authority* (Boston: Benjamin H. Greene, 1832), 403.

14. Gunnison, *The Mormons, or Latter-Day Saints*, 116.

15. Ibid., 117.

16. Governor Thomas Ford, *A History of Illinois from Its Commencement as a State in 1814–1847 Containing a Full Account of the Black Hawk War, the Rise, Progress and Fall of Mormonism, the Alton and Lovejoy Riots, and Other Important and Interesting Events* (Chicago: S. C. Griggs & Co., 1854), 319.

17. Caswall, *The City of the Mormons*, 1.

18. Ford, *A History of Illinois*, 320.

19. Gunnison, *The Mormons, or Latter-Day Saints*, 127.

20. Brown, *Chronology*. users.marshall.edu/~brown/nauvoo/nt-parent.html

21. Ibid.

22. Ibid.

23. Ibid.

24. contentdm.byu.edu/cdm4/item_viewer.php?CISOROOT=/RelEd& CISOPTR=2499&CISOBOX=1&REC=20

*And of course not all discoveries of natural history
turn out to be true or even natural.*

The Cardiff Giant

*In ancient days as we are told
Noah marched the animals into the fold,
Then closed the door of hickory bark,
Of which material he made the ark.*

*He shipped a man of monst'rous size,
Who was noted for his wond'rous lies.
There was but one of his race to be found,
And he was so wicked Noah had him bound.*

*After three days amid the flood,
Noah called the man of Giant blood,
And brought him on the dock of his ship,
As he wished to talk to his Giantship.*

*"Pooh!" said the Giant, "the water ain't deep."
(This like most of his lies was rather steep.)*

Noah said, "it was both," he could make it plain,
It was over the head of this monst'rous man.

"Noah! won't you believe?" The Giant was mad;
He would show him the truth of what he said.
So into the water he jumped with a thud—
Went down to the bottom—and stuck in the mud!

The flood subsided, and on Time flew.
Of the Giant that drowned, no man ever knew
Until the matter was lately made clear,
By a man at Cardiff, not far from here.

One day as he was digging a well,
He struck something hard—what it was he couldn't tell;
So he dug all around and there he found
A monstrous man stuck fast in the ground.

Soon threw [sic] the country the news it flew,
And people flocked round the Giant [illegible].
Some were dubious, and others would tell,
That someone had made it to get up a sell.

But the wise believe this story they say,
He was a Giant of Noah's day
Who sunk to the bottom and got stuck in the clay
Because he was stubborn, and would have his own way.

                                        —L. Frank Baum

Nestled amid barns and brick buildings that re-create a nineteenth-century village in upstate New York, a curiosity lies in a hole in the ground. People walk up to the edge and peer down at the stone figure at the bottom. Larger than life, it sits, gray and weather-beaten, a silent testament to an earlier era. The features are rough and one can only guess what sort of expression it displays. Those with fanciful imaginations can clearly hear a voice cry out to the throngs:

Ladies and gentlemen, boys and girls. Step right up and take a close look at the last giant to have walked the earth. He's ten feet tall if he's an inch and was found right here in Cardiff. Step right up, buy a ticket, and take a look.

A barker must have called something like this in 1869 after two men, digging a well on William C. "Stub" Newell's property, encountered the petrified remains of a giant. Once word spread, everyone wanted to come and see for themselves, with Newell charging a modest fee for the privilege.

"The roads were crowded with buggies, carriages, and even omnibuses from the city, and with lumber-wagons from the farms—all laden with passengers. . . . [We] found a gathering which at first sight seemed like a country fair. In the midst was a tent and a crowd was pressing for admission. Entering, we saw a large pit, or grave, and, at the bottom of it . . . an enormous figure. . . . It had a color as if it had lain long in the earth, and over its surface were minute punctures, like pores. . . . Lying in its grave, with the subdued light from the roof of the tent falling upon it, and with the limbs contorted as if in a death struggle, it produced a most weird effect. An air of great solemnity pervaded the place. Visitors hardly spoke above a whisper," wrote Andrew Dickson White, cofounder of Cornell University.

A poster advertising the find declared the following specifications:

HIS DIMENSIONS.
Length of Body, 10 feet, 4½ inches.
Length of Head from Chin to Top of Head, 21 inches.
Length of Nose, 6 inches.
Across the Nostrils, 3½ inches.
Width of Mouth, 5 inches.
Circumference of Neck, 37 inches.

Shoulders, from point to point, 3 feet, 1½ inches.

Length of Right Arm, 4 feet, 9½ inches.

Across the Wrist, 5 inches.

Across the Palm of Hand, 7 inches.

Length of Second Finger, 8 inches.

Around the Thighs, 6 feet, 3½ inches.

Diameter of the Thigh, 13 inches.

Through the Calf of Leg, 9½ inches.

Length of Foot, 21 inches.

Across the Ball of Foot, 8 inches.

Weight, 2990 pounds.

Geological Hall, Albany, November 29th, 1869

Over time, though, the Cardiff Giant's origins were exposed and the world learned of what has come to be called the "greatest hoax of all time."

It all began with an argument over religion. Tobacconist George Hull, an atheist, got into a heated debate with Turk, a fundamentalist minister. Turk, it seems, believed the Bible to be literal, including the notion that giants once lived among us. Hull couldn't believe that people in the modern age could believe such nonsense.

Not all that long before, Hull had heard of a report in a newspaper, *Alta California*, of a prospector who had been petrified after drinking the liquid found in a geode. The report turned out to be a hoax, but other papers around the country had reports of similar finds. So inspired, in 1868 he hired people in Fort Dodge, Iowa, to carve a 10-foot-long, 4½-inch-thick block of gypsum. The stonemasons thought they were helping create a statue of the recently deceased president, Abraham Lincoln. The block traveled east to Chicago, where Hull then hired a German stonecutter to shape it into a human form. The artisan used various liquids to age the stone so that it would appear ancient. Next, to further the aging, he beat the statue with steel knitting needles embedded in a board. Having chosen his cousin William Newell's Cardiff, New

York, farm, Hull had the statue shipped by rail, having now invested $2,600. The next investment was time.

After waiting a year he hired two local men to dig a well on the farm, despite the questionable location for such a project. As a result, on October 16, 1869, the innocent workers found the statue, saying, "I declare, some old Indian has been buried here!"

Such a find was sure to cause a sensation, and it did, as people flocked from all around the state to take a look. Newell began charging a dime a peek, and then upped the price a mere two days later to two bits in response to the growing demand.

Amid the gawkers were the skeptics who couldn't believe the Newell Giant was really a fossilized human being. There were those who said it had to be a statue, perhaps, as suggested by Dr. John F. Boynton, one given by a Jesuit missionary to impress local Native American tribes in the seventeenth century. The "petrifactionists," as they were known, said it proved the accuracy of Genesis 6:4: "There were giants in the earth in those days."

Regardless of the speculation, more and more came to Giantville, as the farm was dubbed. The head count averaged nearly five hundred people daily, earning Hull an estimated $30,000, and he wasn't the only one to see the profit inherent in such a find. A syndicate out of Syracuse, headed by David Hannum, quickly offered Newell $37,500 for a three-quarters interest, clearly turning Hull's investment into a huge profit.

The Giant left Cardiff and was relocated to Syracuse, and as people ponied up hard-earned cash to look, more sophisticated analysis proved it to be a hoax. Chisel marks were noted by authorities. Yale paleontologist Othniel C. Marsh not only declared it a hoax, but also a humbug, using the term coined decades earlier by Charles Dickens. When Marsh died in 1899, *The New York Times* paused to recall the hoax, and noted that it had taken Marsh all of ten minutes to make his declaration.

When confronted Newell and Hull admitted the truth, on December 10. Even when word spread people were willing to pay to see the statue, now nicknamed "Old Hoaxey."

As word continued to crisscross the country, it acted as a siren song to Phineas T. Barnum. The world's greatest showman offered to buy the statue from the syndicate, according to his memoirs. He had publicly declared his intention to just rent the stone man for three months. Either way, his $60,000 offered was rebuffed and, infuriated, he promptly returned to New York City. He commissioned someone to craft a wax mold, and then a plaster replica of the false man was created.

With completely straight face he declared to those paying admission that they were about to feast their eyes on the one, true Cardiff Giant, not the fake up in Syracuse. An incredulous Hannum heard of Barnum's success and told the press, "There's a sucker born every minute." The classic line was repeated again and again, and in time was erroneously attributed to Barnum.

The owners of the true fake man sued and were countersued in turn.

At one point a judge told Hannum to have his giant declare itself the genuine fake. Finally, a reasonable judge, on February 2, 1870, declared that since both were fakes he was tossing both suits.

There were several suits involving the Giant, including one filed in Boston, nowhere near it. For example, the May 11, 1874, edition of *The New York Times* reported a libel suit being filed against the *Boston Herald*. C. O. Gott of Fitchburg, Massachusetts, then the owner of the statue, said the *Herald*'s story from the previous year had claimed that the statue had been sold for a mere eight dollars in New Orleans. The November 1873 *Herald* article went on to say that the alleged sale

recalls the palmy days of that ingenuous humbug. We well remember the learned remarks made by connoisseurs in this city, when it was exhibited in a vacant store quite near our office. While the vulgar herd looked on in silence, seeing a colossal figure which excited their curiosity but which they did not attempt to explain, the Harvard professors, and other

learned men traced its pedigree by their knowledge of artistic
history, and constructed theories as to its origin which at once
displayed their erudition and helped to sell the "show." But
our professors and learned men were not the only victims of
the sell. A distinguished professor of Yale [Reverend Alexander McWhorter] discoursed learnedly upon it in the *Galaxy*
magazine. He demonstrated beyond a doubt that the statue
was authentic, that it was antique, and that it was a colossal
monolith. He ciphered it down that it was a Phoenician image
of the god Baal and found no difficulty in proving to his own
satisfaction that it was brought to America by a Phoenician
band of adventurers who sailed in one of the "ships of Tarshsh"
and that it was buried by the isolated to save it from being des-
ecration [*sic*] by the hordes of savages who overpowered and
destroyed the Phoenicians. He accounted for several marks and
symbols upon the image which were unmistakably Phoenician.
Not long afterward the man who brought the "colossal monolith" to light confessed that it was a fraud, and the learned gentlemen who had indorsed [*sic*] its authenticity were left as
naked as the statue itself.

That particular lawsuit was settled quietly.

The fakes proved popular enough to inspire other fakes over
the years, beginning with 1876's Solid Muldoon, supposedly
found in Beulah, Colorado.

Also inspired were the authors of the day, starting with Mark
Twain, who turned the Giant into a character in his 1870 work
"A Ghost Story." There, the real Giant pays a visit to haunt the
Barnum replica. A year later L. Frank Baum wrote the poem
quoted earlier, "The True Origin of the Cardiff Giant," pub-
lished in *The Rose Lawn Home Journal* (volume 1, number 3).
His most recent fictional appearance was in Stephen King's
From a Buick 8.

Along with the lawsuits being tossed, public interest also
waned, and the syndicate sold the statue. In fact, it was sold

multiple times, being relocated with each sale. When it was displayed at the 1901 Pan-American Exposition, it hardly generated a ripple. Later it wound up owned by an Iowa publisher, who kept it as an oddity in his home. Eventually he sold it, after much bargaining, to the New York State Historical Association for thirty thousand dollars. In May 1948, it was installed at the Farmers' Museum in Cooperstown, New York, near that other museum, the Baseball Hall of Fame.

Barnum's replica has also survived, and tourists can find it at Marvin's Marvelous Mechanical Museum in Farmington Hills, Michigan.

Farmers' Museum
5775 State Highway 80 (Lake Road)
Cooperstown, NY 13326

Robert Greenberger

In a less open-minded time, one man's lifestyle or culture could easily become someone else's attraction or specimen.

The 1897
Living Eskimo Exhibit

Sir Martin Frobisher, seeking a Northwest passage on behalf of England in 1576, was the first man to explore the Arctic extensively. He went on three separate expeditions during which he kidnapped two of the Inuit and brought them back to England. Thus began a trend of using Native American people as artifacts, to put them on display for the curious.

The trend continued into the early twentieth century, with mostly bad results. Perhaps the most notorious such story was the case of Minik, the young boy kept on display at New York's American Museum of Natural History.

One would expect famed explorer Robert Peary to have treated the people he studied better, but that was not the case. Peary initially arrived in Greenland in search of Inuit who could help him get to the North Pole. His hunger for fame led him to the Inughuit, the northernmost band of Inuit on the land. He also traveled carrying a note from anthropologist Franz Boas. The leading scientist at the American Museum of Natural

History had petitioned the explorer to bring at least one Eskimo to stay in America over the winter.

Peary, over time, had employed members of the Inughuit on his expeditions, so in 1897 he decided to try to entice members of the tribe, housed at Qaanaaq, Greenland, to come to New York with him. Peary promised that they would come home after a short time and some accepted, because they were curious to see the world. Others came unwillingly, reluctant to be parted from their families. He never indicated that they would be objects of study, essentially living specimens no different than the animals caged at the Bronx Zoo.

The press, the curious, and other onlookers greeted his ship when it docked, all craning their heads for a glimpse of the three men, a woman, and two children, a boy and a girl. The sextet was whisked away to their new home, the museum's basement, which provided little that would allow them to learn about the city.

While poked, prodded, and observed, the Eskimo suffered, with four of the six dying from tuberculosis within a year. One survivor, the little girl, was shipped back to Greenland, while Minik was adopted by a museum officer.

Minik was only six when he came to America. When his father, Qisuk, died from disease along with Nuktaq, Atangana, and Aviaq, the little boy begged his captors for the right to give his father a proper burial. He alone knew the right rituals, but the officials had other plans for the body. Instead, they filled a coffin with stones and a stuffed dummy and staged a fake burial. Minik attended the service, which occurred by lantern light, the shadows helping to cover up the indignity.

As for Qisuk's corpse, it was autopsied, with the brain being pickled "in the interests of science." The body then went to William Wallace, the museum's superintendent of buildings and chief curator. Wallace ran a workshop, a "bone house," to have all four of the Inuit skeletons cleaned off. Once complete, they were returned to the museum and were stored.

Wallace adopted Minik and never told the six-year-old what had become of his father's body. In 1906, though, word reached the newspapers and Minik discovered the shocking truth when he heard of it from classmates. An upset young man demanded his father's bones, and Wallace finally agreed. Museum director Hermon Carey Bumpus, who hated Wallace, refused the request, and went so far as to never admit to having possession of the bones, despite reports to the contrary.

Overall, Minik briefly had enjoyed a middle-class existence, until the Wallace family sank into financial ruin after financial irregularities and accusations of impropriety were revealed in 1901. Wallace's wife left him and his biological son was sent to live with relatives; Wallace and Minik were reduced to living in a tenement. Wallace continually asked Bumpus for financial help in raising the boy, but was rebuffed each time. Bumpus never wanted to draw attention to the shoddy care given the living exhibits under his watch.

Minik wanted to go home, and Peary refused to pay, so a Manhattan lawyer took up his cause, calling it a national disgrace. Here was Peary raising more than $100,000 for his next Arctic expedition, but no funds could be spared for the boy he had transported half a world from home. Surprisingly, President Theodore Roosevelt, a naturalist, refused to apply pressure on Peary or contribute funds to help the youth. When Peary was ready to travel in 1909, Roosevelt asked him to bring the boy. Peary rejected the request, claiming his boat was already crowded. The truth was, the publicity-mad explorer didn't want to lose time to a rival expedition.

Determined to find a way home, Minik set out on foot, writing letters from Canada. His cause was not forgotten, and seeking to protect her husband's reputation, Peary's wife finally arranged Minik's passage back to Greenland. She did this while extracting a promise from the lad never to return.

Peary made a great show of saying Minik was being returned home "laden with gifts," but apparently that was far from the truth. Research later proved he arrived in Greenland with little more than his clothing.

The youth finally made his way back home, only to discover he needed to relearn the language and customs of his people. It was a tough assimilation, but he worked hard and managed to be reaccepted. In fact, he became respected for his hunting skills, and worked as both a guide and translator for tourists. In 1913, he was hired by the American Museum of Natural History to act as the guide for what became known as the ill-fated Crocker Land Expedition. The party was in search of the island known as Crocker Land, but they were ill equipped and undisciplined, which led to more disasters than research. The group did not finally return home, without Minik, until four years later.

Working once more with Americans helped the young man decide to return to America, a fateful decision that led to his death a mere two years later, on October 29, 1918, a victim of the great influenza epidemic. When he arrived back in America, he headed north, becoming, among other things, a lumberjack in North Stratford, New Hampshire. At the lumber camp he was practically adopted by his employer, Afton Hall. Minik came to live with the Hall family until the epidemic took many lives in the home.

He was buried in Pittsburg, New Hampshire's Indian Stream Cemetery.

As for Qisuk's bones, they did not lie forgotten. Canadian writer Kenn Harper first became interested in Minik's short life around 1977, when he was living in Qaanaaq. Many outlandish embellishments had been given to the boy's story, so Harper set out to uncover the truth, and he told Minik's story in *Give Me My Father's Body*, first published in 1986. His research brought him to New York, where members of the Explorers Club gave him the cold shoulder, but he did access Peary's papers, which contained quite a bit of information about the boy. The book was a dispassionate review of what occurred, complete with newspaper article clippings, some of Minik's correspondence, and many photos from the era. Harper began a public campaign to force the museum to release the bones. At first the museum officials wouldn't budge, embarrassed by their predecessors. Finally, though, they relented, and then Harper helped work through two countries' worth of red tape before all the bones were returned to Greenland. They were given a proper burial and service in 1993.

There, a small plaque reading NUNAMINGNUT UTEQIHUT (They Are Home) marks their graves.

The story has refused to die, and a 2000 edition was printed with a foreword by Kevin Spacey, who optioned the book for a film that has never materialized. "When you get to the end of a great story, there comes a moment of silence," he wrote. "The lights in the theatre come up, or you turn the last page in a book as good as this one, and you sit stunned. There is nothing to say. And in the next heartbeat, you think of a million things to say."

Since that time museums have been more sensitive to the living who have participated in collections and research. Minik's story certainly helped in that change. These days, though, there's a global wave of countries insisting that their artifacts be brought back to their place of origin.

One such claim was settled in 2006 and brought Minik's story back to mind. The British Museum finally returned the remains of several Aborigines to Australia some 160 years after they were first obtained.

George Augustus Robinson, the chief protector of Aborigines in the Port Phillip district of Tasmania, obtained the bundles of ashes in 1838. They were wrapped in animal skin and used as talismans by the natives to ward off sickness. Robinson apparently took the bundles from very ill and dying Aborigines with little thought as to the impact of his actions. Had the bundles remained, they would have been buried with the bodies of the ill.

The London museum acquired the remains in 1882 from the Royal College of Surgeons. It took twenty years of wrangling for

Britain to finally agree that it was appropriate to return them. A law passed in 2005, allowing public museums to return ancestral remains, paved the way for a final deal.

Eight other British institutions, including the British Natural History Museum, had Aboriginal items that were the subject of demands that they be returned to Australia.

American Museum of Natural History
Central Park West at West 79th Street
New York, NY 10024

Robert Greenberger

Sometimes we have to ask the question "why did they kill?" and all too rarely we are not talking about humans.

Man-Eaters at the Museum: The Lions That Stopped a Railroad

The story of the man-eaters of Tsavo is by far the most remarkable account of which we have any record.

—Theodore Roosevelt

A chill runs down your spine, up your leg, and through your bones the first time you come face-to-face with a Tsavo lion.

I'm not kidding.

It's an instant reaction, a distinctly eerie feeling when you are in the presence of the four-hundred-pound, ten-foot eater of men. Even if it is stuffed and motionless, when you come eyeball to eyeball you get the sense that this huge, powerful predator is, even without the telltale sign of a mane, owner of the moniker "king of the jungle." In short, he can knock your lights out!

His body is sculptured—every muscle contoured to his bone. His hair is short. Not even a mane to slow his pace, his prowl. He is cunning. He is lean. He is mean. He is a killing machine. Workers on the Kenya-Uganda Railway at the turn of the twentieth century witnessed this lion's power firsthand. Two lions are thought to have attacked and killed at least 135 men, 28 of them working for the railroad, and the others unfortunate and uncounted Africans. The lions were named Ghost and Darkness. The workers called them prowling devils.

The two Tsavo lions at the Field Museum in Chicago had a very aggressive, violent, downright brutal past. They struck fear in the hearts of countless men building a bridge for the Uganda Railway in East Africa in 1898. Thousands of Indians and Africans were hired as artisans and laborers. Their job was to link east to west and end at Lake Victoria. The operation came to a screeching halt at Lake Tsavo in Kenya. This part of the job involved bridging the Tsavo River, which ran north to south. The skilled workers were signed up in India and Pakistan before making the journey to Africa. Workers there joined them at the site. All of them signed up for an adventure that some would pay for with their lives.

The two Tsavo lions had a different plan. They had no interest in bridging north and south, east and west, or in expanding commerce in the tropics. What they wanted was an easy target, a meal they barely had to work for. And in this campsite of three thousand men, running two to three miles north and south on each side of this river, the lions Darkness and Ghost acted like they had found what the chief engineer on the project would call "their own personal manna from heaven."

The Ghost and the Darkness

The story is a terrifying one. It got Hollywood's attention. In 1996 Paramount released the movie *The Ghost and the Darkness*. The movie was criticized for not holding strictly to the truth of what happened. On many counts the movie, starring Michael Douglas and Val Kilmer, did not portray the actual events.

The inaccuracies in the script included where it was filmed, in South Africa and not Kenya, where nature placed the Tsavo

River. There are other inconsistencies, including what the lions looked like. The real lions had no manes. And the protagonist was manufactured. In the movie, American big-game hunter Charles Remington (Michael Douglas), who headed to Africa to save the frightened workers, is the hero who hunts and kills the Tsavo lions, but he didn't exist in real life. Actor Val Kilmer played the real-life protagonist, Lieutenant Colonel John Henry Patterson, though his role did not live up to the profoundly influential one Patterson played in 1898.

Lieutenant Colonel John Henry Patterson

Lieutenant Colonel John Henry Patterson was the chief engineer on the bridge project of the Uganda Railway construction. He tracked, hunted, and stalked Darkness and Ghost over the course of nine months, from the first attack on the campsite to the final shooting of the second lion. Truthfully, he was not very well liked by many of the camp workers. Maybe it was his rigid, portraitlike demeanor; I'm just guessing here. Nevertheless, he was a British military man who was an excellent marksman. And after his heroics, he was forever revered by many who had been frightened to the core by the two animals that were terrorizing them, and ran them from their jobs, vowing never to come back unless the lions were gone. In the Africa Protectorate, Patterson was the superhero of 1898.

Nine-Month Reign of Terror

Darkness and Ghost were responsible for a nine-month reign of terror. Thousands of workers were camped along both banks of the Tsavo River. Those thousands of workers would go to bed each night fearing the attack of the man-eaters. They had good reason. At first the workers didn't know what was going on. Later there would be an all-out hunt for the killer animals. The Tsavo lions would prove to be too cunning, too strong for most of the men. Scores and scores of workers fled in fear, vowing not to come back until the lions were killed. The two beasts shut down the building of the Uganda Railway. Lieutenant Colonel Patterson would kill the lions eventually. But what brought him and his workers to that point chilled them to the bone, as they were the prey for two lions that nightly had their pick of the campsite. This story begins in March of that fateful year.

During the course of nine months, the two Tsavo lions attacked and ate at least 135 workers. Some say as many as 144. What brought these lions to become the stalkers and eaters of men? Why were the workers so helpless and at the animals' whim? Why do these lions not have a mane like other lions? We'll answer those questions. And we'll tell you why the workers referred to the animals as devils. And why they ran in fear from their jobs and their livelihoods. The story unfolds on the first floor of the Field Museum.

The Tsavo Sideshow

As you walk into the museum, the lions are not on display for immediate viewing like Sue, the largest, most complete *T. Rex* ever, anywhere. Sue is placed prominently on the south end, as you enter this palace of a museum in Chicago. Sue stands on a stage on the marble floor and reaches toward a ceiling that seems to top off at heaven's gate. The Tsavo lions are not placed in this kind of a showcase. There are no big, bold, lettered signs telling you how to get to the lion exhibit. I can't say that these lions are hidden, but they are an interesting sideshow to the larger extinct-animals exhibit here. Interesting, because that's exactly how they would have felt comfortable in real life—apart from the main stage, watching, prowling, and waiting to pounce.

You can find the Tsavo lions in a side room on the first floor. The lions are in a glass case in the west wing in the Rice Wildlife Research Center. They are next to the African antelopes and other wildlife. It's quiet here, not unlike the quiet the railway workers might have felt on those dark nights so long ago. The Tsavo lions are speechless today, much like they were more than a century ago, when they were quietly stalking before grabbing their victims. You do get a hint, here in this dark corner of the museum, of what it must have been like for the men who were the prey of the beasts, the men who were picked off one by one, night after night, until finally they ran in fear, stopping production of the railway altogether.

The First Attacks

It's 1898. Thousands of men are camped along the river and nearby work sites. They are grateful for a night of rest after working long hours in the hot sun. While the dark skin on these men may not show the full effects of the sun, the heat is draining them of their strength; their bodies lay resting happily on the cool ground. The silent night of rest is shattered with a cry in the darkness. A brutal scream and a ruckus in one of the tents arouse some of the men. But most of them are too tired to get up and investigate what brought the screams. It would be another night and another attack before the workers fully understood what had happened. They would learn soon that they were no match for the "prowling devils."

The next morning an investigation turned up nothing of note. Lieutenant Colonel J. H. Patterson heard from a few of the workers that a lion was responsible. Lieutenant Colonel Patterson did what any warm-blooded British regent would do— yeah, he disregarded the stories of the workers and assumed that the first, and even the second, missing worker was a victim of foul play. He was probably robbed of his rupees and then murdered, discarded out of the campsite, thought Patterson. Nothing would be further from the truth. And one morning, after another vicious attack, Lieutenant Colonel Patterson learned of the real problem firsthand, when one of his first hands, a platoon commander, met his fate.

The Death of Ungan Singh

It was dawn. Lieutenant Colonel Patterson was awakened by the terrified voice of a worker who was actually in the commander's tent when the lion stealthily pushed his head inside and snatched the Sikh, named Ungan Singh. Through the worker's gasps and gulps, the scenario became clear. Without wasting a moment, the lieutenant colonel grabbed his shotgun and headed toward the commander's campsite. He found the evidence he needed to size things up. Pug marks were visible in the sand. There was a trail of dragged feet leading away from the tent. He heard from an eyewitness, who said that his heart had turned to water at the sight of the lion that had invaded their canvas home. He was face-to-face with the Tsavo lion. And unlike our own encounter in the museum, this was the real deal. He had frozen in fear and watched the lion grab the commander by the throat. The officer struggled with the powerful beast all while he lay stunned in silence and gripped in terror. The officer cried out, "Let Go!" and grabbed at the huge animal. The struggle continued outside the tent. It was a fight to the finish. But, he would implore the lieutenant colonel, what chance would a human have against the lion?

That scene would play out over and over and over again. The lions grew in confidence as each kill was made. It seemed as if the kings of this jungle were toying with the workers, attacking at one side of the camp one night, another side another night—using the workers as food just as we would pick an apple from a tree. It was dehumanizing and terrorizing. No one knew where Darkness and Ghost would attack next. The British military leader would say that the two treated the thousands of workers as if they were a personal gift from God—food given to the lions that had only to choose a victim, stalk, pounce, and eat.

Nightly Terror Continues

Nightly the workers were alerted to the pair of beasts, as they heard the ferocious roars. At first from a distance, and then closer and closer the lions would creep toward the campsites, their roars getting louder and louder as they approached. And then, nothing. Quiet. The quiet was terrifying. All knew the lions had their sights set on their next meal. The Tsavo rulers were stalking in complete silence now. This is the part that was so terrifying. The workers knew the man-eaters had decided on their prey and were now stalking, waiting for the kill. The quiet would last anywhere from one to two hours, enough time for the campers to use their imaginations to wear down the nerve next to their chilling bones. They were sitting ducks for the powerful devils they imagined them to be. Then, the attack.

All at once you would hear uproar: cries of terror in the night. Which campsite held the latest victim? Whatever campsite it was, Lieutenant Colonel Patterson headed that way, armed with a rifle and a shotgun. He had both a .303 caliber and a 12-bore shotgun. The .303 was relatively new; it was developed just ten years before, using a black powder round. The shotgun was a popular firearm used for hunting—this one would fire and then spray pellets. Both tools would eventually prove useful in lion hunting.

Nightly the lieutenant colonel would head immediately to the site of the latest attack. He'd camp there and wait for the next attack. He would remark in his book, *The Man-Eating Lions of Tsavo*, Patterson's account of the horror, that it was almost as if the lions knew where he was and would next attack on campsite just across the river. Patterson many times would camp in a nearby tree and sit awake, waiting for the man-eaters. But every time the lions chose a different campsite for their next victim. The lieutenant colonel remarked that he was beginning to feel like the lions were watching him, playing with him, choosing a campsite farther away from him so as to avoid his powerful arms. Were they that intuitive? This hunter believed they were.

Fast forward. Today, at the Field Museum of Chicago, there is another Patterson who has felt the magnificence of a Tsavo lion. He is a scientist. His name is Bruce Patterson. Ironically, there is no known familial relationship between the two. But clearly they share an interest in the wild beasts. Dr. Patterson is the MacArthur Curator of Mammals in the Field Museum's Department of Zoology. He's been studying the Tsavo lions for ten years. When I asked him what he felt for the beasts, he simply said: "Respect." And then there was a long pause. He said you have to respect an animal that can kill you with a swat of his paw. He studies the lions periodically in their home of Tsavo, but more regularly in his office in Chicago.

Bad Teeth

Now, to answer some of those questions. Why did the Tsavo lions become man-eaters? Why don't they have manes like other lions do?

As to why the workers were so helpless against the beasts, we have already seen how the lions caused them to be paralyzed in fear. Their only recourse was to run. Here's the shocker of this article: Dr. Patterson says the Tsavo lions probably became man-eaters because they had bad teeth.

That's right.

They needed a dentist.

How eerie, nonsensical, and downright sad, to say the least, that something as simple as bad teeth could lead to the deaths of so many men. Dr. Patterson says the lions' mouth problems, along with a disease in the region, combined to become the perfect storm for this tragedy.

Dr. Patterson looked at the skulls and mandibles of the Tsavo lions. One of the man-eaters had broken a lower canine at least two years before, judging from the wear and rearrangement of the remaining teeth. As Dr. Patterson describes it, "This damage had opened the tooth's pulp cavity to infection, and x-rays revealed a root-tip abscess, which would have made any pressure on the tooth extremely painful." That meant no killer bite. According to Dr. Patterson, the lions were not successful hunters of big game, such as buffalo and zebra. And without a killer bite, humans became more attractive prey. The second lion, according to Patterson, had some minor teeth problems, and he says this lion was probably mostly guilty by association.

So one of the lions had bad teeth. This hunting team turned their attention to humans. They couldn't attack big game successfully; what about smaller prey? According to Dr. Patterson, a drought and a wildlife disease in the region wiped out many of the animals near Tsavo. Alternate, smaller prey were not available to the lions. It was then that the railroad crews arrived in Tsavo. The timing couldn't have been more unfortunate. It was a very unfortunate perfect storm for the workers on the Uganda Railway.

Maneless Man-Eater

Why didn't the man-eaters have manes? The fact that they looked mysteriously different from other lions made some of the workers wonder if they were really devils—these lions with no hair. Why were these violent animals maneless? Did it have anything to do with the reign of terror they visited on the workers?

As it turns out, the answer to that question is no. Whether a lion has a mane is more probably linked to climate. That's the finding of Dr. Patterson, as he published in the *Journal of Mammalogy* in April 2006. The Tsavo lions live in the tropics of Africa—at low elevations, a very warm climate. Dr. Patterson says, after a study of zoo animals all across America, it's the cold temperatures that help the king of beasts grow a longer and thicker mane. But, he says, take that animal out of the colder zone and put him in a place like Tsavo, and he, too, will lose the thickness and growth of his mane. So it is local circumstance that made the lions maneless. It had nothing to do with background, history, special powers, or special evilness. No, it had only to do with temperature. To quote the research done by Dr. Patterson and reported by the Field Museum, "Dense manes

retard heat loss as would a scarf or fur hat. Zoo lions in hot cli-
mates adapt with smaller, thinner manes."

The Tables Turn

Now, back to our drama of 1898. The maneless and man-eating
Darkness and Ghost had their own killing fields. The workers
were paralyzed by fear. The workers did what any red-blooded
worker would do when his life was in jeopardy on the job. No,
they didn't form a union. They ran away. Many hopped a supply
train back to the coast. They vowed not to come back until the lions were trapped and killed. The head of the operation had a bigger problem on his hands: He had to answer to the British
government. How did the tables turn? How did man come out the
winner in this tropical nightmare? All the credit goes to the
hunter, Lieutenant Colonel Patterson, who finally shot and killed
both animals. The first victory came after many near misses.

It was tough to track the brutal beasts. By now the fame of the
man-eaters had spread around the country and beyond. Scores of
police from Africa, India, and Britain descended on Tsavo to help
in the hunt for the killers. Men kept watch in trees near the
mostly empty campsites. A makeshift cage was used to try to trap
them, but to no avail. Once one of the lions actually did make it
to the cage, but the soldiers guarding it were so frightened, they
fired randomly, and the shots succeeded in freeing the animal accidentally. In due time the extra men on hand to help dwindled.
Many were called back to their jobs. Now Lieutenant Colonel
Patterson was mostly on his own. He had to use his own cunning
against the man-eaters. Eventually he would take them down. But
not without more trials and tribulations.

There was the time when Patterson planned a distraction to
corner his prey. He had some men gather tin pans and pots to
make a continuous loud, distracting noise. When they did, the
lion came out of its lair, slowly and cautiously. Behind the lion
stood Patterson. But for circumstantial reasons, he was carrying

the rifle of a friend. This proved to be a mistake. Patterson drew the rifle, pulled the trigger, and snap. Nothing. The gun did not fire. Luckily the lion was distracted by the noise of the pots and pans; otherwise, this story would never have been written—at least, not by Patterson.

It finally happened. One day the British hunter found a dead donkey, half eaten. The lions had moved down a notch on the food chain when the workers abandoned the work site. Patterson decided to have a perch erected some twelve feet tall, and to sit up there waiting for the lion to come back to finish his meal. The structure was made of four poles intersecting at the top, with a piece of wood that served as a lookout bench. After several hours and nightfall, Patterson's patience paid off. The lion returned. But it wasn't the donkey he had an eye for. It was Patterson himself.

The lion was decidedly more interested in the fresh meat on the perch than that which lay on the ground. Slowly the lion circled around the perimeter of the structure, moving closer every time. He let out a few grunts and growls that sent a shiver down the lieutenant colonel's spine. After more than an hour of stalking, the lieutenant colonel would wipe his sweaty palms one more time before picking up his rifle, aiming, and boom!

A loud, ferocious growl, and then an attempt to escape. The lion was hit this time, and he was in pain, if not dying a quick death. Lieutenant Colonel Patterson called out to others a quarter of a mile away that he was all right and that he had hit his target. The remaining workers turned on their campfire lights and made their way to the makeshift perch. All the while, singing gleefully. The lieutenant colonel dispersed the crowd, because he knew there was more work to be done. He would return the next morning to search for the wounded lion.

After dawn they found out they had true reason to celebrate. The dream was a reality: They found the carcass of the lion. It measured nine feet eight inches and was three and a half feet high.

According to Patterson's account, it took eight men to carry it back to camp. There was dancing, celebrating—Patterson was carried on the workers' shoulders—they shouted "Savior!" and accolades that made Patterson feel a little uncomfortable.

It would be another two weeks before the group was completely out of harm's way, when the second male was shot and killed.

The Second Lion Is Finally Stopped

It was several days later that the second lion showed up at an inspector's bungalow. And it was several follies later before man's cunning and firepower put an end to the reign of terror. Lieutenant Colonel Patterson killed the second lion near two weeks later.

Two days after the killing of the man-eater, his companion snoops around a bungalow, and the chief is called in. The man-eater couldn't get inside so, as Patterson put it, he satisfied himself with a goat outside the barn. By the time Patterson got to the bungalow, he could see the goat meal, still unfinished. Like the donkey, he used the goat as his bait. This time he hid out in a shack near the bungalow, waiting for the return of the lion. He tied several goats up to a railing and lay low in the shack. I told you there were a few follies before trapping this lion. The lion returned, and Patterson drew his gun, fired, and managed only to draw out the beast's anger. He was shot, but not seriously enough to be stopped. The lion left, and Patterson and a few of the men followed his path.

It was an easy one because the animal was bleeding, and he grabbed a goat, which slowed him down. In the brush, Patterson saw the lion, raised his rifle, and shot. But that didn't stop the man-eater from charging toward Patterson and the men, who quickly climbed the nearest trees to get out of the beast's path. The lion sneaked away beyond the rocks, where again the trail ran cold. It was a full ten days before the lion showed up again.

Patterson again built a structure on which to perch himself and wait for the animal to return. He placed the goats as bait. The man-eater returned. But it wasn't the goats the beast was after. He caught sight of Patterson in the perch and stalked the lieutenant colonel. Round and round the perch he prowled, getting closer and closer. Finally within range, Patterson fired—he hit the lion in the chest. A fierce growl, and then Patterson fired three more times, with another hit to the lion. He could tell that he had struck him because of the second loud growl.

All was quiet until morning. Patterson and two assistants followed the trail through the jungle in daylight. It was easy to follow, as there were patches of blood. An angry growl startled them. Patterson saw the lion through the bushes; the lion saw him as well. The beast made a charge, and Patterson fired three more times, hitting him once in the leg. The lion still wasn't stopped, and the two assistants ran to the nearest tree. Patterson was forced to do the same. From the tree Patterson fired another shot, and the lion dropped. He quickly jumped down from the tree and charged toward the lion. But the lion wasn't finished; he charged back. Patterson fired two more shots, hitting his chest and his head, finally stopping the man-eater's reign of terror.

Word of the lion's demise spread. The men eventually surrounded the dead beast. In their jubilation they wanted to grab the dead animal and tear it up. Patterson did all he could to keep it intact. (If he had not there would be no Field Museum exhibit to write about.) And since Patterson was by now revered, he had greater influence on the workers than he had before this terrible ordeal.

In fact, many of the men looked to their leader now as though he was a god. They called him Savior. They said god had killed the Devil. Today you can see these two ferocious animals that closed a railway in Africa in Chicago, Illinois. Why Chicago?

Why the Field Museum?

How did the Tsavo lions wind up at the Field Museum? The year
was 1924. Colonel Patterson came to Chicago to give a public
lecture on the infamous lions at the Field Museum of Natural
History. At that time he told the museum's president, Stanley
Field, that he still had the skins of the man-eaters. Mr. Field then
bought them from Patterson for five thousand dollars and presented them to the museum.

It took a while to repair and mount the skins. The taxidermy
experts are credited with doing a remarkable job. There were
scrapes from the brush of the jungle and bullet holes. Not only
that: Patterson had used the skins as rugs for more than twenty
years. They were old, dusty, and dried out. You would not know
that today. The two man-eaters look as threatening now as back
then. It is a remarkable work of re-creation. So these two man-
eaters are now in a place where they can't do damage. But if you
walk up to this exhibit at the Field Museum in Chicago, you can
feel the terror they wrought on thousands in Africa. You can feel
it. We don't want these two lions to *ever* come back to life.

So, I end this with a plea to Ben Stiller and his movie people:
Stay away from the Field Museum. These lions are not your av-
erage animals. We do not want, under any circumstances, the
Tsavo man-eaters to come back to life.

The Lions' Den Today

Today the Tsavo lions are under the watchful eyes of scientists in
Africa, and of those from other countries who visit the site. Scientists are studying the social system of the lions in the Tsavo
area. A pack of lions are threatening livestock there today, and
they want to find out how to eliminate the risk to the animals
while not destroying the Tsavo lions.

Research is ongoing in the area of dental trauma and the
pathologies of lions in the Tsavo area.

(Note: *For more information on the Tsavo lions, read Dr. Bruce*

Patterson's book, The Lions of Tsavo: Exploring the Legacy of Africa's Notorious Man-Eaters, *New York: McGraw-Hill, 2004.* bpatterson@fieldmuseum.org.)

———

The Field Museum
1400 S. Lake Shore Drive
Chicago, IL 60605

———

Gerardette Hearne

A chink in a piece of heroic armor is sometimes only visible after the fact . . . and then may be present only in the smallest of details.

Lindbergh's Swastika

Good luck.

Bad luck.

Charles Lindbergh had both.

The great American hero became intertwined with an odd, crooked cross.

Today that sign is associated with evil.

In the 1920s, it was a good luck sign. It's called the swastika.

Would you like to see one?

Go to the Smithsonian National Air and Space Museum in Washington, D.C. In the great hall, Lindbergh's plane, the *Spirit of St. Louis,* hangs from the ceiling like a model. Go to the second-floor gallery opposite the plane. In a corner by the hall's entrance is a glass case. Inside it is the prop spinner from the *Spirit of St. Louis.* Inside the spinner are the names of the workers who built the plane, and a hand-painted swastika put there for good luck.

The superstitious will say the swastika worked, though Lindbergh's flying skills and shrewd judgment of aircraft may have had more to do with it. In 1927, Lindbergh was attempting the impossible—flying from New York to Paris nonstop, long before such air service became common, safe, and routine. Adding a dash of good luck couldn't hurt.

That flight would catapult Lindbergh to near immortal fame as a great American hero, probably the biggest before Neil Armstrong first set foot on the moon or the Beatles setting foot in New York. Yet in a span of fifteen years, Lindbergh the hero nearly became Lindbergh the traitor when he urged the United States to stay out of World War II, blaming the British, the Jews, and the Roosevelt administration for their eagerness to intervene.

And then there was that little Nazi medal pinned to his jacket by Luftwaffe head Hermann Göring; you know, the one with the German eagle surrounded by four little swastikas?

Coincidence?

Read on and judge for yourself.

Charles Who?

There was nothing that bespoke a famous destiny when looking at Lindbergh's life prior to his epic flight. He put in some time on the barnstorming circuit as a wing walker and skydiver. He worked for a while as a plane mechanic. He bought a JN-4 Jenny trainer and returned to the barnstorming circuit as a pilot. He made a few rough landings that required repairs. He even earned a commission in the Army Air Corps Reserve. He flew the mail. The only thing Lindbergh didn't do was get killed—a common hazard facing many pilots in the early days of aviation.

What Lindbergh was doing was exceptional at a personal level. His love of flight coincided with the growth of aviation as the high-tech industry of the 1920s and 1930s. It took some courage for the pilots of the day to fly higher, faster, and farther than ever before. But it also took some smarts. To go higher, farther, and faster required advances in technology. Pilots were quick to spur advancement through advocacy on the stump and practice at the stick.

Had Lindbergh stayed on his original path, he probably would have had a long career as an excellent, prosperous pilot with many good stories to tell. He would have been one of the thousands who first took to the sky in canvas-covered open-cockpit biplanes and ended at the controls of jetliners.

Obscure Charles Lindbergh was aiming higher.

Charles, Why?

There were twenty-five thousand reasons why anyone would have wanted to fly nonstop from New York to Paris, and each one had a dollar attached to it. New York hotelier Raymond Orteig put up the prize money in 1919, willing to pay anyone who could make the flight in either direction.

It was common in the 1920s for rich enthusiasts to put up prize money to reward record-breakers in aviation. Back in the day, the money came with fame, though the practice stopped once air travel became commonplace. Many risked all to win. Some were already famous.

French World War I ace René Fonck tried in 1926 in a Sikorsky S-35. Overloaded with fuel, the plane's landing gear collapsed on takeoff at Long Island's Roosevelt Field. Fonck did not die in the flames, though his two crew members did.

In April 1927, two naval aviators tried to get off the ground at Langley Field, Virginia, in a trimotor Keystone Pathfinder biplane. They crashed on takeoff and died.

Two weeks later, French World War I ace Charles Nungesser and navigator François Coli left Le Bourget Field in Paris in a Levasseur PL 8. They disappeared. (The plane may have crashed in Maine, but that is the subject of a separate controversy.)

Commander Richard Byrd, the first to fly over the North Pole, placed his bet on the reliable Fokker trimotor. And why not? The same type of plane had gotten him over the pole. Well, it crashed on a practice takeoff shortly before Lindbergh's flight, severely injuring pilot Floyd Bennett.

So far the Orteig Prize excelled at getting pilots killed and injured.

Why should it be any different for Lindbergh?

Charles, How?

If God had meant man to fly, He would have given him wings.

Lindbergh had to purchase his.

February 1927 found Lindbergh at Ryan Airlines in San Diego. There he would work closely with designer Donald Hall and factory manager Howland Bowlus to modify a Ryan CAM-2 mail plane. St. Louis businessmen Harry Knight and Harold Bixby put up most of the $15,000 Lindbergh needed to buy the plane. Lindbergh kicked in another $2,000 from his savings, while his former employer, Frank Roberstson of RAC, an air mail carrier, kicked in another $1,000.

Here Lindbergh the aviation geek came to the fore. Engine failure was a common risk in the 1920s, so Lindbergh figured on minimizing the problem by relying on a single-engine aircraft. Streamlining would cut drag and increase fuel efficiency. Putting the massive gas tank in front of the pilot seat removed the risk of it plowing through the pilot if the plane crashed. That meant sacrificing the windshield for a periscope to provide a forward view. It was that or leaning his head out of the side window. The wingspan was lengthened by ten feet, again to provide more space for extra fuel tanks.

In the two months that it took to build the *Spirit of St. Louis,* some things could not be done for lack of time. Redesigning the tail to suit a larger aircraft fell by the wayside, resulting in an unstable plane that would require some attention from Lindbergh during flight. Discomfort would help the pilot stay awake, so Lindbergh purposely chose an uncomfortable wicker seat for the cockpit.

For navigation, Lindbergh would rely on an earth-induction compass that would take into account any deviations in the magnetic field, thus allowing him to fly a true course. In the days before autopilot or global positioning systems, a pilot had to follow a compass heading without making any mistakes that could throw him miles off course after many hours in the air.

Lindbergh chose the engine with great care. It would be a 9-cylinder Wright Whirlwind J-5C, rated at 233 horsepower. The engine was self-lubricating, allowing forty hours of continuous operation before requiring a mechanic's attention. Any extra range for the plane could be obtained by cutting the plane's weight. Lindbergh would make his flight without a radio. The damn things were heavy and didn't always work anyway.

Between the extra fuel, uncomfortable seat, unstable airframe, and long-range low-care engine, Lindbergh and Hall had assembled a package that could deliver a forty-hour nonstop flight of up to four thousand miles.

In addition to all this high-tech assemblage, there would be one low-tech addition to Lindbergh's plane. The nose cone that was to be mounted over the propeller hub was modified with a swastika painted on its inside, along with the painted signatures of all the employees at Ryan who worked on the plane.

Prior to the rise of Adolph Hitler and his Nazi Party in Germany, the swastika was a good luck sign found in many places around the world, from Boy Scout badges to key fobs, architectural adornments, and logos. In World War I, American pilots flying for France who served in the Lafayette Escadrille adorned their Nieuport fighters with an Indian head emblem featuring the swastika as part of its feathered war bonnet.

It was a given in the 1920s that pilots had short life spans. Lindbergh knew that and really did his homework when pulling a plane together that would not fail him. A good luck charm certainly would not hurt.

Charles, When . . .

On the morning of May 20, 1927, Charles Lindbergh climbed into the cockpit of his Ryan NYP, fired up the Wright engine, taxied to the end of Roosevelt Field, and pushed the throttle to the fire wall. The little plane gained speed slowly—half of its 5,100-pound takeoff weight was fuel. It still cleared the power lines at the end of the field by twenty feet. Hardly anyone saw him take off.

It took about 33.5 hours for Lindbergh to fly to Paris. He flew as high as ten thousand feet, to avoid storm clouds, or as high as ten feet, to avoid waves. There were times when he had to fly by instruments, due to fog. Between taking star fixes and dead reckoning, he finally arrived at Le Bourget at 10:22 P.M. on May 21.

About 150,000 Frenchmen saw him arrive.

They gave him a hero's welcome.

The *Spirit of St. Louis* was nearly torn to pieces for souvenirs, and would have been were it not for some quick-thinking French military pilots, who surrounded the plane. Then the assorted policemen and soldiers at the airfield got Lindbergh out of view before he was torn up for souvenirs as well.

From that moment on Lindbergh would be the most famous man on the planet—before the arrival of John, Paul, George, and Ringo.

Today you can fly the same route from New York to Paris in about six hours, at about 580 miles an hour at an altitude of about forty thousand feet. Your seat will be comfortable (we hope). You will get a free meal. The worst that can happen is your luggage getting lost. No total stranger will give a damn about your departure or arrival at either end. Be sure to hail your own cab to get into town. And if you just happen to be carrying a swastika, expect lots of dirty looks from any Frenchmen you meet—or from any Americans, for that matter.

Charles, What?!

Ten years later Charles Lindbergh, the most famous man in the world, pretty much ignored the anniversary of his flight while the rest of the world celebrated and commemorated it. He had ducked out to Great Britain, using his self-imposed exile to live in privacy after being lashed in an unending whirlwind of publicity.

Returning home to a hero's welcome in 1927, Lindbergh endured the ticker-tape parade, the numerous publicity flights in the *Spirit of St. Louis,* and the cheering millions. The upside was standing there as the face of the infant aviation industry. His fame propelled public interest in learning how to fly, either as a pilot or a passenger. He fell in love with Anne Morrow, the rich, beautiful daughter of the U.S. ambassador to Mexico. He taught her how to fly. They surveyed the Great Circle route together in a Lockheed Sirius. Adventure later yielded to a home life. The Lindberghs came back to earth to start a family, settling in Hopewell, New Jersey, with little Charles Jr. in the crib.

Happiness did not last long.

In March 1932, the child was kidnapped and murdered. Charles and Anne Lindbergh had to endure a trial in the court of public opinion, caught like deer in the unremitting spotlight of publicity. The accused killer, Bruno Richard Hauptmann, received his trial in a court of law, also suffering heavy coverage by newsreel cameras until he was convicted, sentenced, and then executed.

In polite obscurity, Charles and Anne Lindbergh rebuilt their lives in England, far away from the unceasing American publicity machine. More kids were born. Lindbergh continued to promote aviation, going through several consulting gigs with Pan American Airways and Sikorsky, and then making seaplanes for passenger service. With a geek's faith in technology, Lindbergh promoted the aviation industry, preaching the gospel of higher, farther, faster. The 1930s saw a massive shift in aviation technology, transitioning from open-cockpit biplanes chugging along at 200 mph to low-wing all-metal monoplanes featuring enclosed cockpits and airspeeds approaching 400 mph.

That was aviation's smiley face.

The airplane's use as a tool of war was the growing shadow.

Lindbergh spent the late 1930s touring Europe as an "honored guest" and taking the measure of that shadow by sizing up the air forces of Britain, France, Germany, and the Soviet Union. In late 1938, he accepted for a third time an invitation from Nazi Germany to visit, see nice new airplanes, and talk aviation. Major Truman Smith, U.S. military attaché in Berlin, made the arrangements for the trip with one eye on using Lindbergh to collect intelligence on the Luftwaffe.

Lindbergh got a good tour. He saw the Messerschmidt ME-108 and ME-109, the latter being Germany's main fighter plane. He checked out the Junker JU-90 transport and was the first non-German to see the then secret Junker JU-88 twin-engine medium bomber.

The tour was capped with a dinner at the U.S. Embassy in Berlin. Among the honored guests was Luftwaffe Reich marshal Hermann Göring. In his hand was a little box containing a medal Hitler wanted to bestow on Lindbergh. It was a German cross. In each corner was a German eagle, each bird perched upon a little swastika. Lindbergh accepted the medal, perhaps all too used to accepting honors, perhaps too polite to give his host offense by turning it down.

This medal did not make Lindbergh a Nazi. In the years to come his critics would argue otherwise. The Nazi medal generated little ink in the American press when it was awarded. *The Chicago Tribune* took greater notice of a protest lodged by Soviet aviators against Lindbergh for disparaging the strength of their air force during the Czechoslovakian crisis. They alleged that this remark influenced Prime Minister Neville Chamberlain to surrender Czechoslovakia to Nazi annexation, in his attempt to appease Hitler.

Lindbergh made his findings known in a report to the U.S. government. Germany's Luftwaffe was way ahead of rivals France and Britain. The German aviation industry would certainly equal that of the United States by 1942, though in later comments he rated it ahead of America's. Knowing that air power would be the decisive factor in the next war added weight to his estimates. France estimated the Luftwaffe had 6,000 frontline aircraft, plus 2,000 to 3,000 older planes, plus a productive capacity of up to 20,000 aircraft per year. Britain had 2,000 aircraft, of which 700 were modern, but it could build 10,000 planes a year. France could produce about 5,000 planes a year, but presently had only 540. Lindbergh crunched the numbers and was impressed with Germany's advantage.

Not all experts agreed with Lindbergh. C. G. Grey, coeditor of *Jane's All the World's Aircraft,* reacted to Lindbergh's claim of a 3,000-plane Luftwaffe as "bunk." Britain's RAF had force totals competitive with the Luftwaffe, while the United States has at least 1,500 aircraft plus a rearmament program that would do some good, he said.

Privately, Lindbergh believed that war in Europe could be avoided if Britain and Germany could arrive at an understanding. Failing that, if war came to Europe, the United States must stay out of it. He kept his views private—for the present. But before making his views known, Lindbergh would do his duty.

Charles Warns

In April 1939, Lindbergh the reservist was recalled to service as a colonel with the Army Air Corps. His mission: Inspect and assess about twenty aviation research facilities run by the federal government, various universities and aircraft companies.

Testifying before the House Foreign Relations Committee two months later, Colonel Lindbergh told it like it was: Germany was ahead of the United States in basic and applied aviation research. "A few years ago, we led the world in both military and commercial aviation, but in the last five years that lead in military aviation has been taken away from us, so that today we stand far from the top," he said. The United States needed to improve how it applied quality to advancing aircraft design, and clearly lacked the means to produce as many aircraft as Europe.

So long as Lindbergh was serving his country, he kept his opinions to himself. That changed once his duty was done. Lindbergh came out against the Roosevelt administration in September 1939, shortly after World War II began. His attitude toward the growing likelihood of war in Europe reflected the isolationist mainstream of American conservative public opinion. "If we enter fighting for democracy abroad, we may end up losing it at home," Lindbergh said in a speech broadcast by all three national radio networks. The two oceans are protection enough for American interests, he added. "If we enter the quarrels of Europe during war, we must stay in them in time of peace as well. It is madness to send our soldiers to be killed as we did in the last war if we turn the course of peace over to the greed, the fear, the intrigue of European nations. . . . We must either keep out of European wars entirely or stay in European affairs permanently."

Lindbergh was not alone. About two thirds of all Americans favored neutrality or nonintervention. By the fall of 1940, an organization called America First had been formed to lobby and agitate against U.S. involvement in World War II. Naturally the group turned to Lindbergh as a spokesman, since he could command radio time for his speeches on the basis of his celebrity, which could also fill arenas.

The Fight for Freedom Committee, a New York–based organization, managed to score equal time on the radio with speakers James Warburg, a well-known banker, and mystery book author Rex Stout. "When Colonel Lindbergh speaks of the past German successes in Europe in the past twenty months . . . he stresses, and quite properly, the enormous importance of air power and the past and present superiority of Germany in that arm," Stout pointed out. "But when he [Lindbergh] speaks of

the ease [with] which we can defend America from attack, he
talks as if he had never heard of the airplane. He leaps backward
to the nineteenth century. He scorns any attempt by any foe—
to do what? To send three million men three thousand miles in
three thousand ships, land them at the Battery, and march them
up Broadway. That isn't the way it's done today, Colonel."

Lindbergh took none of it lying down. In a May 1941 broadcast speech given at New York's Madison Square Garden, Lindbergh spoke to a packed house. Looking at things from a
different angle, he said he feared that the current administration
would commit the United States to war before the next election.
Entering into the war would cost the U.S. millions of lives with no
guarantee of victory, he said, and with no promise that American
freedom and democracy would survive such an ordeal. The alternative was defending America's shores from invasion without
getting involved in a war.

Throughout 1941, President Roosevelt successfully prepared
the United States for war, but he had to do it in increments that
did not go unseen by his opponents. Many in America First
feared one-man government, arguing that American involvement in a foreign war would make such a thing possible. Some
even went so far as to use conspiracy theories to illustrate such a
threat, with one senator contending that the radio and movie in-
dustries were run by "small oligarchies" using their power to
spread prowar propaganda before an audience of one hundred
million Americans.

Lindbergh followed suit. In a September 11, 1941, speech in
Des Moines, Lindbergh alleged that three groups were pressing
for war: the British, the Jews, and the Roosevelt administration.

They planned: first, to prepare the United States for foreign
war under the guise of American defense; second, to involve
us, step by step, without our realization; third, to create a series of incidents that would force us into conflict. . . . Only

the creation of sufficient "incidents" yet remains, and you see
the first of these already taking place.

(Among these "incidents" had been a recent attack by a German sub against the destroyers *Greer* and *Kearny,* which had
been escorting merchant ships bound for Britain that were
carrying cargoes of weapons and supplies purchased under the
United States' Lend-Lease program. Roosevelt ordered the
Navy to "shoot on sight" should German U-boats fire again at
U.S. ships.)

Lindbergh pointed out that Jews "enjoyed large ownership
and influence over our motion picture, our press, our radio and
our government." But he also urged Jewish groups to oppose
the war, because they would be among the first to "feel its consequences."

This was a tough line of reasoning to sell. How could Jews in
America not suffer from war by seeking peace when an unfet-
tered Nazi regime was busy killing millions of Jews in Europe?
Columnist Dorothy Thompson had referred to Lindbergh as a
"pro-Nazi recipient of a German medal" months before Lindbergh's fateful Des Moines speech. Now the charge was going
to stick with a vengeance.

Public opinion began to change.

Almost a week after the Des Moines speech, isolationist senator Burton Wheeler (Democrat-Montana) was egged at an appearance in Billings as soon as he mentioned Lindbergh's name,
and later that month he was heckled in Los Angeles. Jewish
groups rallied against Lindbergh's resort to Nazi-like tactics that
threatened to stir up "religious and racial hatreds" that set "group
against group." America First denied that Lindbergh was anti-
Semitic. Senator Claude Pepper (Democrat-Florida) accused
Lindbergh of being among a small group of "doubters" and "in-
ner enemies" who were "as ruthless and heartless as Hitler himself." Lindbergh's play of the "race card" was not getting him any

support. Other antiwar activists resented being associated with anti-Semitism. Senator Gerald Nye asserted as much at a speech at the Brooklyn Academy of Music, an appearance guarded by five hundred cops in heavily Jewish Brooklyn.

Once Roosevelt committed the Navy to shoot U-boats on sight, Americans did what they always do in such situations: rally around their flag and their president. Midwestern isolationism began to crack. An American Legion convention in Milwaukee voted to endorse Roosevelt's foreign policy and condemn European tyrants. One leader of the Illinois Republican Party came out in support of "the national defense effort." The Indiana Democratic Party's state committee voted to repudiate the isolationist views of Senator Frederick Van Nuys, the Democratic senator from Indiana. The Michigan state legislature had approved an isolationist resolution in May, only to repeal it in October. Only in heavily German Wisconsin did popular opinion remain unchanged.

In October, the Gallup Organization published a poll showing only one in sixteen Americans agreeing with Lindbergh that the Jews had anything to do with getting the United States involved in a European war. Those same respondents also listed Lindbergh as most active in trying to keep America out of war, with America First coming in second.

Lindbergh and America First staged another massive rally at New York's Madison Square Garden in late October. The New York Police Department deployed over seven hundred cops to restrict passage through the security perimeter to ticket holders only. A few blocks away activists handed out handbills touting the facts about "America's number one Nazi," Charles Lindbergh.

Speaking to a full house, Lindbergh recounted his 1938 European tour assessing the air forces of the nations now fighting. Lindbergh explained that if war came to Europe, Germany would win, or the continent be destroyed. "[I] therefore advocated that England and France build up their military forces with utmost rapidity, but that they permit Germany to expand eastward into Russia without declaring war." Now the misguided American idealists who were calling for intervention were allied with the communist Soviet Union against European Germany, Lindbergh explained, implying that this was the world turned upside down.

"If the issue of intervention had been placed openly before our Congress and our people, a decision could have been reached in the traditional American way. But this was not done because the interventionists knew the American people would not agree to war," he said. Lindbergh then turned his guns on Roosevelt's foreign policy, accusing the administration of achieving intervention on the sly, through Lend-Lease and the U.S. naval escort of British convoys. This after FDR was elected to an unprecedented third term by promising to not send Americans to war.

The cost of such a war would be quite high. Lindbergh pointed out that it would require an army of ten million men, plus a navy and merchant fleet large enough to transport the force across the Atlantic and invade Europe. Then he compared this unknown capability against current practice, with England failing to maintain its foothold in Europe in Norway, Flanders, and Greece against the mightiest army and air force in the world. Lindbergh cast victory in stark terms: the loss of freedom at home and U.S. armies abroad for another generation to police the world without any gain for America.

Lindbergh then reached his rankling conclusion: "The most fundamental issue is not one of war and peace but integrity." If Roosevelt would only put the war question to an honest vote, after explaining to the American people why the nation needed to fight, everything would be okay. Left unsaid was that many Americans, like Lindbergh, saw no need to fight in the war. Left unseen was all the evil Nazi Germany stood for.

Not fooled by this long-winded reasoning, Sergeant Alvin York, a Medal of Honor winner and hero of World War I, slammed Lindbergh in an Armistice Day speech in Evansville, Indiana. York blamed Lindbergh for making speeches that are "making this country so overconfident that unless we wake up, we'll be easier for Hitler than France was." York, the plain-spoken Everyman, was taking an ax to Lindbergh's lengthy arguments. "Charles Lindbergh . . . and every other leader in the America First movement, is an appeaser of Adolph Hitler. That is not an accusation. That is a simple statement of fact," said York. Hitler was so bad he had even invaded Russia, betraying his most loyal ally, Soviet dictator Joseph Stalin. Don't assume that Germany's difficulty in Russia meant Hitler was licked, the old soldier said. "Now is the time to beat him [Hitler] down."

"I'm not afraid of war," York said. "I went through one, and I hated every minute of it. No one who lived through the last war could possibly have any other feeling. We all hated it. And yet we cannot avoid this new war, unless like Lindbergh, we value our present security more than we value liberty and freedom and democracy."

By early December 1941, America First was still gaining membership, and its leaders were contemplating backing anti-war candidates in the 1942 primaries against prowar senators and congressmen.

Then something happened.

On December 7, the threat America First never contemplated attacked the United States in the Philippines, Wake Island, Guam, and Hawaii.

While Lindbergh and his colleagues ranted about Germany, Japan struck first.

War came, courtesy of the Rising Sun and not the swastika.

On December 9, America First ceased feuding with Roosevelt.

In a public statement Lindbergh declared his loyalty to America first: "Whether or not that policy [of Roosevelt's] has been wise, our country has been attacked by force of arms and by force of arms we must retaliate. . . . We must now turn every effort to building the greatest and most efficient Army, Navy and Air Force in the world. When American soldiers go to war, it must be with the best equipment that modern skill can design and that modern industry can build."

In the end, Lindbergh's long, logical reasoning was shattered by harsh reality. Roosevelt, exercising his power as commander in chief, had perched America at the edge of harm's way, knowing that another war was coming. Lindbergh had argued that this was one-man government as a threat to democracy, as Congress had not voted to approve Roosevelt's order to occupy Iceland or provide British ships with U.S. naval escorts. While eloquent and well reasoned, Lindbergh's arguments were an abstraction pushing against a current reality, one that many Americans understood once Nazi U-boats began shooting at Navy ships. Many in politics would make this mistake in the future, though Lindbergh's error makes a good example to ponder.

Charles Was . . .

Lindbergh was half right about World War II.

The United States did build a military machine numbering more than ten million men and built a thousand-ship Navy and massive merchant fleet to move it across the Atlantic—and the Pacific. In 1944 alone the United States produced almost 100,000 aircraft, and trained the pilots to fly them and air crews to service them. The United States did win the war, and became enmeshed in European politics for the next half century, thanks to the cold war.

Lindbergh was still willing to put his country above his beliefs. He threw himself into serving the war effort any way he could. He wanted his reserve commission reactivated, but this offer found no takers in Roosevelt's cabinet.

In 1942 Lindbergh served as a consultant to the Ford Motor Company, helping it set up its massive Willow Run assembly plant to manufacture the B-24 Liberator heavy bomber. Once up and running smoothly, the milelong Willow Run plant could stamp out one B-24 every 25 hours. In 1943 Lindbergh shifted his consulting services to the Chance Vought division of United Aircraft, makers of the F4U Corsair fighter plane. He managed to wangle a civilian assignment to the Pacific theater as Chance Vought's technical representative, spending six months studying the Corsair's performance in combat. He also got to fly about fifty combat missions, either in the F4U or the Lockheed P-38 Lightning, downing one Japanese aircraft. More important, he showed pilots how to get more performance out of their aircraft than their training had taught them.

But he did his service flying against the Rising Sun and not the swastika, perhaps a cruel irony the political Roosevelt deemed just. The canny president always kept political trouble far away from home—whether it was Lindbergh or MacArthur.

In his postwar years Lindbergh was considered as having redeemed some of his prewar honor. He still did consulting work for Pan Am. President Eisenhower restored his reserve commission, promoting him from colonel to brigadier. He wrote a memoir, served on a panel that helped set up the Air Force Academy, and even chatted with the Apollo 8 astronauts before they blasted off to orbit the moon. He led a full life until his death in 1974.

But it was a life caught between two swastikas.

The first was a good luck sign, the one painted inside the spinner of his *Spirit of St. Louis.* The 1916 *Encyclopedia Britannica* describes the swastika as a "symbol of prosperity and good fortune" that was found all over the world throughout time. It was found struck in ancient Mesopotamian coins, Scandinavian folklore, early Christian and Byzantine art, stone carvings in Central and South America, and even among America's Navajo.

The second became a sign of evil during and after World War II. Hitler was a loud, obnoxious dictator in the 1930s, heading a political party that found a useful logo in the swastika. After the 1940s the swastika's ill repute was well earned, as Hitler started and lost a war that killed thirty-five million people in Europe, among them six million Jews who were turned into smoke and ashes, in addition to ruining a continent.

Lindbergh would always be associated with the swastika, both its good and bad meanings, becoming a cautionary tale for heroes who dabble in politics.

And in today's world, no amount of explanation can redeem the swastika.

National Air and Space Museum
Smithsonian Institution
On the National Mall
Independence Avenue at 6th Street SW
Washington, DC 20560

William Terdoslavich

*There was a time when these displays were a mainstay
of all natural history museums. Now they seem
to be relegated to less cerebral surroundings. Believe
it or not!*

Shrunken Displays:
Three Heads Are Better
than None

The size of a man's fist, blackened and with eyes and lips stitched shut, long hair hanging and wooden beads draped here and there—these are the memories from childhoods spent traipsing through the halls of museums or the tents of circus and carnival sideshows. And they are the stuff of stories and controversy.

Shrunken heads have been displayed for decades in museums and carnivals, written about—such as in Melville's *Moby Dick*—and featured in films, such as the one hanging from Jack Sparrow's belt in *Pirates of the Caribbean: At World's End*.

But nowadays people have to look very closely to spot one, or look in the right collections. And, if they chance to see one, they might hear the head talk.

Indeed, the objects look grotesque and supernatural, and seem to be filled with a "presence." Museum workers throughout the country have noted visitors speaking to the heads, as if they were alive—that is, when the heads were regularly displayed.

Three types of shrunken heads are held by various museums in the United States and around the world:

- genuine shrunken heads that once belonged to South American Indians: the ones that were gruesomely made small through an elaborate, ritualistic practice;
- fake shrunken heads: made to look like the real thing to send some shivers down the spines of museum visitors and unwitting collectors;
- monkey and goat heads: made to resemble human ones.

While museums have all three varieties, and while visitors ask to see them, an increasing number of institutions are taking the heads off the shelves and putting them in storage. Museum officials say they don't want to offend the people who wander through the various exhibits.

Reportedly two shrunken heads were displayed at the Buchenwald concentration camp (which was later turned into a museum) specifically to offend the prisoners. Photographs taken after the camp's liberation depict freed prisoners in front of a table filled with oddities that had been gathered from the various buildings at the camp. The two shrunken heads, allegedly belonging to slain Polish prisoners, are seen clearly in the photo. One of the heads was introduced as evidence during the Nuremberg trials.

Heads in New York Museums

The Smithsonian's Museum of the American Indian in New York City displayed two shrunken bodies from the 1920s until 1990, when they were moved into the museum basement because of a law prohibiting the display of Native Americans' remains. Originally labeled as the work of the Jivaro, it was later learned that they had been crafted by a Peruvian medical doctor, Gustaye Struve. Dr. Struve had spent time with the Jivaro in Ecuador and studied their techniques of shrinking skin. There was a surplus of unclaimed bodies in South America because of yellow fever and malaria, so Dr. Sturve had plenty of corpses to work with. He made quite a bit of extra money by selling his wares to tourists and collectors.

Dr. Robert Carneiro, a curator at New York's American Museum of Natural History, is considered one the world's experts on shrunken heads. He has been quoted as saying that although headhunting likely continues to this day, only the Jivaro, or Shuar, were known for shrinking the heads of their enemies, and that the practice supposedly stopped forty years ago.

The Ripley's Believe It or Not Museum in Times Square proudly displays its shrunken heads.

"We have twenty-four," says Ripley's employee Joan Vargas. "We have the largest collection in this country. All are Jivaro shrunken heads." She said the museum opened in late 2007, and the heads are the most popular exhibit. "People come here just to see them."

She adds that the heads are the final display visitors see before exiting the museum. "We want them to leave seeing something memorable."

Believe It or Not Some More

Ripley's Believe It or Not museums are scattered across the globe, and several of them boast one or more shrunken heads, which they still display, despite other museums' locking away their collections. In the 1930s and '40s the Ripley museums printed three different postcards for sale featuring shrunken heads. Some of the postcards become available from time to time on eBay and in antique stores, and are considered quite collectible.

In a Ripley's museum in Queensland, Australia, a shrunken head on display came from the Quick Scissors Hair boutique in Miami.

At Ripley's Orlando Odditorium, a single shrunken head from a Shuar tribe is one of the major draws. Museum employee Kevin Chang said a lot of people call specifically asking about the head: "People come up to the desk and ask about [it], too. It's in the middle of the museum. It's a big attraction. People are intrigued by it." He said there are no plans to put it in storage.

Several years ago the Ripley's museum in Niagara Falls, Ontario, lost one of its heads. A thief broke into a display case and took the shrunken head of a South American Indian valued in excess of sixteen thousand dollars. It was considered especially valuable in part because its hair was unusually long—nearly three feet. The head was historically important because it was one of the first items acquired by Robert Ripley in 1926. It had been exhibited at the Chicago World's Fair in 1933 before it was moved to the Ripley's museum in St. Augustine, Florida. It was later moved to Ontario.

Heads at Other Museums

Two heads used to be displayed at Chicago's Field Museum. They were donated by a nearby elementary school. Children too often stuck gum in the heads' hair, and so the school decided to part with the oddities. Now the heads are off-limits to everyone. The museum's Web site (fieldmuseum.org) says the following:

Why were the shrunken heads from South America taken off display? The shrunken heads from the Shuara (Jivaro) culture of lowland Ecuador were taken off display when the South America Hall was recently converted into the new Museum store. However, the exhibit in which the heads were showcased was outdated and needed to be revised. Today, we now know that headhunting was a part of the complex religious belief system of the Shuara, who placed a strong emphasis on creating a rich mythology and used shamanistic practices to unify the real and supernatural worlds. From ethnographical research conducted by anthropologist Michael Harner, we also know that the Shuara shrank heads not only of enemies caught in battle, but also of revered members of their community as a way to incorporate their spirits into those of the living.—Alaka Wali, Associate Curator, Anthropology

Shrunken heads still can be found at Penn State University's Earth and Mineral Sciences Museum and Art Gallery. At one time the heads were considered the school's mascots. An article in the *Daily Collegian*, the school's newspaper, stated: "The heads are the museum's most popular exhibit, according to curator Andrew Sicrec." One of the heads has hair more than two feet long; the other has short hair and has a crack running down the center of its face, which was caused by humidity from the air conditioner. The museum acquired the heads during the 1930s.

The South Florida Museum in Bradenton displayed among its shrunken heads one that did not have its lips sewn shut. The museum removed the heads in 2007.

The Charleston Museum in South Carolina removed its collection of shrunken heads in the 1980s. The public did not consider it appropriate, according to museum curators. Museum officials cited the Native American Graves Protection and Repatriation Act as an example of the sentiment justifying the desire to keep the heads in storage. The law, passed in 1990, requires U.S. museums to return the remains of descendants upon request.

Oxford, England's famous Pitt Rivers Museum still displays shrunken heads, though controversy swirls around them because some museum officials question the ethics of displaying human remains. The heads attract hundreds of visitors daily and are especially popular with children. Children's author Philip Pullman, who featured the museum in his best-selling *His Dark Materials* trilogy, has been quoted as supporting the display. Some visitors also argue that the heads should stay because they are educational. As of this writing the museum was conducting a review of the issue, including studying museum visitors' comments about the heads.

The museum, near the Oxford University Museum of Natural History, was founded in 1884. Lieutenant General Augustus Pitt Rivers donated more than 18,000 archaeological objects he'd collected from around the world—including the heads.

More than 500,000 objects are on display, including the remains or partial remains of 2,000 people.

"The Treatment of Dead Enemies" shadowy exhibit on the first floor houses the shrunken heads. They are from the upper Amazon River basin, from the Shuar, Achuar, Huambisa, and Aguaruna tribes, and are considered the museum's most famous display.

In 1987, the museum took down its exhibit of tattooed heads from the Maori—following complaints from the Maori community. Three years later they returned the skeletons to Australian Aboriginal communities, following a request by the Aborigines. No one from Ecuador or Peru has asked that the shrunken heads be either returned or taken down.

A shrunken head that was on display for three decades at the Alberni Valley Museum in Port Alberni, British Columbia—one of the museum's most popular curios—was taken off the shelves nearly ten years ago by the curator. The head had been donated to the museum in the 1960s by a local resident, who had bought it while in South America during the 1920s. Museum officials did not believe a counterfeit head merited display, and they were unsure if what they had was genuine. Fakes lack details such as puncture marks around the lips and eyes where wood pins were inserted, the officials said, and lack a hole at the top of the head where it would have been strung on a cord so the warrior could wear it around his neck. The Alberni shrunken head lacked such a hole. In addition, the neck was left open, another feature that questioned its authenticity.

A Shrinking Practice

Anthropologists and archaeologists are unsure when or where head-shrinking began, though some experts believe it dates back at least two thousand years, and possibly began in South America as an outgrowth of man's ability to skin and cure hides. Shrunken heads appear in Incan art, and early Spanish explorers who saw some of the heads thought they belonged to a race of tiny men. Africa and Borneo were also known for their headhunters, and some tribes supposedly practiced head-shrinking, though not to the extent of the Ecuadorean tribes. In addition, according to some historical accounts, ancient Celts preserved decapitated heads.

Ritual decapitation dates back to at least 200 B.C. in South America. Ancient Nazca and Moche pots depict trophy heads, and some appear to display head-shrinking. The Jivaro, or Shuar, lived in the same lands as those early civilizations. The majority of authentic shrunken heads in museums and curiosity shops come from the Jivaro.

Shrinking detached human heads was practiced in the Ecuador and Peruvian jungles until the early part of the twentieth century. Considered both trophies and works of art, some heads are as small as an orange, the best of them having long black hair. The eyes and lips were sewn closed with fiber from jungle plants, and almost all of them have skin made dark from the shrinking process or because charcoal had been rubbed thoroughly into them, giving them the appearance of roasted meat.

Hunting for Headhunters

The Jivaro were described as "crueler than nature." They resisted conquest by the Spanish in 1599, and killed more than twenty thousand in one day when raiding two Spanish settlements. Because they suspected the Spanish governor of cheating them on a gold transaction, they publicly slew him by pouring molten gold down his throat, reportedly saying: "Have you had your fill of gold now?"

A head taken in battle and later shrunken was called a *tsantsa*.

Although many other cultures throughout the world practiced headhunting, the Shuar clan of the Jivaro tribe became famous for their practice of shrinking and preserving human heads. Headhunting was outlawed initially by the Spanish in the mid-1800s, and later in the century by the Ecuadorean government. However, the practice continued for quite some time.

Trapping and Slaying Souls

In Shuar society, natural deaths were unheard-of. The clansmen often died in battle. Even deaths from illnesses, accidents, and old age were blamed on the enemy. Death was basically considered murder, and every death, therefore, needed to be avenged. If a death was not avenged, the closest relative would have an unhappy life.

To determine which enemy was responsible for a death, a Shuar shaman would divine the culprit during a religious ceremony. Once the murderer was revealed, revenge would be sought—sometimes for generations, resulting in continuous intertribal wars.

When a Shuar tribesman slew the offending individual, the head would be cut off with a sharp instrument. The eyes and lips were sewn shut to keep the spirit, called a *muisak,* from being unleashed. The skin was blackened with charcoal so the spirit could not see out through a crack or other imperfection. The Shuar feared the enemy spirits more than they feared their living foes.

The clan's warriors celebrated their victories and the taking of heads by drinking chichi, a beer made from fermented jungle yams, dancing, singing, and taking various hallucinogens. Further, they would undergo many magical rites intended to protect them from their victims' ghosts, which they feared lingered in the heads. A later, more elaborate celebration would be planned in secret so their enemies could not see them and wield any magic against them.

A young Shuar male was considered a warrior when he took his first head. The tribe believed that a warrior acquired the strength of his victim, and so those warriors with the most kills were revered. A warrior who gained three or four kills was given the title of *kakaram,* or powerful one.

The head was not considered magical until it was shrunken according to tribal rituals. Heads were usually processed within a day or two—after they were taken a safe distance away from the village.

The tribesmen believed that to possess a *tsantsa* was to carry around good luck and the blessings of their murdered, and now avenged, ancestor.

Shrinking to Fit

The warrior would make a vertical slit at the back of the head, peeling the skin away from the skull. The skull would then be tossed into a nearby river. Next the skin was turned inside out and the fatty tissue scraped away. The skin was boiled in hot water and chinchipi juice for a few hours, which shrunk it to half its normal size. The lips and eyelids were pierced with wood pins and sewn shut with fiber from jungle plants. Hot pebbles filled the head cavity, and it was rolled, molded, and kneaded to tighten it and prevent the features from becoming distorted. Hot sand was added to further shrink the skin, and to harden it. Finally, the shrunken head was hung above a fire to dry and cure, then it was washed and rubbed so it would shine. The entire process took twenty to twenty-four hours.

In the following festival, the head taker would wear his trophy around his neck, and the other warriors assembled would curse and insult the head so the spirit would be suppressed. Finally, the head would be placed on display on top of a long spear, and the tribe would feast in its presence. The spirit would be slain afterward during a "soul-killing dance," which everyone in the village would join. Blood-smeared warriors cavorted around the head, role-playing the kill. Some of these celebrations would last up to five days.

The head usually lost its value after the celebrations and would be given to children to play with or tossed to animals to eat.

Gathering Heads

When an increasing number of outsiders visited South America in the nineteenth century, shrunken heads became a valuable commodity. Real and fake heads were brought back by explorers, missionaries, and tourists. The Jivaro began to trade the heads for muskets. This allowed the tribe to hunt better, and to more efficiently kill their enemies—which in turn led to more shrunken heads.

Because the demand for shrunken heads grew, others tried to duplicate the Shuar recipe. Beginning in the late 1800s, counterfeit shrunken heads came out of Peru, Colombia, Ecuador, and Panama.

An American, Harvey Lee Boswell, who operated curiosity shops and sideshows, bought his first shrunken head in the late 1840s with twenty cartons of cigarettes, which had cost him about ninety dollars. A few years later he purchased another for thirty dollars from a back-alley shrunken head dealer.

In the October 1921 issue of *National Geographic*, an article by H. E. Anthony states:

> Because of the interest aroused in the outside world by tales concerning these headhunters, there has been in the past a lively trade in human heads. The Jivaros, learning that there was this demand which could be capitalized into muskets, quickly gave a ready response; so that it became necessary for the Ecuadorean government to forbid the traffic in the objects.

The Business of Counterfeiting

Many shrunken heads held in museum collections and by private individuals are considered counterfeit. While some are indeed real human heads, they were not made by the Shuar or other Indian tribes; they are simply the result of a clever use of taxidermy. Telltale signs include a head looking too good, as fake shrunken heads are made using more modern methods that preserve more details. Imposters also are usually not as thoroughly shrunken, the facial and nose hair has not been singed away, and the skin lacks the shiny, polished quality of the originals.

A second kind of fake involves passing off the heads of monkeys and goats as human. A taxidermist typically fitted goatskin over a form, shaving the hair except for eyebrows and eyelashes—such heads do not have ears. Monkey heads more closely resemble human ones.

Another sort of forgery is made with resin or rubber. In the 1950s, magazines advertised rubber shrunken heads for $1.50.

An expert with New York's American Museum of Natural History examined more than fifty shrunken human heads and found that only two or three of them were actually prepared by the Jivaro, or Shuar. The Indians were known to occasionally provide shrunken heads on order, and while these are not considered wholly counterfeit, they are not as rare or as valuable as the trophy heads taken in battle.

Some shrunken heads are advertised as outright fakes. For example, the Internet business Salangome (salangome.com) sells heads "made in Ecuador by indigenous artisans, crafted from animal skin using traditional methods." They range in price from about $50 to $80, though a random assortment of five can be bought for as little as $100.

The Business of Collecting

Canadian entrepreneur William Jamieson at one time had sixty shrunken heads, some of which he donated to museums. Jamieson, considered the world's most avid head collector, made trips to the Amazon River basin to meet with Shuar Indians and learn the culture. Jamieson reportedly gained his first few pieces by placing an ad in a Canadian newspaper and speaking on radio talk shows. He bought one from a woman in Florida for twelve hundred dollars, and paid a few thousand for another stored in an antique shop a few blocks from his home. The third one had belonged to a child.

Although many auction houses today refuse to sell them openly, shrunken heads can still occasionally be acquired through tribal art dealers around the world. The Internet always has a few ads posted.

The price of shrunken heads is escalating. One was recently sold on the Internet site artareas.com for more than ten thousand dollars. The description of the item read:

> This Ecuadorian Shrunken Head is from the jungles of South America. The headhunters from this region believed that the soul lived inside the head. Therefore, by possessing an enemy's head, a warrior would also possess the deceased's spiritual power. Shrunken heads were used for trade purposes as well. For example, one shrunken head would be traded for one musket. A rare white man's shrunken head would be worth at least 2 muskets. These trophies were prepared in a slow process of boiling and heating with hot sand and stones. Don't miss this rare chance to own the ultimate in exotica.

A search of eBay revealed a variety of listings, from nine-dollar plastic replica shrunken heads intended to hang from car rearview mirrors, to handmade goatskin and hair miniature heads from South America, to "museum quality mummified skulls" selling for hundreds of dollars.

Jean Rabe

*Judge Crater, Ambrose Bierce, and this
lovely lady of the skies.*

So Where Is Amelia Earhart?

Amelia Earhart disappeared into thin air on July 2, 1937.

No one knew for sure how it happened.

She did leave some of her stuff behind.

Again, go to the Smithsonian National Air and Space Museum. There is a second-floor gallery opposite Lindbergh's *Spirit of St. Louis.* There you will find a red Lockheed Vega, with its single engine and single high-mounted wing. *Old Bessie* was the plane Earhart flew solo across the Atlantic from Newfoundland to Ireland, becoming the first woman to equal Lindbergh's feat. Her leather flight jacket is also on display next to her plane.

In a life of many firsts, this was not enough for Earhart. She was never one to rest on her laurels. Why settle for an ocean when the world beckoned?

In 1937, Earhart set her sights on becoming the first woman to fly around the world along the equator. The toughest leg of the trip was across the Pacific, from Lae, New Guinea, to Howland Island, a speck of land in the middle of a watery nowhere. She was trying to do this years before the global positioning system was invented. Her plane had no computerized autopilot or navigational aids. All Earhart could do was follow a compass heading, flying a straight line as close as possible for hour after monotonous hour, until she'd get close enough to make radio contact with a Coast Guard cutter near Howland. There she could get a bearing to follow via radio direction finding.

In later years many followed the same course in their own planes. All made it. Journalists, writers, and theorists have all speculated about her fate. Maybe she came down farther south than Howland, still able to make landfall. Maybe she flew north to overfly the Marianas, crashed, was captured by the Japanese, and executed as a spy.

Maybe she survived the crash, changed her name, and settled down as a suburban housewife.

Maybe, maybe, maybe . . .

Amelia Flies

In the 1930s, aviation was new.

Feminism was newer.

Women acquired their right to vote in 1920. Afterward a few daring women pushed back the boundaries of propriety, just to show they could do things as well as men. Earhart came into these heady decades after living a life unconventional for her time. She grew up as a tomboy, not a girl. She sought out a high school with a good science program. She went to work and saved up her dollars to pay for flying lessons. She got her pilot's license, bought her own plane, and logged about five hundred solo hours at the stick by the time she was "discovered."

The year was 1928. Lindbergh had just flown solo across the Atlantic, covering New York to Paris in just 33.5 hours. Socialite

Amy Guest was eager to become the first woman to fly across the Atlantic—as a passenger. She had purchased Commander Richard Byrd's Fokker trimotor for the feat, and had lined up a pilot and mechanic to fly and maintain the plane. G. P. Putnam, who handled publicity for Lindbergh, only heard about the stunt secondhand from Byrd, and asked his friend Captain Hilton Railey to find who had bought the trimotor.

Railey traced the project to Guest via her attorney, David Layman. From him Railey found out that Guest was being pressured by her family not to undertake such a dangerous and foolish stunt. Could Railey find a woman who could take Guest's place? Railey started working his network of friends. Chatting with retired admiral Reginald Belknap, Railey heard about a young social worker named Amelia Earhart who worked at a Boston settlement house and did a lot of flying on the side. Acting on the tip, Railey got on the phone and called the settlement house. Once Earhart was on the line, Railey came quickly to the point: "How would you like to be the first woman to fly the Atlantic?"

Earhart asked for details, then made it clear she did not want to be just a passenger. She wanted some time at the controls of the trimotor during the flight.

Behind the scenes, Guest bowed out in Earhart's favor, and also allowed Putnam to act as the flight's backer. Taking off from Newfoundland on June 17, 1928, the trimotor *Friendship* made it to Wales in twenty hours, forty minutes. Pilot Wilmer Stultz flew the plane, mostly on instruments; Earhart got no time at the controls. "It was a grand experience," she told Railey, "but all I did was lie on my tummy and take pictures of the clouds. We didn't see much of the ocean. Bill [Stultz] did all of the flying—had to. I was just baggage, like a sack of potatoes." Railey pointed out to Earhart that technically she became the first woman pilot to cross the Atlantic. "Oh well, maybe some day I'll try it alone," she replied. Stultz and his mechanic, Lou Gordon, went on to be upstaged by their "passenger," who

reaped the lioness's share of fame under the guidance of
G. P. Putnam. Earhart and Putnam would later marry—her
first, his third. She kept her own name and viewed the marriage
as one between equals. This is not unusual today, but was quite
radical in the 1930s.

In the years that followed Earhart would become the first
woman to fly solo across the United States, from the East Coast to
West Coast and back again. She set an altitude record of over eighteen thousand feet piloting an autogiro, a hybrid that was half
helicopter, half airplane. Then, in 1932, piloting a single-engine
Lockheed Vega, she flew from Newfoundland to Northern Ireland, becoming the first woman to fly solo across the Atlantic.
The flight lasted almost fifteen hours, earning her a Distinguished
Flying Cross and putting her on par with Lindbergh. With the
same plane Earhart was first to fly from Hawaii to California,
and then she set a new record flying nonstop from Mexico City
to New York.

The plucky red Vega was too slow for air racing, so Earhart
retired *Old Bessie.* The plane now sits on the second floor of the
Smithsonian National Air and Space Museum, beside a glass
case displaying Earhart's flight jacket and within view of Lindbergh's *Spirit of St. Louis.*

(Note: Earhart's Vega is also near the glass case displaying the
prop spinner belonging to the *Spirit of St. Louis,* with its controversial swastika good luck sign painted on the inside.)

Having lived a life of many firsts, Earhart now had her heart
set on flying around the world—along the equator. This flight
would run close to twenty-nine thousand miles. Others had
flown around the world before, but the equatorial route featured
more time over water once the Pacific was reached.

It was a special challenge.

A different plane would be needed.

Earhart settled for the Lockheed Electra L-10E. The twin-
engine twin-rudder plane could carry anywhere from ten to
fourteen passengers at about 190 miles per hour, with a range of

about 800 miles. It was just entering service in 1934 with North-west Airlines, Pan Am, and Delta.

Earhart's Electra, however, would need a lot of modifications. To double its range, the passenger seats were stripped out and re-placed with extra fuel tanks. A Bendix radio direction-finding loop antenna was added to aid navigation. A chart room for the navigator was placed in the plane's tail section. Sticker price on the airplane was eighty thousand dollars. Earhart could fly, but she needed a master navigator to plot the course for her historic flight. On her first attempt she chose Captain Harry Manning, who had skippered the passenger ship *President Roosevelt* dur-ing Earhart's 1928 voyage back from Europe. He would navigate for the bulk of the flight, leaving the difficult Hawaii–Howland Island leg to Fred Noonan as second navigator.

Like many aerial navigators during aviation's infancy, Noo-nan got his start at sea. After twenty years aboard various ships, Master Mariner Noonan transferred his navigation skills to avi-ation when he was picked up by Pan Am in 1930. Five years later Noonan navigated the first Pan Am Clipper flight from San Francisco to Honolulu, a crucial linchpin route that allowed air service to reach out from the continental United States to Manila in the Philippines. Noonan also was navigator for many Pacific survey flights that later laid out Pan Am's trans-Pacific air service. He also penned several technical articles on aerial navigation.

In March 1937, Earhart piloted her Electra from Oakland to Honolulu. She made the flight in 15 hours, 51½ minutes, break-ing the previous record, set by Pan Am's Hawaii clipper, by over an hour. The Electra's propeller bearings ran out of lubricant during the flight, thus forcing a delay while the problem was serviced. Had the problem not been discovered, Earhart's Elec-tra would have gone down between Hawaii and Howland, mak-ing history in a different way.

On March 20, Earhart resumed her quest. With Earhart at

the controls, the trio was going to cover the eighteen hundred miles to Howland but got no farther than the runway. During takeoff Earhart's fuel-laden plane hit a wet patch, causing it to skid. She applied power to one engine to compensate, but this did not straighten the Electra, which continued to veer right. The right tire then blew out, and was followed by the collapse of the left landing gear. The Electra flopped onto its belly, grinding into the concrete runway in a screeching right turn that bent back the propeller blades. The wrecked plane finally came to a stop. One of the fuel tanks had ruptured. Earhart had the good sense to cut off the engine switches, preventing an explosion. The trio emerged from the aircraft unscathed, but damage to the Electra was extensive. The right engine had been pushed into the wing, which had also buckled. The twin rudders were bent. The left wing was canted upward.

The Electra would have to be dismantled, crated, and sent back to Lockheed to be rebuilt.

Earhart was unfazed. "This accident means postponement only," she told the news reporters. "It is my full intention to go ahead with the adventure as soon as possible." With that said she boarded a ship back to Los Angeles.

Amelia's determination would have fatal consequences.

Writing just months after her disappearance, Hilton Railey questioned the value of Earhart's final flight:

Why . . . did she attempt that hazardous expedition? She had to. She was caught up in the hero racket, which compelled her to strive for increasingly dramatic records, bigger and braver feats that automatically insured the publicity necessary to the maintenance of her position as the foremost woman pilot in the world. She was a victim of the era of "hot" aeronautics, which began with Colonel Lindbergh and Admiral Byrd, and which shot "scientific" expeditions across continents, oceans and polar regions by dint of individual exhibition.

Railey had a point, though he overlooked the positive consequences. The aviation heroes and heroines of the 1920s and
1930s popularized flight, inspiring a generation to look to the
skies. By the end of the 1930s airlines would begin scheduled
service across the Atlantic and Pacific. Earhart specifically inspired women to seek careers rather than marriages, including
some who went to flight school to earn their wings.

So what was wrong with a little record-setting and all-
American hype on the side?

The Last Flight

Due to changes in weather patterns, Earhart would make the
next attempt to circle the globe by flying west to east. In late
May, she flew the repaired Electra from Oakland to Miami, announcing the start of her second attempt on June 1, this time
with Noonan alone as navigator.

By easy stages, Earhart made her way to Brazil, crossing the
narrow South Atlantic from Natal to St. Louis, Senegal. Then it
was across Africa via Dakar, Fort Lamy, El Fasher, Khartoum,
then Assab in Eriterea. The stages got longer. Earhart flew a
1,900-mile leg from Assab to Karachi on June 14. Three days
later a 1,390-mile flight was made to Calcutta. From there Earhart
flew shorter stages from Calcutta to Rangoon, then to Singa-
pore, on to Bandung, to Surabaya (both in present-day Indone-
sia), and then on to Port Darwin, Australia, and from there to
New Guinea. By the end of June the duo had reached Lae, New
Guinea. Howland Island, a patch of coral and dirt measuring
two miles long and a half-mile wide, was about 2,500 miles eastward. As one newspaper described it, "no plane has ever ven-
tured that route."

It was going to be a very long leap of faith.

On Friday, July 2, Earhart took the controls of the Electra,
heading eastward. But the flight may have been compromised at
the start by several factors. An antenna mounted underneath the
Electra may have been torn off during taxiing and takeoff.

While newsreel footage suggests this possibility, no antenna was found on the runway. Earhart and Noonan had discarded a retractable wire antenna during earlier stages on the way to Lae; cranking the antenna back in after every transmission had been getting to be a pain. The Coast Guard cutter *Itasca* and the U.S. navy tugboat *Ontario* were stationed near Howland. Both the *Itasca* and the Electra had radio direction-finding gear, thus allowing Earhart to fly into Howland by "following the beam" once radio contact was made with the ship. Earhart planned to check in with *Itasca* via radio every thirty minutes during the flight.

The *Itasca*'s communications log tells the story of how routine turned to disaster. At 2:45 A.M., Earhart's voice is recognized, but her words come through garbled: "Cloudy weather. Cloudy" was all that was heard.

One hour later, Earhart asks *Itasca* to broadcast every hour and half hour at 3,105 kilocycles; weather overcast.

At 4:43 A.M., five listened in the ship's radio room to Earhart's garbled voice, making out nothing.

Then, at 5:12 A.M. Earhart radios: "Want bearing on 3,105 kilocycles on hour. Will whistle in microphone." At least whistling into the mike would avoid the garbling problem, giving the radio crew on the *Itasca* something to lock on to.

At 5:15 A.M., the crew picked up the sound of Earhart's whistling over the radio speaker. She estimated her position at two hundred miles out from Howland.

Then, at 5:45 A.M., the next message: "Please take bearing on us and report in half hour. I will make noise on the microphone. About 100 miles out."

The plane had a cruising speed of close to 200 miles per hour.

Earhart should be arriving at *Itasca*'s position in about thirty minutes.

Six fifteen A.M.: Nothing.

Six thirty A.M.: Nothing.

Six forty-five A.M.: Nothing.

Seven A.M.: Nothing.

Seven fifteen A.M.: Nothing.

At 7:30 A.M., Earhart broadcasts again: "We must be on you but cannot see you. Have been unable to reach you by radio. We are flying at 1,000 feet."

Next call comes in at 7:57 A.M.: "We are circling but cannot see island. Cannot hear you. Go ahead on 7,500 kilocycles with long counts either now or on schedule. Time on half hour."

At 8:03 A.M.: "Earhart calling *Itasca*. We received your signals but unable to get minimum. Please take bearings on us and answer on 3,105 kilocycles." Using the Morse key, Earhart made "long dashes," which were noted on the *Itasca*'s communications log, but the radio direction-finder could not "cut her in" at 3,105 kilocycles.

Then, at 8:44 A.M. came the message: "We are online, possible 157–337. Will repeat this message on 6,120 kilocycles. We are now running north and south."

Then silence.

Followed by more silence.

A second radio direction-finder had been set up on Howland Island prior to Earhart's final leg as a backup for the *Itasca*. Though manned and operating overnight, it could not establish a bearing on the fated Electra due to Earhart's brief voice transmissions.

Itasca fired up her boiler to pour out thick, black smoke in the hope that Earhart and Noonan could spot it.

The only thing left to do was weigh anchor and search the most likely place where Earhart might have made her last radio call.

Prior to the flight Earhart was advised by *Itasca* that the ship's direction-finder had a frequency range from 270 to 550 kilocycles, and Earhart's radio could broadcast at 500 kilocycles, within the *Itasca*'s frequency range. Yet repeated signals from *Itasca* asking Earhart to switch her frequency to 500 kilocycles were never acknowledged.

The Coast Guard had itself covered, putting the blame on Earhart for miscommunication. It did not help that Earhart's 50-watt transmitter was attached to a less than great V-shaped antenna. While 3,105 kilocycles was the frequency the Federal Communications Commission had allotted for civil aviation in the United States, it was not the best for long-distance communication.

Search Is a Lost Cause

Blame game aside, a rescue mission still had to be mounted. The north-south line 157–337 degrees intersected with Howland's location (0 degrees, 48 minutes, 28 seconds north latitude, 176 degrees, 37 minutes, and 6 seconds west longitude). *Itasca* steamed along that line to the north–northwest and found nothing, then widened its search area to the northeast of Howland, still finding nothing. The Coast Guard believed Earhart's plane came down about one hundred miles north of Howland.

President Franklin Roosevelt committed the Navy to the search mission. On Saturday, July 3, the Navy dispatched the battleship USS *Colorado* from Pearl Harbor. Aboard were three float planes, normally used for scouting. In California, the carrier USS *Lexington*, with over fifty planes onboard, was ordered to make ready for search duty in the South Pacific.

There may have been reason for cautious optimism. Ham radio operators reported picking up Earhart's signals after July 2, following a broadcast by KGMB in Honolulu on 3,105 kilocycles instructing Earhart to use key or voice to "break" the carrier wave at that frequency for one minute, followed by four short breaks. Pan Am also reported the breaks—or dashes—as well, but drew a bearing four hundred miles northeast of Howland. Another interpretation offered by Pan Am radio operators was that Earhart and Noonan might have made it to the Phoenix Island group south of Howland.

Earhart's husband, G. P. Putnam, pointed out to reporters that the plane was well stocked with concentrated food that could keep Earhart and Noonan alive for a while. "I have a hunch they are sitting somewhere on a coral island and sending out their signals. . . . Fred [Noonan] is probably out sitting on a rock now catching their dinner with those fishing lines they had aboard. There'll be driftwood to make a fire. Maybe they could rig up a gasoline stove if there is any gasoline left." He had also paid a visit to Noonan's wife that July 3 to provide her with some reassurance.

Paul Mantz, a technical adviser for the Earhart flight, theorized that Earhart could have made a water landing and drifted back to the Phoenix Islands, which are located south of Howland. Commander Clarence Williams, who mapped out Earhart's route, also theorized that adverse winds may have blown Earhart's plane along a more southerly course, putting the crash site near Baker Island, about forty miles south of Howland. Other experts pondered the possibility of Earhart and Noonan salvaging the transmitter to broadcast an SOS, but without engine power the radio's generator could not work, and battery life would have been limited. The Electra's radio battery was stowed in the plane's underside. If Earhart made a water landing, the seawater would have killed the battery.

There was no way Earhart could use the radio if the plane was afloat.

Skeptics may wonder if there ever was a reasonable chance of finding Earhart and Noonan alive. The concept was not far-fetched. One naval plane that ditched one hundred miles shy of Hawaii in 1925 drifted for nine days before being found and the crew rescued, despite the radio being inoperable. In 1931, the two-man crew of another plane, which was lost in the Atlantic off of South America, was rescued after being adrift for five days. On Monday, July 5, *Itasca* reached a point 281 miles north of Howland, again checking out a report by three radio operators at Wailupe Naval Station who may have received a fragmentary radio signal: "281 north Howland . . . KHAQQ . . . beyond north . . . don't hold with us much longer . . . above water . . . shut off." KHAQQ was Earhart's call sign. But the *Itasca* reported finding nothing.

The Coast Guard was still picking up a weak signal on Earhart's frequency, adding to speculation that the plane had made it to land. Expert calculations by the Navy noted that prevailing winds at the time of Earhart and Noonan's disappearance would have blown the Lockheed Electra on a southeasterly course from Howland.

The *Colorado* launched its three search planes on Wednesday, July 7, from the vicinity of Howland Island. The two-hour flight covered the McKean Island area south of the equator and Winslow Reef southeast of Howland. The air search turned up nothing. *Itasca,* along with the Navy minesweeper USS *Swan,* together had searched 104,000 square miles of ocean by this time. The *Lexington*'s arrival, expected on Monday, July 12, would add more than fifty aircraft to the search, capable of overflying thirty-six thousand square miles in six hours.

By Friday, July 9, the Navy was concentrating its search south of Howland, with a particular eye on the eight islands that make up the Phoenix group. But hope began to fade when the *Colorado, Itasca,* and *Swan* found nothing after covering another thirty-eight thousand square miles in the area where the weak radio signals were supposed to have originated.

Carondelet Reef, Gardner Island, and McKean Island were all overflown.

The searchers spotted a wrecked tramp steamer and abandoned guano works, but no recent plane wreckage. Pessimism turned out to be founded when the source of Earhart's weak radio signals turned out to be a radio dramatization of Earhart's fatal flight that was carried by KGMB in Honolulu and picked up by an overexcited radioman in Hilo who misinterpreted the program. (Millions of Americans would later do something similar on October 31, 1938, by mistaking a radio broadcast of *War of the Worlds* for an actual invasion from the planet Mars. Some people believe everything they hear on the radio.)

Monday, July 12, marked the tenth day of Earhart's disappearance.

The *Lexington* was now on the scene, ready to launch fifty to sixty aircraft at a time to run massive search patterns. The search area had expanded to become a 265,000-square-mile box, with Howland at its center. Weather restricted the first air search by the *Lexington* to just twenty planes on Tuesday, July 13. Once weather had improved, thirty search planes were flown on a bearing parallel to the carrier, each plane flying two miles apart at 120 mph at 500 feet.

The air corridor would cover a path 60 miles wide to a range of 100 to 200 miles. The chances of finding the Lockheed Electra, Earhart, or Noonan were becoming slim to none.

By Thursday, July 15, press reports were describing the search as "increasingly hopeless." The *Lexington*'s air group had to cut the number of search planes by a third due to tropical heat and the harsh challenge of keeping so many planes airworthy. Mechanics were taxed to the limit.

Itasca and *Swan* had already shifted their search pattern six hundred miles west of Howland, toward the Gilbert Islands, again taking into account the possibility that the Lockheed had made a water landing and drifted back.

The next day the air search shifted northward, as the *Lexington* launched another forty-two planes to comb a corridor on either side of the date line to a point 220 miles north of the equator, covering another twenty-eight thousand square miles of ocean.

Still nothing.

Monday, July 19, marked the last day of search. The *Lexington* was finally running out of aviation gasoline. A quarter of a million square miles of ocean had been searched by air and sea, turning up not a clue.

President Franklin Roosevelt justified the $4 million expense by pointing out that the fliers and sailors would have put in the same work had all the ships and planes been out on maneuvers.

By the end of July the only person holding out any hope was G. P. Putnam. He acknowledged that his wife would probably be dead if the plane made a water landing, but he still held out hope that the plane may have landed in the Gilbert, Marshall, or Ellice Island groups. Even so, hope does not last forever. Seventeen months after her disappearance, Earhart was declared legally dead by a Los Angeles probate court. Putnam was named executor of the estate. Earhart's will left the cash portion of the estate to her mother, Amy Otis Earhart, through a trust fund.

Others staged their own search missions.

In October 1939, Eric Hanner pulled out of Honolulu at the helm of a fifty-five-foot schooner to spend a year in the South Pacific looking for Earhart. He was not successful. Another schooner captain, Irving Johnson, searched about sixty specks, reefs, and islands around the Gilbert and Ellice Island groups in the spring of 1940. He found no more than Hanner had.

World War II would put an end to the theorizing, for a little while. Like the Kennedy assassination, the Earhart disappearance would keep going, since no one likes an unsolved mystery.

Now What?

Just as nature abhors a vacuum, every mystery needs an explanation.

During the war years, rumors were rife in America that Amelia Earhart was really a spy whose final flight uncovered illegal Japanese efforts to fortify their Pacific islands, clearly a treaty violation.

Her plane crashed or was shot down, she was captured, then deep-sixed somewhere.

For Hollywood, this angle was too good to be false, so it

deserved a movie! *Flight for Freedom* opened at New York's Radio City Music Hall in April 1943. Though there is no character in the movie named Amelia Earhart, actress Rosalind Russell tried to strike a good resemblance. Fred MacMurray played a rival flier whom she falls in love with briefly. Then duty calls. Rosalind Russell realizes she also loves her country, and off she flies for a cause greater then herself!!!

In 1944, Earhart lore caught its first curveball. U.S. Marines overran Saipan in the Marianas. An American officer attached to the Marshall Islands' military government heard a second-hand tale from a local islander that an American woman pilot was picked up by a fishing boat, forwarded to the Japanese authorities, and taken back to Japan before the war. The story got a brief mention in *The New York Times,* then dismissed. The story seemed as off course as far-fetched. Saipan was due north from Lae, the course perpendicular to the eastward heading for Howland. Earhart might have been off course on her last flight, but not that far off course.

The rumors fueled the spy story, but Earhart deserves no credit here. Pacific spy honors really belong to Lieutenant Colonel Earl H. Ellis, U.S. Marine Corps, who began studying the possibility of war with Japan in the early 1920s.

Ellis played an important role in developing the Marines doctrine for seizing defended island bases through amphibious assault. He supplemented his studies with undercover trips to various Japanese-held island groups in the Pacific. Ellis died mysteriously in Palau in 1923.

With the war over in 1945, the United States had ample opportunity to comb Japanese archives, but found no records about a captured American woman flyer. Earhart's mother believed that her daughter had been spying for Uncle Sam, given her reluctance to talk about the Lae–Howland leg of her flight. In a 1949 statement, Amy Otis Earhart said she believed her daughter had landed on a small island, got picked up by a Japanese fishing vessel, was brought to the Marshall Islands, allowed to broadcast a few messages, and then was killed by an "arranged accident." Unlike her mother, Muriel Earhart Morrissey insisted that her sister Amelia was not a spy.

Speaking at a symposium sponsored by the Smithsonian's National Air and Space Museum in 1982, Morrissey put it this way: "She [Amelia] wanted to be the first woman to fly around the world. She wouldn't have been dishonest with the people who put up the money [for the flight]." As for her sister's disappearance? "I believe she just ran out of gas and went down off Howland Island," Morrissey said.

The Saipan rumor was difficult to slay. In 1960, Paul Mantz, who had played a key supporting role in Earhart's final flight, was trying to run down the serial number of an aircraft generator found on Saipan. Was it the one that was installed in Earhart's Lockheed?

While Mantz was trying to track down his clue, reporter Fred Groener of CBS aired a story citing reports by local people of a white woman and white man who had crash-landed on Saipan, then were captured by the Japanese. Hilton Railey, who "discovered" Earhart, claimed that she died in a crash landing at Saipan, based on his correspondence with several Japanese sources. Captain Paul Briand Jr. (U.S. Air Force) added fuel to the controversy by claiming to have Japanese photographs of Earhart's execution and burial on Saipan. Within a month, the generator clue that Mantz was running down proved false. A Bendix Corp. spokesman said that the company had found a Japanese bearing in the unit. The company had not used Japanese parts in its generators at the time, he said.

Groener revived the story in 1961, claiming to have recovered bone fragments from the two graves that Saipan natives said were those of Earhart and Noonan. The Saipan story quickly went cold in the early 1960s. The assassination of President Kennedy replaced the Earhart disappearance. The second gunman on the grassy knoll displaced Saipan.

The public can only take so many conspiracy theories; the

Navy, still fewer. It released declassified files in 1967, with no mention of Earhart's crash and/or capture on Saipan.

The Earhart story came back from the grave in 1992, but not in Saipan. The clue that started the next round of speculation originated at Nikumaroro (formerly known as Gardner Island), courtesy of the International Group for Historic Aircraft Recovery.

Roughly at the midpoint of Earhart's last flight, Nikumaroro was also the last known position radioed to the *Itasca* by Earhart. Found was a sheet of aluminum with rivet holes and a Cat's Paw shoe heel. But the tray-sized metal piece lacked a serial number that could have been used to make a definitive trace. At best, the evidence is circumstantial. Metallurgical tests done four years later by Alcoa could not ascertain the fragment's age, but experts said that the alloy used in the metal sheet was typically found in 1930s aircraft.

The Navy had searched Nikumaroro/Gardner in 1937 and found nothing.

In 1998, the metal fragment theory was supplemented by a report about bone fragments. The report was uncovered by archival work done by the International Group for Historic Aircraft Recovery. A British doctor based in Fiji, D. W. Hoodless, had measured some bones recovered from Gardner Island by a survey group visit in 1940. Sadly, the bone fragments were lost to history. Two American forensic anthropologists took the British doctor's report and cross-checked it against a scientific database of human remains. In an academic paper the anthropologists noted cautiously that if Hoodless's measurements were accurate, the remains he documented would more likely than not belong to a European woman about five feet six inches in height. Without the actual remains, a DNA check against Earhart's known descendants is impossible.

Again, the evidence remains circumstantial.

Flying Proof Versus Written Fiction

Other flyers tried to gain insight into Earhart's disappearance by retracing her steps. All of them failed to disappear. Howland could no longer be used as a stopping point, having been abandoned after World War II, its dirt-and-coral airstrip reverting back to nature.

If Earhart had been successful, she would have been the first woman pilot to fly around the world. Geraldine Mock became the first in 1964, flying a Cessna 180. Joan Merriam would accomplish the same feat, also in 1964, only this time by retracing Earhart's flight plan, flying a twin-engine Piper Apache. Merriam had to fly due north from Port Moresby, New Guinea, to Guam, near Saipan, a route that had to fill in for the lost Lae–Howland leg of Earhart's flight. The U.S. Navy assigned three aircraft to escort Merriam on this stage. (They weren't taking any chances?) She made it back to Oakland, California, by May 12. Sadly, Merriam lost her life in a crash of a Cessna 180 near Big Pines, California, less than a year later.

In 1967, flight instructor June Pellegrino also retraced the Earhart flight, but she was flying a Lockheed L-10 Electra similar to Earhart's. Her South Pacific route took her from the Canton Islands to Honolulu. Like many experienced fliers, Pellegrino believed Earhart ran out of gas short of Howland.

Another Lockheed L-10 Electra made the trip in 1997, this time with Linda Finch at the controls. Unlike Earhart's $80,000 "flying lab," Finch's plane required a $1 million restoration and was equipped with an up-to-date satellite navigation system. A chase plane flew alongside as well. Pratt & Whitney, an aero-engine maker that sponsored the flight, probably wasn't taking any chances, either.

Authors don't have to be as exact as pilots. One incident proving the point came in 1970, when McGraw-Hill published *Amelia Earhart Lives*. Coauthors Joseph Klass and Joseph Gervais claimed that Earhart was captured by the Japanese while on an aerial spy mission, held prisoner in the Imperial Palace in Tokyo, and then released in 1945 under an assumed name in exchange for Emperor Hirohito staying on the throne. The woman who was alleged to be Amelia Earhart refuted the claim. Irene Bolam had spent her World War II years in suburban Mineola, New York, not in Tokyo, Japan. She dismissed the book's findings as "utter nonsense."

Gervais had run into Bolam at a meeting of the Early Flyers of America and noted her resemblance to Amelia Earhart. "In response to his subsequent letters and telephone calls, I denied in writing and over the telephone that I was Amelia Earhart. . . . He appeared more interested in the fantasy than fact," Bolam told a *New York Times* reporter.

Lost Star: The Search for Amelia Earhart by Randall Brink revived the Saipan/spy mission myth in 1994. Brink repeated the rumor that the captured Earhart was forced to broadcast Japanese propaganda as Tokyo Rose, then was released and returned to the United States with a new identity.

Brink's book even ran a photo of Earhart looking pretty bad, her hands bound behind her back, allegedly taken by a police officer on Saipan and later obtained by Gervais (a dependable source?). Another interview, with a Lockheed technician, claims that two holes were cut in the Lockheed's fuselage to serve as camera ports, but the technician goes unnamed by Brink.

Fiction repeated is not proof, and certainly cannot pass as nonfiction.

Conspiracy theorists used their imaginations to make up the pieces to complete their puzzle pictures, since the real pieces of evidence were lacking. But fiction writers get to paint their pictures using imagination only. Jane Mendelsohn did so in 1996 in her novel *I Was Amelia Earhart.* She touches on the actual details of Earhart's late career to form the picture frame, skipping all the spy story nonsense, to crash her heroine on a tropical island, where she must start over with Noonan alongside. In her fantasy, Mendelsohn has Earhart keeping a diary of her new life, falling in love with the tropical paradise around her, all this time waiting to be rescued. At least Michiko Kakutani of *The New York Times* gave it a good review.

More unromantic is *Amelia Earhart: The Mystery Solved*, coauthored by pilot Elgen Long and his wife, Mary Long, a publicist. The book, which came out in 2000, compiled all the factors that would have worked against Earhart and Noonan. It is a dry catalog of error and sloppiness. The headwinds were too strong, slowing the plane and forcing it to burn more fuel than expected. Earhart and Noonan did not know how to operate their radio direction-finder, thus making it impossible to get a fix on *Itasca*'s radio beam. The cockpit seats lacked shoulder belts, thus raising the likelihood that the pilot and navigator would have been injured or killed in a crash. Then there was that radio control box that was mounted at eye level in the cockpit. Not a good place for that gadget if your unrestrained body were to go shooting out through the windshield. The Longs claim to have spent twenty-five years working on their account, interviewing more than one hundred sources and digging up reports about the last flight, all cataloged in boring detail according to a brief, unfavorable review by *The New York Times*. While theorists get lost in flights of fancy, the Longs simply brought the tale back to earth, concluding that Earhart and Noonan came down one hundred miles short of Howland.

The last word goes to Amelia Earhart's niece, Amy Kleppner, a Maryland high school teacher, who accepts the crash at sea short of Howland conclusion after using Occam's razor to shave down all the other theories.

"I've read everything written and reported about my aunt," Kleppner said in a 1998 interview. "No one has produced credible evidence that their [Earhart and Noonan's] plane crashed on any of the Phoenix Islands, or that they died of starvation, or that they were captured, tortured and killed by the Japanese on Saipan, or any other theories."

"The simplest explanation is the most likely," Kleppner concluded.

National Air and Space Museum
Smithsonian Institution
On the National Mall
Independence Avenue at 6th Street SW
Washington, DC 20560

William Terdoslavich

Who says that serious science can't be icky and gross?

The Mütter of
All Medical Museums

In the words of their mission statement:

> The Mütter Museum was founded to educate future doctors
> about anatomy and human medical anomalies. Today, it
> serves as a valuable resource for educating and enlightening
> the public about our medical past and telling important sto-
> ries about what it means to be human. The Mütter Museum
> embodies The College of Physicians of Philadelphia's mis-
> sion to advance the cause of health, and uphold the ideals and
> heritage of medicine.

Founded in 1849 at the suggestion of Dr. Isaac Parrish to the
College of Physicians of Philadelphia, the Mütter (named after
its first real benefactor, Dr. Thomas Dent Mütter, who gave it
both its first real cash endowment as well as his own personal
collection of instructive anatomical and pathological specimens) was started as a museum of pathological anatomy to

preserve valuable material that might otherwise be lost to science.

According to their official history:

> Dr. Mütter's collection of bones, wet specimens, plaster casts, wax and papier-mâché models, dried preparations, and medical illustrations—over 1700 items in all—joined the 92 specimens from the College's earlier collection in the new quarters. Many of the items which today's visitors find most memorable date from that time: the bladder stones removed from Chief Justice John Marshall by Dr. Philip Syng Physick; and the skeleton of a woman whose rib-cage was compressed by tight lacing. . . . Around this nucleus the museum grew rapidly.

And indeed the collection did . . . and still does.

On the mundane side there is an extensive collection of what can only be referred to as examples of the evolution of medical technology, with an impressive multigenerational lineup of surgical/medical instruments from throughout the ages, including a wooden stethoscope from the early nineteenth century believed to have been made by René Laennec (credited as the stethoscope's original inventor); a battlefield sewing kit belonging to Florence Nightingale; Marie Curie's quartz-piezo electrometer (personally presented to the college by Madame Curie in 1921); and a full-scale model of the first successful heart-lung machine; as well as numerous archival photos of battle injuries that were taken on the battlefield during the Civil War—and that's the boring stuff.

The greatest crowd-pleasing aspect of the Mütter collection lies in its abundance of anatomical points of interests. For example:

The Mütter possesses Joseph Hyrtl's collection of skulls, 139 in all (Joseph Hyrtl, an Austrian anatomist, who was born in 1810 and died in 1894, authored *The Handbook of Topo-*

graphic Anatomy, the first textbook of applied anatomy of its kind ever issued, which went through some twenty editions and has been translated into every modern language); skeletons in all shapes and sizes, including the tallest human skeleton currently on display in America; the Muniz collection of trephined (they have holes cut in them) Peruvian skulls; and numerous brains arranged in size order from frog to man, as well as representative samples from an epileptic and a convicted murderer.

There is also what could be called a celebrity section.

In addition to the aforementioned bladder stones of one of our greatest chief justices of the Supreme Court, there are also VIP body parts from both a former president of the United States and from the accused assassin of a president of the United States.

At the end of June in 1893, the public and the press were informed that then president of the United States Grover Cleveland was on a vacation on a private yacht steaming up Long Island Sound.

The truth about that little boat trip was not to be revealed until a quarter century later, when Dr. William Keen wrote the following account of his experience in the pages of *The Saturday Evening Post.*

From "The Surgical Operations on President Cleveland in 1893," by Dr. William Williams Keen:

> On Sunday, June eighteenth, 1893, Dr. R. M. O'Reilly—later Surgeon-General of the United States Army—the official medical attendant on officers of the Government in Washington, examined a rough place on the roof of Mr. Cleveland's mouth. He found an ulcer as large as a quarter of a dollar, extending from the molar teeth to within one-third of an inch of the middle line and encroaching slightly on the soft palate, and some diseased bone. The pathologist at the Army Medical Museum—who was kept in ignorance, of course, of the

name of the patient—after examining the small fragment which Doctor O'Reilly had removed, reported that it was strongly indicative of malignancy.

Doctor O'Reilly, foreseeing the need for an operation, advised Mr. Cleveland to consult Dr. Joseph D. Bryant, long his medical attendant and intimate friend. Doctor Bryant quickly went to Washington and confirmed the diagnosis. The President, after the examination, with no apparent concern, inquired: "What do you think it is, doctor?"

To which Doctor Bryant replied: "Were it in my mouth I would have it removed at once."

This answer settled the matter.

During the discussion as to what arrangements could be made, "the President would not under any circumstances consent to a time and place that would not give the best opportunity of avoiding disclosure, and even a suspicion that anything of significance had happened to him. The strong desire to avoid notoriety was dwarfed by the fear he had of the effect on the public of a knowledge of his affliction, and on the financial questions of the time."

He decided that July first was the earliest suitable date. Colonel Lamont, the Secretary of War, and a close personal friend, was then informed of the facts, and it was soon arranged that to secure secrecy the operation should be done on Commodore Benedict's yacht, the Oneida.

The next question was as to how soon after the operation the President could probably safely return to Washington.

August seventh was decided on.

Meantime Doctor Bryant had written me, asking for a consultation "in a very important matter." As I was about to go to New England I suggested that I should go to New York at noon and that we meet at three-fifteen on the deserted deck of the Fall River boat, which did not leave till 6 P.M. There, without any interruption, we laid all necessary plans. The living rooms on the Oneida were prepared and disinfected; an operating table and all the necessary instruments, drugs, dressings, and so on, were sent on board. Arrangements were made with Dr. Ferdinand Hasbrouck, a dentist accustomed to giving nitrous oxide, to assist.

My own family were kept in entire ignorance of the facts. To explain my absence I simply said that I was called to a distance for an important operation and would probably be absent for some days.

On June thirtieth I reached New York City in the evening, went to Pier A, and was taken over to the yacht, which was lying at anchor at a considerable distance from the Battery. Dr. E. G. Janeway, of New York; Doctor O'Reilly; Dr. John F. Erdmann, Doctor Bryant's assistant; and Doctor Hasbrouck had also secretly gone to the yacht. The President, Doctor Bryant and Secretary Lamont, at a later hour arrived from Washington, openly drove to Pier A, whence they were taken to the yacht.

At the time when he left Washington, on June thirtieth, Mr. Cleveland issued a call for a special session of Congress on August seventh, with the object of averting the financial danger by the repeal of the silver clause of the Sherman Act.

On arriving on the yacht the President lighted a cigar, and we sat on deck smoking and chatting until near midnight. Once he burst out with "Oh, Doctor Keen, those office seekers! Those office seekers! They haunt me even in my dreams!" I had never met him before; but during that hour or more of conversation I was deeply impressed by his splendid personality and his lofty patriotism. I do not believe there was a more devoted patriot living.

He passed a good night, sleeping well without any sleeping medicine. Before he dressed, Doctor Janeway made a most careful examination of his chest and found nothing wrong.

There was little if any arteriosclerosis. His pulse was ninety. His kidneys were almost entirely normal.

I then examined him myself. He stated that he was sure the

rough place was of recent origin; that it was not there on March fourth, when he was inaugurated, but had been first observed about six or eight weeks before July first. There were no perceptibly enlarged glands. I confirmed the facts as to the ulcer and deemed the growth to be unquestionably malignant. During the morning his mouth was repeatedly cleansed and disinfected.

The anesthetic troubled us. Our anxiety related not so much to the operation itself as to the anesthetic and its possible dangers. These might easily arise in connection with the respiration, the heart, or the function of the kidneys, etc., dangers which are met with not infrequently as a result of administering an anesthetic, especially in a man of Mr. Cleveland's age and physical condition. The patient was 56 years of age, very corpulent, with a short thick neck, just the build and age for a possible apoplexy—an incident which had actually occurred to one of my own patients. He was also worn out mentally and physically by four months of exacting labor and the office seekers' importunities.

Twenty-four years ago we had not the refined methods of diagnosis, nor had we the greatly improved methods of anesthesia which we have to-day.

After canvassing the whole matter we decided to perform at least the earlier steps of the operation under nitrous oxide, and the later, if necessary, under ether. Doctor Hasbrouck was of opinion that we could not keep the patient well anesthetized with nitrous oxide long enough to complete the operation satisfactorily.

Doctor Bryant and Secretary Lamont had spent the night at their homes, but returned to the yacht the next morning— July first. The yacht then proceeded up the East River at half speed while the operation was performed.

So careful were we to elude observation that Doctor Bryant and all of us doctors, who might have been recognized by some of the staff of Bellevue Hospital, deserted the deck for the cabin while we were steaming through the East River in sight of the Hospital at Twenty-sixth Street.

Commodore Benedict and Secretary Lamont remained on deck during the operation, which was performed in the cabin. The steward was the only other person present, to fetch and carry. I have always thought that due credit was not given to him, and to the captain and the crew, for their never betraying what had taken place. It is curious also that the alert and ubiquitous reporters seem never to have thought of interviewing the captain and crew of the Oneida. The captain and crew knew Mr. Cleveland very well, for he had already traveled over fifty thousand miles on the yacht and his mere presence was no novelty.

Any curiosity as to the evidently unusual occurrences was apparently allayed by the statement that the President had to have two very badly ulcerated teeth removed and that fresh, pure air, and disinfected quarters and skilled doctors, all had to be provided, lest blood poisoning should set in—a very serious matter when the patient was the just-inaugurated President of the United States.

Doctor Hasbrouck first extracted the two left upper bicuspid teeth under nitrous oxide. Doctor Bryant then made the necessary incisions in the roof of the mouth, also under nitrous oxide.

At one-fourteen P.M. ether was given by Doctor O'Reilly. During the entire operation Doctor Janeway kept close watch upon the patient's pulse and general condition. Doctor Bryant performed the operation, assisted by myself and Doctor Erdmann.

The entire left upper jaw was removed from the first bicuspid tooth to just beyond the last molar, and nearly up to the middle line. The floor of the orbit—the cavity in the skull containing the eyeball—was not removed, as it had not yet been attacked. A small portion of the soft palate was removed. This extensive operation was decided upon because we found that the antrum—the large hollow cavity in the up-per jaw—was partly filled by a gelatinous mass, evidently a sarcoma. This diagnosis was later confirmed by Dr. William H. Welch, of the Johns Hopkins Hospital, who had also ex-amined the former specimens.

The entire operation was done within the mouth, without any external incision, by means of a cheek retractor, the most useful instrument I have ever seen for such an operation.

This retractor I had brought back with me from Paris in 1866. The retention of the floor of the orbit prevented any displacement of the eyeball. This normal appearance of the eye, the normal voice, and especially the absence of any exter-nal scar, which was the most important evidence of all, greatly aided in keeping the operation an entire secret.

(This cheek-retractor I have deposited with the College or Physicians of Philadelphia together with the portion of tissue removed and photograph of the casts of the mouth on which Dr. Gibson molded the artificial Jaw which he kindly pre-sented to the College.)

Only one blood vessel was tied . . . the operation was done wholly within the mouth thus avoiding any external scar. . . . The large cavity was packed with gauze to arrest the subse-quent moderate oozing of blood. At two-fifty-five P.M. a hy-podermic of one-sixth of a grain of morphine was given—the only narcotic administered at any time.

What a sigh of intense relief we surgeons breathed when the patient was once more safe in bed can hardly be imagined!

Mr. Cleveland's temperature after the operation was 100.8 degrees Fahrenheit, and never thereafter rose above 100 de-grees. His pulse was usually ninety or a little over.

With the packing in the cavity his speech was labored but intelligible; without the packing it was wholly unintelligible, resembling the worst imaginable case of cleft palate. Had this not been so admirably remedied by Doctor Gibson, secrecy later would have been out of the question. . . .

On July fifth, in the evening, the yacht reached Gray Gables and "the President walked from the launch to his residence with but little apparent effort."

And the tumor as well as a laryngeal mirror and the famed cheek retractor are still displayed proudly today with the story of this case of confidential presidential surgery.

The body part from the presidential assassin is a "piece of the thorax of J. Wilkes Booth, assassin of President Lincoln" that was provided to the Mütter by Philadelphia surgeon Joseph Janvier Woodward, who is recorded as having performed the autopsy on the murderer. Yet, it must be said that this is not the most famous autopsy souvenir in the museum.

An article from *The New York Times* for February 8, 1874, reads as follows:

CHANG AND ENG—PREPARATION FOR
THE AUTOPSY ON MONDAY

Special Dispatch to the New York Times

Philadelphia, Feb. 7—The arrival of the bodies, so strangely united in life and death, of Chang and Eng, has given a fresh impetus to the excitement caused by the proposed autopsy which is to take place on Monday, and which will once set at rest that very debatable question in the minds of the eminent surgeons of the last quarter of a century—the question as to the physical and metaphysical relationship of the world-wide celebrated Siamese twins. One week ago last Thursday Dr. Pancoast, Dr. Allen, and Dr. Andrews, gentlemen of high reputations in their profession in this city, left Philadelphia in the company of the brothers Hollingsworth, the local physicians of Salem, en route for Mount Airy, the home of the Chang and Eng families. . . .

On their arrival the arrangements with the family for the transfer of the bodies to Philadelphia were at once completed. The story of the physicians at Philadelphia having agreed to

pay $10,000 for the privilege of making a post-mortem exam-
ination is, I am assured by Dr. Paucoast [sic], utterly devoid
of foundation. He and his two colleagues have not only not
paid anything, but they are not to pay anything to the family.

This they have done: They, as delegates of their professional brethren, have entered into bonds to return the remains
of the twins to the family at such time as the family may call
for them.

Chang and Eng were, of course, the famous Siamese twins
who toured with P. T. Barnum, and despite being joined at the
chest, had been happily married and had twenty-two children
between them (twelve and ten, respectively), living almost normal
lives with scheduled shift times alternating between their two
households.

The postmortem was performed at the College of Physicians
of Philadelphia, and in keeping with their word, the bodies were
then returned to the families—though not before the surgeons
had laid claim to a plaster cast of the torso of the twins where
the two bodies merged in a band of skin and cartilage, as well as
their conjoined livers.

The twins died on January 17, 1874, at age sixty-three, and after the postmortem were buried in the White Plains Baptist
Church Cemetery. The autopsy found a blood clot in Chang's
brain and recorded his cause of death as a "stroke," but it
couldn't resolve the debate over the cause of Eng's death, which
was eventually written off to "fear," or rather to the knowledge,
that his brother's death would lead to his own.

And, finally, the museum has another VIP as well, though the
legal name and background of this subject is still unknown.

This is the body of a woman who supposedly died of yellow
fever back in the 1800s, whose remains were buried in soil, and,
due to some unexpected chemical reaction, whose corpse quite
literally turned into soap (actually a waxy, soaplike substance
called adipocere).

Indeed, she is currently known as "the Soap Woman."

In 1874 a University of Pennsylvania anatomist named Dr. Joseph Leidy donated the body to the museum. He claimed that the Soap Lady, who was discovered by workers removing bodies from an old burial yard, had died in the late 1700s. "The woman, named Ellenbogen, died in Philadelphia of yellow fever in 1792 and was buried near Fourth and Race Streets," according to the original label attached to the exhibit. Leidy's explanation stood until 1942, when museum curator Dr. Joseph McFarland determined that the Soap Lady had actually died in the 1800s, and that her name had been lost to history.

A CT scan done in 2001 and covered by the Associated Press revealed some organ tissue, raising hope that researchers might be able to learn how the woman died. A previous x-ray had shown eight straight pins and two four-hole buttons manufactured in the nineteenth century.

Who she was and what exactly happened to her still remains to be seen.

———

The Mütter Museum
The College of Physicians of Philadelphia
19 S. 22nd Street
Philadelphia, PA 19103

———

Sometimes certain subjects fall outside of those realms normally studied under such topics as science or history. The unanswered questions or inscrutable truths examined leave these exhibits squarely in the realm of . . .

THE UNCANNY

*Though he has been embraced by purveyors of the
literary fantastic, the legendary magician John
Dee was a real person. If you have any doubts, just
have a look at a few of his trinkets in the hallowed
halls of the British Museum.*

The Mysterious Dr. John Dee

The hideous *Necronomicon* of the mad Arab Abdul Al-
hazred...
    Wilbur had with him the priceless but imperfect copy
of Dr. Dee's English version, which his grandfather had
bequeathed him...
    [A] close survey of the *Necronomicon*...seemed to sup-
ply new and terrible clues to the nature, methods, and de-
sires of the strange evil so vaguely threatening this planet.

**—H. P. Lovecraft,
"The Dunwich Horror"**

These quotations from H. P. Lovecraft's famous tale suggest that
Dr. John Dee, scholar and magus of the sixteenth century, had a
startling familiarity with the legendary book *The Necronomicon*, which contained secrets of the supernatural better left unknown. Lovecraft's words also have contributed to the view that
Dr. Dee was a sorcerer, a warlock, or a wizard.

Others consider him an extremely pious and religious seeker of truth and the word of God whose quest was to bring the material human world closer to the spirit world, so that we creatures of God would know how to serve our God better.

Which was he?

And why does no less eminent an institution than the British Museum display several artifacts belonging to him, as well as provide safe custody for his estimable library collection?

Conflicting accounts of the incidents of his life and work make Dee an exceedingly curious subject. However, please read on, ye seekers of knowledge . . .

There are people who believe one rather well-known cliché that suggests that there is a fine line between genius and madness. Then there are people who think there is a fine line between the worlds of science and magic. This latter group was probably more prevalent centuries ago, and the further you go back in time, the more subscribed to was that belief.

During Shakespeare's time—commonly referred to as the Elizabethan era—one finds the areas of science and magic in frequent battle. And at the very center of this concern was Dr. John Dee. His studies and writings were varied, and quite often crossed from the "legitimate" sciences into the world of magic, or "witchcraft," as some would have called it back then.

Dee's life and studies are fascinating. He was often praised by Queen Elizabeth herself and many of her royal circle, yet there were others who pronounced Dee a charlatan and a warlock, and persecuted the man for his studies, and particularly for his "experiments" with the supernatural.

John Dee was born in 1527. From a very young age Dee was a brilliant student and scholar, and for several years during the 1540s and 1550s he studied on the Continent and acquired a vast knowledge of mathematics and cartology. When he returned to England he brought with him a unique collection of mathematical and astronomical instruments and gadgets, many of them unseen in Britain before. Dee's knowledge and reputation as a scholar ultimately was brought to the attention of the queen herself, as was his skill not just in astronomy, but also in *astrology*. Indeed, Dee was asked to consult the stars and choose a "fortunate" day for Elizabeth's coronation, which he did, to great success. As his reward he became the queen's adviser on all matters astrological and scientific (one foot planted in science, one in *meta*science). A few years earlier, Dee had been far from rewarded for his astrological predictions: In 1555, he had been charged with "calculating" the horoscopes for (then) Queen Mary and Princess Elizabeth and dragged before the Star Chamber, although ultimately he was released. Accusations against him for his studies in science and "magic" would continue for the rest of his life.

While Elizabeth was alive, though, Dee flourished. At one point he amassed a collection of more than four thousand rare books and manuscripts that he had picked up in England and on the Continent, a collection that outshone the libraries of many of England's universities at that time. (Many of these are housed today in the British Museum.)

By 1581, Dee's studies expanded in what many (then and now) thought an unusual direction. He believed he was not receiving the proper credit for his studies and was dissatisfied with his status as a scholar. So since his astrological skills had become famous, and he had an extensive clientele, he began to experiment with crystal gazing (crystallomancy) in order to make contact with the higher spirits. By his own account, one of his attempts proved wildly successful. In his writings he mentions how one evening Uriel, the heavenly angel, appeared in a flash of bright light. This spirit, it is said, handed him a crystal as big as an egg; furthermore, Uriel told him that the "shew-stone" could be used to communicate with the spirits of the "other" world. His experiments/meditations continued in this direction after the angel's visit, but to little success. "Scrying"—conversing with the spirits—was not going very well for Dee, who became obsessed with his attempts to the point of exhaustion. Hoping

fortune would smile upon him if he employed a different mode
of operation, Dee recruited other scryers to work with him.
These assistants would do the actual scrying—looking into the
stone, and perhaps talking to the denizens of the spirit world—
while Dee would jot down notes and observations.

Then into his life came one Edward Kelley, who had changed
his name to Edward Taylor. He became the scryer who would
assist Dee for the longest time. Not much is known about Kelley from before he teamed up with Dee, but what *is* known
about him does not cast him in a favorable light: He had been an
unscrupulous lawyer, then an apothecary claiming to have alchemical skills that had been implemented with the assistance of
a mysterious red powder; he had been convicted of counterfeit-
ing and had his ears cut off; he had been accused of necromancy;
and he was known in some quarters as a sensualist. These are
not, one might notice, good qualifications for someone whose
future employment would deal with speaking with angels, and
one can only speculate as to whether Dee was aware of any part
of Kelley's background.

But Kelley, if not a genuine scryer, was certainly a convincing
showman. Dee, clearly not a stupid man, somehow was convinced that Kelley had the ability to communicate with the spirits. Kelley, acting as Dee's intermediary with the spirits, would
gaze into Dee's stone, and virtually every time the feat was attempted, he would contact the spirits (or vice versa). Kelley convinced Dee that he could see a fire in the stone, a flame that put
him in touch with otherworldly spirits, particularly angels. Kelley, clearly no fool himself, further persuaded Dee that these
spirits were relating a "language" to him, a system of words in
the "Enochian" language, which they would be able to use to
communicate with and learn from the angels. Dee and Kelley
spent innumerable dark nights in the grounds outside his home
praying, fasting, and then learning the language that Kelley
blurted out and Dee recorded meticulously for his own use and
knowledge, and for posterity. On some occasions, perhaps to

make his "presentations" all the more realistic and convincing, Kelley claimed to be in contact with devils, evil spirits whose mission was to destroy the two men and prevent their acquisition of "heavenly" knowledge and the Enochian language of the spirit world.

In Dee's written record of these sessions, *Mysteriorum Liber Primus,* he tells of a communication with the spirit Uriel through the use of his "shew-stone."* Kelley would gaze into the stone, Dee would speak, and the spirit would answer through Kelley. In an early "encounter," Dee writes,

> Than presently cam in one, and threw the brave spirit down by the sholders: and bet him mightyily with a whip: and toke all his robes, and apparell of him: and then he remayned all heary and owggly: and styll the spirit was beaten of him, who cam in after him. And that spirit, which so bet him, sayed to the hearing of my scryer, Lo, thus are the wicked skourged . . .

A few minutes later, the spirit reappears with a comrade:

> my scryer saw Uriel go away: and he remayned out of sight a little while. Then he cam in agayn: and an other with him . . . the other did set down in the chayre, with a sword in his right hand: all his hed glystring like the sonne. The heare of his hed was long. He had wings: and all his lower parts seamed to be with feathers. He had a robe over his body: and a great light in his left hand.

This companion, Kelley told Dee, was the archangel Michael.

Dee and Kelley's scrying sessions continued, and Dee recorded the occurrences and conversations meticulously. (There are several volumes of *Mysteriorum Liber.*) Chronologically, they grow more dramatic, more intricate, and more cryptic, filled with symbols

---

*All *Mysteriorum Liber Primus* quotations are from the John Dee Society.

and symbols. By the third volume, *Mysteriorum Liber Tertius*, Dee was transcribing Kelley/Taylor's actual words verbatim. The "visions" had grown much more spectacular:

E.T.: After a long time there cam a woman: and flung up a ball like a glass: and a voice was hard saying, "Fiat." The ball went into the darknes, and browght with it agreat White Globe hollow transparent. Then she had a Table abowt her neck, square of 12 places. The woman seamed to daunce and swyng the Table: Then cam a hand out of the dark: and stroke her and she stode still, and became fayrer: She sayd, "Ecce signum Incomprehensibilitatis;

E.T.: The woman is transformed into a water, and flyeth up into the Globe of Light.

And a few minutes later:

E.T.: A sword cam out of the Dark: and clave the woman a sunder, and the one half becam a man, and the other a woman, and they went and sat upon the Ball of cley or erth.

Dee, no doubt, took all of this seriously, and thought he was performing a great service for mankind. The benefits, he must have thought, that the wisdom of the angelic world could bring to mankind! How this wisdom—and even the method of gaining this wisdom—would reinforce Dee's philosophical view of the inherent unity of all creation! But Kelley was a different matter. Clearly his aim was his own success—as measured by the contents of his purse.

Dee met Prince Albert Laski, a Polish aristocrat visiting England, in 1583. Laski became intrigued with the scholar's "spiritual" work and invited Dee and Kelley to accompany him back to Poland, but the scholar was reluctant to go. However, one night, the spirits told him to go; the spirits, through the "filter" of one Edward Kelley, seeing an opportunity for a financial windfall, persuaded Dee to make the journey.

Dee and Kelley and their families left for Poland that year, anticipating that their studies in and talents with the spirit world would make them celebrities and lead them to comfortable lives for some time. But for a man supposedly so skilled in astrology, Dee should have known that the wheel of fortune would turn. Upon their arrival in Poland, they in short time discovered that Laski had gone bankrupt, and had fallen out of favor with the aristocracy of his own nation.

Forsaken and becoming desperate, Dee and Kelley and their families wandered through Central Europe for some time. Eventually Dee was able to arrange meetings with two great leaders, Emperor Rudolf II and King Stefan of Poland. Dee and Kelley attempted to convince these men of the importance of their spiritual work, but neither man was impressed. According to some reports, Dee scolded the men for their lack of interest in what he considered monumentally auspicious and important research.

Nothing seemed to be going very well for Dee and Kelley. Dee most likely felt rejected and misunderstood; Kelley, on the other hand, probably resented the lack of financial success their undertaking was having. Perhaps that is why Kelley gradually lost interest in scrying for Dee. And perhaps that is why Kelley regained his interest in alchemy, which he began to practice with some modest success in Europe.

By 1586, Dee and Kelley were settled temporarily near Bohemian count Vilem Rožmberk, and Rožmberk wealth supported the two men for a while. The count found Dee's studies of interest, but something apparently interested him far more: the claims that Kelley had made regarding his alchemical skills. Kelley spent most of his time not scrying for Dee, but playing with various elements and his "mysterious" red powder.

During one of Dee and Kelley's then declining number of

scrying sessions, Kelley informed Dee that the spirits had made a very unusual demand: that Dee and Kelley pool all of their research, their assets, and everything else that they possessed. That order included "pooling" their wives, a most unusual order coming from angels of God! For a time, it seems, Dee complied with this command, but he apparently knew deep in his soul that something was not right.

Dee discontinued the spiritual sessions and conferences with Kelley. Eventually, he ended his "partnership" with Kelley altogether. He never saw Kelley again, and, disheartened and weary, he returned to England in 1589.

Many have speculated that Kelley came up with this "order from the angels" as a method of disassociating himself from Dee, since it was evident that the Europeans were much more interested in Kelley's alchemy. This is not hard to believe, for during one of Dee and Kelley's early scrying sessions, an angel had instructed Dee (through the voice of Kelley) to fire another scryer named Barnabus Saul whom Dee had in his service, because the other scryer—Kelley's competition, as it were—was "accursed" and would harm Dee's family. It seems, therefore, that the "angels" always made demands that in one way or another worked for the benefit of Kelley.

Kelley, at least for a while, thrived under Rožmberk's patronage. For some time he sold many people of prominence—including Emperor Rudolf—that he, with the aid of his red powder, could make gold from other elements. Kelley was even made a "baron" at one point by the emperor. But time—and red powder—eventually ran out. Kelley was locked up in a prison near Prague for what appeared to be to Rudolf a reluctance to cooperate. Kelley was imprisoned a couple of times—the final time on a charge of heresy—and gradually his luck and his powers of selling himself and his abilities dissipated. He died from injuries trying to escape from a German prison in 1593.

Much money had been invested in Kelley by Rožmberk and the emperor, much the way a great deal of time had been invested in him by Dr. Dee. No investment in Kelley ever really paid off.

Dee's life upon returning to England did not fare very well either. He returned to his home after being abroad and found something that may have shocked him as much as some of the revelations of the spirits who had communicated with him: His home had been ransacked during his time away, and many unique and rare items from his collection of scientific and occult instruments had been stolen. A sizable portion of his library was missing also. To Dee this must have been a crushing blow; much of his life's work had disappeared.

Dee tried to return to his studies and his scrying sessions, despite his losses. He found a couple of new scryers to help him, but neither of them had a genuine feel for the sessions, and, perhaps worse, didn't even have Kelley's knowledge or gift of showmanship. They did nothing but deplete the meager finances that Dee had left. In desperation, Dee petitioned Queen Elizabeth for help. After a number of letters, the queen responded. He was given a relatively minor appointment in Manchester—"Warden" of the Collegiate Chapter—a position he held until his health began to deteriorate.

Some view the queen's appointment as less kind and generous than perhaps it should have been for a man she had held in such high regard in the past. Sending him to Manchester was tantamount to a form of minor exile, the thinking behind it being to get an embarrassing man away from London, the same way years later British clergyman and savage satirist Jonathan Swift, author of *Gulliver's Travels,* would be given an appointment as dean of Trinity College in Dublin by Church of England officials. On the one hand, "reward" them; on the other, keep them away.

Dee was forced to resign from the position and return to his home when his health gave out. Worse, Queen Elizabeth was now dead, so Dee really had no one of influence to help him anymore. The new king, James I, had little use for anything or anyone who was even marginally tainted by "witchcraft." So Dee was left to fend for himself. Several of his children died from the plague. And his beloved wife died during this period also.

Poverty forced him to do something to survive that must have truly pained the man: To earn *some* income, he was forced to sell rare manuscripts from his already damaged and depleted library. And to make matters even worse, under James I a series of witch hunts had begun. Needless to say Dee's name was among those on the list of those to be interrogated. Matters grew so dire that in 1608 Dee began preparing to leave for Germany. But he never got there; Dr. John Dee died that year, and at last achieved the "oneness" he had sought with the spirit world.

So what are we to make of Dr. John Dee? William Shakespeare, it has been suggested, used Dee as the model for his character Prospero in his play *The Tempest*. Seventeenth-century historians considered him a man who consorted with demons, an evil sorcerer, a view of the man that continues today in some quarters. Other things have probably contributed to this view. In 1873, Dee—from beyond the grave—communicated with his earthly fellow practitioners of the occult; at least, that was the claim of medium Stainton Moses, though these claims were discredited. And even later, Anton LaVey and his Church of Satan used Enochian language in their rites.

Unquestionably, Dee dabbled in the occult. During the period of time in which he lived, there was no clear line drawn between science and magic. (In fact, one can ask, is there a clear line between them *today*?) Dee was far from the only mathematician, scholar, or other category of man of learning who sometimes crossed over into what one might regard as the occult.

Like many other great men's legends, Dee's reputation has changed over the years, though the common view even today is that he was everything from a charlatan to a grave robber to a Satanic conjuror. Dee's search for knowledge *did* cross over into the occult. (Discussions with angels? Use of a crystal to see them?) Few would deny that. But there is no evidence that Dee ever danced with the devil, or any other evil spirit.

That, of course, has not stopped classical authors or modern fantasy and horror writers from using Dee as a character—mostly mysterious, often malevolent—or at least as a reference in their works. As mentioned earlier, Shakespeare supposedly based Prospero, the wizard of *The Tempest,* on Dee. The spirits mention Dee by name in Ben Jonson's *The Alchemist* only two years after his death. Charles Maturin, the influential Gothic novelist, mentions Dee in his classic *Melmoth the Wanderer* (1820). And, of course, as the opening quotations of this essay indicate, H. P. Lovecraft's "The Dunwich Horror" suggests that Dr. Dee had a copy of *The Necronomicon* in his collection of rare, arcane manuscripts, and translated the book into English from its original Middle Eastern language. Lovecraft referred to *The Necronomicon* in several of his works—*The Case of Charles Dexter Ward* being another fairly well-known one—and thereby helped perpetuate the myth that Dee had some connection to this dangerous book of otherworldly knowledge. And several films of the 1990s—Sam Raimi's *Army of Darkness* (1992) and *Necronomicon* (1993) by Brian Yuzna et al.—feature the terror-inducing book as well, although there is no direct mention of Dr. Dee. In one novel by Peter Ackroyd, *The House of Doctor Dee,* the title character haunts his former residence in the modern era. Dee is a central character in Umberto Eco's novel *Foucault's Pendulum,* and he is a character in Michael Moorcock's "alternate history" of Elizabethan England, *Gloriana.*

There is little doubt that his scryer Kelley's reputation was the greatest contributor to this view of Dee; but if he is guilty of anything, it is of naïveté, for falling for Kelley's displays of scrying. (Reports state that before he met Dee, Kelley *did* once unearth a corpse, and through his talents as a ventriloquist got that corpse to "talk" in order to scam another unsuspecting "patron.")

However, Dee, far from being some evil, spooky character, was instead a very devout man who made major contributions in his era. The Rosicrucians, who take exception to the portrayal of Dee as a malevolent sorcerer, point to the following prayer, presented here with modern spelling, as evidence that Dee was instead a man of God:

> Among others thy manifold mercies used, toward me, thy simple servant John Dee, I most humbly beseech thee, in this my present petition to have mercy upon me, to have pity upon me, to have Compassion upon me: Who faithfully and sincerely, of long time, have sought among men, in Earth: And also in prayer (full often and pitifully) have made suit unto thy Divine Majesty for the obtaining of some convenient portion of True Knowledge and understanding of thy laws and Ordinances, established in the Natures and properties of the Creatures: by which Knowledge, Thy Divine Wisdom, Power and Goodness . . . Being to me made manifest, might abundantly instruct, furnish, and allure me (for the same) incessantly to pronounce thy praises, to rend unto thee, most hearty thanks, to advance thy true honor, and to Win unto thy Name, some of the due Majestical Glory, among all people, and forever.*

According to the Rosicrucians, who feel that Dee was among those who led the way to the founding of their movement, this was part of a prayer that Dee said regularly. It very clearly indicates, in its almost John Dunne–ish presentation, that Dee's purpose in his studies—occult or not—was not self-aggrandizement, and they certainly were not for any malevolent purpose. They were to learn how to give greater glory to his god, and to teach others to do the same.

*Schrigner, Linda S., "The R+C Legacy: Dr. John Dee." From the Rosicrucian Library. crcsite.org/dee1.htm

Dee's accomplishments far outshine other aspects of the man, yet, sadly, many of them are forgotten, if they were ever known. Among them are the following.

• He was one of the first modern mathematicians and scientists. He wrote the "Mathematical Preface" to *Euclid's Geometry*, a groundbreaking treatise that helped bring real science to the average person. He was also the first scholar to apply the work to navigation.

• He coined the word "Brittania," envisioning the British Empire, and referred to the New World as "Atlantis" well before Sir Francis Bacon used the term as the title of his work *The New Atlantis.*

• He correctly determined the weather when the Spanish fleet threatened the shores of Britain. His meteorological calculations forecast that mighty storms would destroy the armada, as they did.

• He was the author of forty-nine books, many of which contain important contributions to modern scholarship. Besides the works mentioned in this essay are also *De Trigono* (1565), *Monas Hieroglyphica* (1564), and many others, mostly devoted to the areas of mathematics, science, philosophy, and religion.

And today some of his belongings reside in open display at the British Museum.

Among John Dee–related objects in the British Museum are:

• A speculum (mirror), an Aztec object, once owned after Dee's death by Sir Horace Walpole.

• A large wax support—"The Seal of God"—which Dee used to support his crystal "shew-stone," the crystal stone he used during scrying sessions.

• A gold amulet with an engraving of a vision from one of the scrying sessions.

- A globe, crystal, which may have belonged to Dee. (Its authenticity is still questionable.) This is supposedly the object given to him by the angel Uriel.
- Wax seals used to support Dee's "table of practice" during his scrying sessions.

British Museum
Great Russell Street
London
WC1B 3DG

Allen C. Kupfer

. . . and speaking of that unholiest of manuscripts
that is rumored to have driven anyone who
dared to read it insane . . .

The Enigmatic
Voynich Manuscript

The year was 1912. Rare-book dealer Wilfrid Voynich was excited. He had just gotten his hands on a rare batch of books
from a Jesuit library near Rome. The library, in need of funds,
had decided to sell off some of its holdings. Voynich, a Polish
expatriate then living in London, was one of the bidders. He
ended up with thirty items, all from the private collection of
Petrus Beckx, the former head of the Jesuit order.

He couldn't have guessed that one of those items—a six-inch
by nine-inch handwritten manuscript apparently from around
1600, was destined to become the most famous book he ever
owned. But when he began to delve into it, he became fascinated. Its odd illustrations, its even odder writing—unlike any
other he'd ever seen—and its apparent connection with some of
the most curious figures in history, all called out for answers.
Alas, he went to his grave in 1930 without having found more
than hints.

Nearly a century later his little manuscript is still the most enigmatic book ever written. It is known, appropriately, as the Voynich manuscript.

The world's most mysterious manuscript consists of 240 pages covered with strange handwritten symbols. It looks more like a Western alphabet than, say, Chinese or Japanese—some of the symbols resemble the numeral 6 or the letter g, for example. But taken as a whole, it's clearly unlike any known writing system. And, despite the fact that it is lavishly illustrated— with pictures of plants, astronomical objects, groups of bathing women, and geometric designs—nobody really knows what it's about, although there have been plenty of guesses.

Is it a secret code? An ancient alphabet that has somehow survived in only this single example? A work of nonhuman provenance? An elaborate hoax? A modern forgery? All these have been proposed at some point or another—with more or less authority—and the jury is still out.

Voynich thought it to be the work of Friar Roger Bacon, the celebrated medieval English scholar, and he convinced several others of his theory. Nowadays experts say the author's identity is at best a guess.

It has baffled the world's best cryptographers, including some of those who broke the Nazis' Enigma code in World War II. Some claim that at least one prominent scholar went mad while spending years trying to penetrate its secrets.

And those are just a few of the mysteries surrounding the famous—or should we say infamous?—Voynich manuscript.

Even apparently simple questions about the Voynich, such as its length, turn out to have ambiguous answers. For example, its 240 six-inch by nine-inch vellum pages are apparently the remnant of a longer work, which may have been 272 pages—bound in 17 signatures of 16 pages each. There is also reason to believe the pages were once in a different order. But until somebody can read what's on the pages, the question of their order can't be answered.

Fortunately, there is at least one indisputable fact about the

Voynich: It currently resides at prestigious Yale University in New Haven, Connecticut. It has been there since 1969, when it was donated to the school by antiquarian book dealer Hans P. Kraus. After he obtained it from Voynich's widow—she and her husband had moved to New York in 1914—Kraus tried and failed to find a buyer for it. It is now item number MS 408 in Yale's Beinecke Rare Book and Manuscript Library. You can see samples of its writing and illustrations at several places on the Web (one good source is www.voynich.nu, which also offers a good overview of the problems the manuscript presents).

Before its arrival at Yale, the history of the Voynich is a bit more complicated. One of the major problems is that nobody really knows just when it was written. Judging from the styles of hair and clothing in the illustrations, as well as the style of the drawings, scholars guess that it dates from sometime between 1450 and 1520—a date that would eliminate Bacon, who died in 1294, as the author. Of course it might be a copy of an earlier work, now lost, but that, like many things about the mysterious book, is pure conjecture.

In any case, the manuscript first appears in the historic record in 1639, when an alchemist living in Prague, Georg Baresch, wrote to Jesuit scholar Athanasius Kircher, then living in Rome. Baresch asked Kircher for help translating an odd manuscript he had in his possession. Kircher had a reputation as a linguist, having published a dictionary of Coptic. Kircher also believed (wrongly) that he had discovered the secret of reading Egyptian hieroglyphics. (They remained undeciphered for another three centuries.)

Kircher's reply to Baresch has not survived, but apparently he tried to buy the manuscript, of which the alchemist had sent him a few copied sample pages. Baresch declined the offer, and instead bequeathed it to his friend Jan Marek Marci, rector of Charles University in Prague.

Ironically, Marci was a long-time friend and correspondent of Kircher's, and in 1666 sent him the mysterious manuscript,

along with a letter summarizing what he knew of it—and a few
guesses to fill in what he didn't know. What Kircher did with
it—or what he made of it—is unknown, but after his death in
1680 all his papers, including the mysterious manuscript, ended
up in the Jesuits' library at Collegio Romano. And there, for
some two hundred years, it sat—apparently unnoticed and un-
read. Well, if anybody did notice it, they didn't bother to record
their impressions of it. And it seems unlikely anybody could
have read it then, any more than now.

The manuscript reappears in history after 1870, when Rome,
up until then an independent state, was invaded by troops loyal
to King Victor Emmanuel II of Italy. The new government,
which needed money, made it a policy to confiscate church
property. (This also weakened the church, which had been a
strong rival to the new king's plans to unify Italy.) However, the
personal libraries of faculty members were exempt, and so the
Jesuits took many of the most valuable items home for safekeeping. Petrus Beckx, head of the Jesuit order and rector of
the university, took the Voynich; it still bears his personal *ex lib-
ris* stamp.

For better safekeeping, Beckx's books, including the Voynich
manuscript, were moved out of Rome to Villa Mondragone, a
country estate the Jesuits owned. There it lay in obscurity until
1912, when Collegio Romano ran short of funds, and decided to
sell some of its holdings. And that's how Voynich bought a
batch of them—including the one that now bears his name. And
at that point, we might say, the manuscript's real history
begins—along with the tantalizing questions.

Voynich's curiosity was piqued by a comment in the cover
letter by Marci. Marci said that he believed the manuscript had
once been owned by the Holy Roman emperor Rudolf II, who
had paid 600 ducats for it—about $30,000 in today's currency.
Also, according to the letter, Rudolf had believed that the
manuscript was written in the late thirteenth century by Friar
Bacon, who is generally considered the greatest scientist of the

Middle Ages. Based on that belief, Voynich jumped to the conclusion that Rudolf had acquired the manuscript from the famous English mathematician and astrologer Dr. John Dee. Dee, who had previously gained the patronage of Elizabeth I of England, lived at Rudolf's court in Prague for a while, and Dee had a large collection of Bacon's works. Incidentally, Rudolf died in 1611, so if he really did own the Voynich, that gives a solid date before which it was written.

However, the story of the Voynich is never quite as simple as it seems. We've already noted that, on the evidence of the illustrations, the Voynich is from a period a couple of centuries after Bacon's time. Of course, there is no real way to judge whether either the style or the contents are consistent with Bacon's authorship until someone manages to translate it. Also, Dee kept a journal in which he carefully recorded his doings, and experts say it does not mention the sale of any such manuscript.

An alternate theory is that the manuscript is a forgery—a hoax, concocted either by Dee or by his assistant Edward Kelley, to bilk their noble client of whatever they could convince him to pay. Dee seems generally to have been honest, but Kelley's track record is full of shady dealings—enough to cast doubt upon almost anything he had a part in.

Conceivably Kelley created the manuscript without Dee's knowledge, and convinced his master—who was inclined to believe almost anything Kelley told him—that the manuscript was authentic. Still, if that were so, Dee would likely have recorded the sale in his journal—unless he knew it to be fraudulent, and avoided mentioning it for that reason. But we're multiplying "ifs" again.

Baresch, who asked Kircher to translate it for him some fifty years later, and Marci, who finally sent it along to the Jesuit translator, have also been suggested as possible forgers. However, neither seems to have tried to get money for it—Baresch, at least, apparently turned down Kircher's offer to buy it. Possibly the forger had some deeper motive—it's been suggested that

Marci concocted the manuscript to baffle the Jesuits in revenge for some slight. But if Marci had some reason to deceive the Italian Jesuits, or to discredit the learned Kircher, no record of it has survived. The only reason to think so is the hope that it might explain away the otherwise incomprehensible manuscript. Of course, if you make enough assumptions you can get to almost any conclusion you want, without the inconvenience of having to prove them to anyone's satisfaction. That's happened a lot with Voynich scholarship over the last century.

Besides, if Baresch or Marci concocted the manuscript in the 1660s in order to fool someone, neither seems to have made any effort to drop the other shoe and expose the hoax for what it was. To go to all the work of creating a phony manuscript and then just let the matter sit seems odd. Especially when there's no money involved. Much of the point of such a game is to expose the victim as a dupe who couldn't recognize a forgery.

Some have raised the possibility that the forger was Voynich himself. As a dealer in rare books, he might have had the knowledge to cobble up a convincing fake, and a fair number of opportunities to cash in on it. The best evidence against that supposition is the letters by Kircher and Marci mentioning the manuscript—although some have suggested that Voynich could have manufactured those, as well.

However, he apparently made no great effort to sell it, eliminating the most likely reason for creating a fake. Also, Voynich was sufficiently well established that he didn't need to come up with a "find" to make his reputation. If anything, his advocacy of the Baconian theory probably hurt his reputation with some authorities. And if he created the manuscript to expose some rival as a fool, he never sprang the trap. To all appearances, he himself genuinely believed in its authenticity.

But there are still other reasons to believe the manuscript is authentic. For example, there's that weird writing system. Analysts have determined that the writing can be broken down into twenty to thirty distinct characters—just the right amount for an alphabetic system. (In addition, there are a small number of other characters, a couple of dozen at most, that appear just once or twice in the text. Perhaps they are numbers?) The total length of the manuscript is some 170,000 "letters," which appear to be broken into about 30,000 "words." There is no punctuation.

But while individual characters resemble familiar letters or numbers, taken as a whole they don't match any known alphabet—even assuming they're from the sixteenth century or earlier. Perhaps the Voynich is the only surviving example of some ancient writing system—but that seems highly unlikely. If it was written in a language used by any large population, there ought to be other examples somewhere. Granted, there are a few extinct languages known only from one or two written examples, but most of them use some variation of an otherwise familiar writing system, like the Roman or Hebrew alphabets. Once again, that makes the Voynich very much an oddball, which is why so many experts believe it must be a hoax—gibberish dressed up to look like a real book in an unknown language.

However, there are several reasons to believe the manuscript really is written in a natural language, rather than being cunningly constructed gibberish. For one thing, the frequency of words follows a statistical linguistic principle known as Zipf's law. Stated simply, Zipf's law says that the most common single word—in English, that would be "the"—occurs about twice as often as the next most frequent, and so on down to the least common words, which might appear only once in a text the length of the Voynich. Of course, any real language has words that don't appear in a given sample, even a large one—for example, you won't find "telescope" in very many chemistry textbooks, even though the authors undoubtedly know the word and use it in other contexts. But the law's general frequency principles hold for a reasonably large text in any natural language.

There are other characteristics of natural languages that appear to hold true for the manuscript as well. For example, certain subsets of the letter system appear in each word, like the vowels in European languages. Some characters appear doubled (like the p in "appear"); others never do (like q in most, but not all, European languages). Some sequences of letters never occur. All these appear to suggest that the manuscript is not just a random hodgepodge of symbols, but was created according to a real system—even if we haven't a clue just what that system is.

On the other hand, some features of the text seem to contradict the idea that it's in a natural language. At some points, the same common word appears three times in a row—the equivalent of "man man man." That could be explained if the passage is some kind of incantation or spell, but short of that it doesn't fit the pattern of most European languages. The lengths of words are also odd: There is a distinct shortage of either very long words (ten or more letters) or very short ones (one or two letters), which goes against the pattern of most European languages. Of course, that doesn't rule out non-European languages; for example, the tripled word pattern can be found in Asian languages such as Chinese.

In other words, if the manuscript is a hoax, it's a fairly sophisticated one. For example, Zipf's law wasn't described before 1939. It seems unlikely that Marci—or Dee, or anyone else of his era—could intuitively have followed it in creating something meant only to fool the Jesuits, or Emperor Rudolf II, or whomever the Voynich was trying to deceive. Even Voynich himself, who died in 1930, becomes less likely as a suspect. In short, Zipf's law suggests that the manuscript is unlikely to be pure gibberish concocted by one of the earlier owners—if we can take Voynich's word for its antiquity. And that's another unsolved problem.

In fact, the age of the Voynich is at best an educated guess, based largely on Marci's say-so and the style of the drawing. None of the sophisticated modern chemical analyses that could determine the age of the ink or vellum of the Voynich have been performed, probably because experts are generally content that it comes from the era it has been purported to be from. One assumes that a blatant modern forgery would have been detected years ago.

But it's worth asking why the Yale library hasn't taken the obvious step of authenticating one of its most intriguing holdings. The cost can't be a factor; surely there are many wealthy patrons who would contribute to settling the true age of the Voynich. With today's technology, only a small portion of the manuscript would have to be submitted to the tests—and with today's copying technology, the contents can be preserved easily. Whether Yale believes it to be genuine or not, it can't have much to lose in settling one of the biggest questions: Just when was it created?

The problem is, there's not much independent evidence that it really does come from the 1600s or earlier. None of its earlier owners described it precisely enough to establish its existence before Voynich bought it. Baresch, the first person we know to have owned it, seems to have copied a few pages for Kircher, the prospective translator, to read. But neither those nor any other copies of the manuscript can be found previous to Voynich's photocopies in the 1920s. That could be explained, of course, by the amount of work needed to copy anything before photocopy machines came into use. But it does leave us lacking independent verification of its age.

Also, despite the apparently full detail accompanying the history of the Voynich, plenty of questions remain. For example, the only evidence we have of the existence of Georg Baresch consists of the letter he wrote to Kircher inquiring about the manuscript, and the two that Marci later wrote mentioning him as the former owner. Could someone—anyone from Marci to Voynich is a possibility—just have invented him to give the manuscript an air of authenticity?

Also, we can't ignore the problem that none of the early references to the manuscript can be proven to apply to the one now in the Yale library. For all we know, the volume that rested in the Jesuits' library for two hundred years was something entirely different from the one at Yale. A stamp in the Voynich says otherwise, but stamps can be forged, too—and Voynich, for one, probably had the ability to do so.

Actually, considering that the book was unreadable, it's somewhat surprising that it has survived at all. Only the fact that its Jesuit owners probably felt uncomfortable discarding any book—except perhaps obvious heresies or blasphemies—may have saved it from oblivion. The illustrations give some hint of its subject—for example, the first section appears to be a botany text; other sections apparently relate to alchemy or astronomy. So it could have been preserved for possible use, pending its deciphering. After all, texts in Arabic and other unfamiliar languages were known to contain materials that European scholars had not yet discovered.

Of course there are plenty of explanations that haven't been disproven—and probably can't be by anything short of a convincing translation or solid proof that the Voynich is a hoax. The manuscript could be written in one of the exotic European languages, such as Basque or Finnish, a Middle Eastern language such as Hebrew, or something from even further afield—Mongolian has been suggested—despite its apparent origin in Central Europe and its rediscovery in Italy. And that still doesn't account for the writing system, though it would explain the difficulties in making sense of it.

The superficial appearance of the Voynich manuscript might lead you to believe it to be a textbook on several useful sciences. As noted, the illustrations appear to refer to astronomy, botany, alchemy, and perhaps health or hygiene—but, on the other hand, some of the plants illustrated are described elsewhere by botanists as "fanciful." Granted, those subjects might have seemed less than innocent in an era when even mathematics was sometimes confused with conjuring. Possibly the Voynich, like Leonardo da Vinci's mirror-written notebooks, was a coded set of research notes the author intended for his eyes alone.

For a long time the most popular theory was that the Voynich is written in some sort of code, and there are good arguments in favor of it. The use of codes goes back to ancient times, as far back as the need to conceal information. Governments, mystics, inventors, businessmen—all have reasons to record information in a way that only they—or their trusted associates—can read.

But if it's a code, it's managed to stump all the experts. Among the world-class cryptographers who have taken a crack at the Voynich are John Tiltman, a British brigadier general who headed up the Bletchley Park operation that broke the German U-boat codes in World War II, and William Friedman, who led an American team that did much the same with Japanese ciphers. Both eventually retired from their attempts to read the Voynich—without convincing results. More recent efforts with high-powered computers haven't yielded any definitive decodings either.

The earliest decoders assumed that the Voynich is written in a substitution cipher of some kind—the text being some known language, with the letters of the alphabet replaced according to some system that allows a person with the key to read them. For example, one character stands for A, another for B, and so on throughout the alphabet. A variant would use symbols for sounds, such as a single symbol for ch or th. (A familiar fictional example is the code in Edgar Allan Poe's story "The Gold Bug." The difference here would be that instead of the replacement letters being from our familiar alphabet, they are apparently arbitrary symbols, as in the Sherlock Holmes story "The Adventure of the Dancing Men.")

However, simple substitution codes are fairly easy to crack, especially if the writer doesn't complicate the text by changing word lengths or including bits of nonsense. This is especially true if the original language is known. But cryptographers have tried reading the Voynich assuming it's a substitution cipher, and that the plain text is in any of a number of the European and Middle Eastern languages common at the presumed time of composition—from Latin to Welsh to Hebrew. None have produced convincing results.

Also, handwriting experts say the letters were written smoothly, from left to right (the right margin is slightly ragged, as you'd expect with handwritten text beginning on the left side)—very much as if they were written without having to stop and look up each letter or word from some kind of code table. That suggests that the scribe (or scribes—some say there is evidence of two writers) must have learned the writing system so thoroughly that it was second nature—like a natural language. If the scribe had to stop to look each word up in a book of substitutions, the writing would likely be less flowing. Of course, if the scribe had plenty of practice, that objection might not apply.

That leads to the assumption that the manuscript is written in a more sophisticated code, with which the scribe was thoroughly familiar, to the extent that he could write in it as smoothly as in plain text. In fact, Raphael Missowski, an older friend of Jan Marek Marci and a member of the court of Rudolf II in the early 1600s, was reported to have created an unbreakable code. Could the Voynich be an example of his work? Having no other examples to compare it to, it's hard to tell. Once again, the uniqueness of the Voynich prevents us from following up a potential lead.

However, there are several possibilities it is impossible to rule out. For example, the manuscript may use a "book" code, in which each word in the plain text is arbitrarily assigned a substitute—in the case of the Voynich, the substitute would not even be a recognizable word. The substitution doesn't have to be one for one: One word could stand for an entire sentence, for example. The problem with this kind of code is that the book of substitutions—the key—needs to be available to anyone the writer wants to be able to read the messages—and no such book has survived for the Voynich. That could be an unlucky accident, of course. But lacking the key, the chance of deciphering the manuscript is vanishingly small. Also, book codes tend to be very slow going, both to write and to read, and so are mostly used for short messages.

Other complex cryptographic techniques were certainly familiar to the thinkers of the era in which the Voynich appears to originate. Meaningless symbols, rearranged word lengths, deliberate misspellings, anagrams, use of multiple languages, and the omission of vowels can make even a simple substitution code forbidding to decipher. Use of one of the polyalphabetic ciphers—which were invented in the mid-fifteenth century—is also a possibility, although they didn't become common until after Marci's time. Some experts argue that a text using such codes would not display some of the natural language features the Voynich displays.

Another possibility is the use of steganography—a technique that hides a meaningful text inside another apparently innocent one. A simple example would be using the second letter of every word in something like a shopping list to spell out a secret message. However, the use of an eye-catching alphabet and apparently meaningless words—not to forget the decidedly odd illustrations—is guaranteed to pique the curiosity of anyone coming across the manuscript—which more or less defeats the purpose of the steganographic technique, which depends in part on the innocent appearance of the document in which the plain text is concealed. Why make somebody look closely at something you're trying to hide?

That raises the question of what the author was trying to hide, and there have been plenty of suggestions on that score—many of which depend on unprovable assumptions as to who the author was. One of the more intriguing suggestions was made during Voynich's lifetime by William Romaine Newbold, a professor of philosophy at the University of Pennsylvania. Newbold argued that the letters of the manuscript are actually meaningless; each is instead made up of tiny forms derived from Greek shorthand. Newbold claimed that these forms, visible only under a microscope, revealed the manuscript to be the work of Friar Bacon (a theory favored by Voynich himself). He claimed that Bacon had built microscopes some four hundred years before they are usually supposed to have been invented, and offered "translations" of several short passages that showed Bacon to have made several other discoveries far in advance of his age. Until his death in 1926, Newbold's translation was widely believed to be the authoritative answer to the manuscript's mysteries.

Nobody has been able to duplicate Newbold's results, however, and they are now generally discredited. (One major problem is that he took the license to rearrange the text until he got something that seemed to make sense.) Also discredited are his reports of discovering the whereabouts of the tombs of St. Peter and St. Paul, and his claim to have deciphered ancient writings found in a cave. Some claim that Newbold—like those unlucky scholars of the works of H. P. Lovecraft, who stumble upon the forbidden (and fictional) *Necronomicon*—was driven mad by his study of the Voynich. Others believe he was already well on his way. At this distance in time, the argument seems moot.

The wildest suggestions about the origin and meaning of the Voynich have come, predictably, from writers of fiction. The most entertaining strategy has been to treat it as an equivalent of the *Necronomicon*—an alien work containing dark secrets "that mankind was not meant to know." Colin Wilson took that approach in several Lovecraft-inspired works, including his novel *The Philosopher's Stone*, where it plays an important role in the conclusion. Wilson has also suggested that Lovecraft himself may have been aware of the Voynich, and based his creation of the *Necronomicon* on it—but that, like so much else about the Voynich, remains unknown.

The Voynich also figures in the novel *Indiana Jones and the Philosopher's Stone* by Max McCoy. Here a mad scientist has deciphered the manuscript and learned that it contains the alchemical method for turning base metals into gold. He steals it, and Indy is called in to retrieve it before disaster strikes, and, of course, other complications follow.

The most recent trend in Voynich studies, demonstrated in articles by computer scientist Gordon Rugg (in *Scientific American,* 2004), and by cryptographers Andreas Schinner and Claude Martin, leans back toward the hoax theory, although the experts differ in their reasons for believing so, which raises some doubt about their conclusions. It may be that one of them is correct; perhaps, in spite of all the arguments to the contrary, the enigmatic document that has puzzled readers for centuries—possibly as far back as Shakespeare's day—is no more than a cunning farrago of gobbledygook. Clever, well-wrought gobbledygook, perhaps, but still utterly without a crumb of meaning.

That would be too bad. The world needs unsolved mysteries, and the Voynich manuscript remains one of the all-time puzzlers.

———

Beinecke Rare Book and Manuscript Library
Yale University
121 Wall Street
New Haven, CT 06511

———

Peter J. Heck

Fall River's favorite "found innocent" female may have finally made a killing—in the bed and breakfast trade.

A Museum That Takes Overnight Reservations

The town museum is located at 451 Rock Street, and its bio is as follows:

> Founded in 1921, the Fall River Historical Society's mission is to preserve and protect all manner of artifacts relating to the rich and varied history of the city of Fall River, Massachusetts. The Historical Society is housed in a granite mansion, built in 1843 in the Greek Revival style for Andrew Robeson, Jr., a prominent businessman. A one-time station on the Underground Railroad, the house was to change hands several times over the next quarter century.

> Its collection includes artifacts and chronicles of town history, as well as genealogical records and an extensive local manuscript and photograph collection.

> It is also the home of the so-called Borden collection, about

Fall River's most famous citizen, Lizzie Borden, immortalized in infamous ditties and local folklore.

Most folks know the popular poesy:

Lizzie Borden took an axe
And gave her mother forty whacks.
And when she saw what she had done
She gave her father forty-one.

or the following bit by Bixby:

There's no evidence of guilt,
Lizzie Borden,
That should make your spirit wilt,
Lizzie Borden;
Many do not think that you
Chopped your father's head in two,
It's so hard a thing to do,
Lizzie Borden.

You have borne up under all,
Lizzie Borden.
With a mighty show of gall,
Lizzie Borden;
But because your nerve is stout
Does not prove beyond a doubt
That you knocked the old folks out,
Lizzie Borden.

But the real facts of the case were as follows:

Lizzie and her older sister, Emma, resided with their father, Andrew, and his second wife (along with a housekeeper named Bridget Sullivan) at a house befitting the well-to-do banker and his family, at 92 Second Street in Fall River, Massachusetts.

Both girls were considered unmarriageable spinsters past their prime, and rumors pervaded the town that there was a significant amount of friction between the girls and their father's second wife.

On August 4, 1892, while Emma was out of town, Mr. and the second Mrs. Borden were found, slain, by Lizzie and the maid.

Lizzie quickly notified the authorities and sought help from the neighbors before approaching the bodies (it should be noted that none of the witnesses at the time ever noticed or recalled any bloody traces on Lizzie's hands or dress, as might befit someone who had just engaged in a berserker-like homicidal fury resembling the one that had been brought to bear on the victims).

A coroner's inquest revealed that the two victims had been cleaved cranially and bludgeoned by an axlike weapon, and that there was apparently a gap of close to two hours between the murders, suggesting that the assailant was not pressed for time nor worried about being interrupted or discovered by some other member of the houschold.

Suspicion immediately fell on the "odd woman spinster," Lizzie, and a case was mounted against her, largely on the basis of circumstantial evidence and prejudice.

The trial was convened on June 5, 1893, and lasted two weeks, and was filled with gory demonstrations, exhibitions, and innuendos.

The jury deliberated for a little over an hour and came back with a verdict of not guilty, at which point Lizzie returned home with her sister, sold the family house, and they moved into another mansion in the town, where she spent the rest of her days.

Despite her being cleared in the court of law, there seems to have always been a presumption of guilt surrounding Lizzie, and a cloud of suspicion that always followed her.

Lizzie Borden died of complications from gallbladder surgery in 1927, at the age of sixty-six, thirty-four years after her acquittal. Her estate was divided among those friends and servants who had stayed loyal to her over the years, along with a considerable donation to the Animal Rescue League of Fall River, as per her last will and testament.

The historical society has on display most of the artifacts associated with the case, including the handleless hatchet that was believed to be the murder weapon; Lizzie's prison lunch pail; the police photographs taken at the scene of the crime; the billy club the arresting officer carried; the pillow shams from the bedroom that Abby (the second Mrs. Borden) was murdered in; the photographs of Andrew's and Abby's crushed skulls that were introduced as evidence; and the braided hairpiece that Abby was wearing when she was attacked.

The case is covered tastefully yet completely with a mix of Joe Friday–esque "just the facts" information tempered by a bit of the Grand Guignol sensationalism befitting a homicide that at the time was considered to be the crime of the century.

But Fall River is also home to another museum that deals with this famous case, one located at 92 Second Street (also now called 230 Second Street) at the so-called scene of the crime.

The Lizzie Borden Bed and Breakfast and Museum is open to the public with tours daily from 11:00 A.M. to 3:00 P.M., commencing on the hour every day except major holidays.

According to its proprietors:

Since the murders on August 4, 1892 the house has been a private residence. Now for the first time the public is allowed not only to view the murder scene, but is given an opportunity to spend a night (if you dare) in the actual house where the murders took place. . . .

We offer two two-bedroom suites, Lizzie & Emma's Bedrooms, and Abby & Andrew's Bedrooms (this suite has a private bath); the John Morse Guest Room, Bridget's Attic Room and two additional spacious attic bedrooms (the Jennings &

Knowlton Rooms), each of which offer a double bed in a room with Victorian appointments. Guests are treated to a breakfast similar to the one the Bordens ate on the morning of the murders, which includes bananas, jonny-cakes, sugar cookies and coffee in addition to a delicious meal of breakfast staples.

This accessibility to the general public has lead to numerous overnight investigations for paranormal activity surrounding this crime scene—and as often occurs when such scrutiny is brought to bear, weird occurrences have been recorded.

There have been publicized events sponsored by *Haunted Times* magazine and representatives from the so-called Ghost Hunters University, as well as a sleepover by some members of the Horror Writers of America and a Halloween night séance.

Guests who have stayed overnight in Lizzie's room have reported instances of the closet door opening and closing during the night, as well as hearing crying and weeping; other things going bump in the night; and on more than one occasion Lizzie's bed vibrated with guests in it.

Psychic Jane Doherty did her own investigation of the premises and related a vision she experienced prior to arriving at the site: "Whenever I thought of the Lizzie Borden house, a vision of a bearded man came into view. The man in the vision carried an ax and entered the house through the back entrance. He appeared to be a woodsman or outdoor type man. I didn't receive any information about his identity. I just knew he had something to do with the murders." And once she arrived at Lizzie's room, she reported,

A picture on the wall caught my eye. I walked towards the picture and reacted. My stomach responded, but I also felt agitated. The face of the picture haunted my memory. Startled, I realized this was the image of the man in my vision. This man's image created a sick feeling in the pit of my stomach.

Nauseated, I needed to turn away from the framed image on the wall. Before turning in a different direction I asked our tour guide Kathy Gunslov, "Who is the man in the picture?" She responded, "Oh, that was Lizzie's Uncle . . . Uncle John. He was Lizzie's real mother's brother. He was a suspect at first, however, he had a solid alibi at the time of the murders."

Which, of course, did not necessarily clear him of being involved with the murders, perhaps hiring someone else to "bury the hatchet" on his relations.

A séance hosted by a local psychic named Liz (and sponsored by Ghost Hunters University) recorded numerous unexplained psychic manifestations, ranging from table levitation to tilting and rotation—even when there was no one near the piece of furniture.

The landlord also has suspected that a pair of children haunt the upstairs Knowlton bedroom, and can occasionally be heard playing with toys well past their bedtime (a supposition of the management being that they are the drowned offspring of Andrew's uncle that might have been attracted to the psychic energies of the place).

Needless to say, the presumed heightened emotional states of the murder victims and the wrongly accused, and the savage murderers themselves, are more than enough rationalizations for their spectral dwelling at that location beyond their mortal lives.

And if the ghosts of the "found innocent" Lizzie and her parents, and other spectral visitors of the former human sort, were not enough, some guests who have stayed in the Abby and Andrew Suite have told the proprietors that they felt cat's paws walk across their covers at night. One explanation could be from a story in the Knowlton letters: A friend of the Borden family visiting from New York told Lizzie she was being bothered by their cat. Lizzie allegedly picked up the cat, left the room, and said that the cat would "never" bother her again.

Perhaps Lizzie was indeed a murderess after all, and that poor little kitty has taken up permanent residence in that house.

———

Lizzie Borden Bed & Breakfast/Museum
92 Second Street
Fall River, MA 02721

———

New Orleans, despite its pummeling by the elements,
is still a city breathing with history—and some of its
former residents may still be hanging around even
after respiration has ceased.

A Museum Dedicated to
More than Just Dolls and Pins

A simple definition of what we refer to as voodoo is

> a religion practiced throughout the Caribbean, especially
> Haiti, that is a combination of Roman Catholic rituals, ani-
> mistic beliefs, [and] magic and involves rituals resulting in
> possession and/or communication with spirits or ancestors.

According to their Web site, the New Orleans Historic
Voodoo Museum is believed to be the only museum in the world
dedicated to voodoo, and its primary purpose is to represent the
traditional practices of the voodoo religion in New Orleans,
bringing together ancient and modern day voodoo practices.
The museum places an emphasis on understanding voodoo as

• a religion, in which the practitioners understand the gris-gris
  magic comes via supernatural powers;

- a superstition, in which the practitioners believe the object, such as a doll or a candle, has a power in itself;
- folklore, which is the oral traditions handed down from generation to generation, either by culture or locality (the voodoo queen Marie Laveau and the Rougarou swamp zombie are examples); and
- folklore that is misappropriated either for financial gain or personal aggrandizement.

Indeed, New Orleans is the perfect place in the United States for this museum, as it is both the original stomping grounds for an original voodoo priestess and only a short walk from her final resting place.

A former hairdresser, the great voodoo queen of New Orleans, Marie Laveau, was born there in 1794 and died in 1881, and became known as the most famous and powerful voodoo queen in the world. On the occasion of her death, *The New York Times* ran the following under the headline of THE DEAD VODOU QUEEN:

New Orleans, June 21—Marie Laveau, the "Queen of the Voudous," died last Wednesday at the advanced age of 98 years. To the superstitious creoles Marie appeared as a dealer in the black arts and a person to be dreaded and avoided. Strange stories were told of the rites performed by the sect of which Marie was the acknowledged sovereign. Many old residents asserted that on St. John's night, the 24th of June, the Voudou clan had been seen in deserted places joining in wild, weird dances, all the participants in which were perfectly nude. The Voudous were thought to be invested with supernatural powers and men sought them to find means to be rid of their enemies, while others asked for love powders to instill affection into the bosoms of their unwilling or unsuspecting sweethearts. Whether there ever was any such sect, and whether Marie was ever its Queen, her life was one to render such a belief possible. Besides knowing the secret healing qualities of the various herbs which grew in abundance in the woods and fields, she was endowed with more than the usual share of common sense, and her advice was oft-times really valuable and her penetrations remarkable. Adding to these qualities the gift of great beauty, no wonder that she possessed a large influence in her youth and attracted the attention of Louisiana's greatest men and most distinguished visitors. . . .

Lawyers, legislators, planters, merchants, all came to pay their respects to her and seek her offices, and the narrow room heard as much wit and scandal as any of the historical salons of Paris. There were business men who would not send a ship to sea before consulting her upon the probabilities of the voyage. . . . She was by no means backward in delivering her opinions, and as her predictions nearly always came true, and the course she suggested generally proved the wisest, Marie soon possessed a larger clientele than the most astute and far-seeing legal counselors. . . .

People were not all as enlightened and unprejudiced as they are now, and failing to understand how she arrived at her conclusions, they could imagine no better source than Voudouism. . . .

She died without a struggle with a smile lighting up her shriveled features. She was interred in her family tomb . . . in the old St. Louis cemetery, and with her is buried the most thrilling portion of the unwritten records of Louisiana.

The museum itself was established in 1972 by Charles Gandolfo, who, like Laveau, prior to this calling ran a hair salon. Of Haitian descent, he brought a sense of native pride and real-world proximity to the subject.

Though modest and cramped in floor space, the storefront

museum tracks the religion's migration to the United States through the slave trade from the islands to the port of New Orleans. A separate room display in the Gris-Gris room explains the spirit pantheon of the faithful, and features the accoutrements of the practices of the faith, including charms and talismans, as well as the necessary tools required for the legendary process of zombification.

The museum also conducts a combination New Orleans voodoo history and cemetery walking tour that puts the humble exhibits into greater context by leading the tourist right up to the tomb of Marie Laveau, where numerous newcomers to the faith have often left sacrifices and offerings in hopes of incurring her favor in matters of the heart, whether they involve love or revenge.

According to Troy Taylor at prairieghosts.com,

Today, Marie and her daughter still reign over the shadowy world of New Orleans Voodoo from the confines of St. Louis Cemetery No. 1. Both are entombed in this cemetery in two-tiered, white stone structures. The tombs look like so many others in this cluttered cemetery, until you notice the markings and crosses that have been drawn on the stones. Apart from these marks, you will also see coins, pieces of herb, beans, bones, bags, flowers, tokens and all manner of things left behind in an offering for the good luck and blessings of the Voodoo Queen. Many believe that Marie returns to life once each year to lead the faithful in worship on St. John's Eve. It is also said that her ghost has been seen in the cemetery and one man claimed that he was slapped by her while walking past one day. The ghost is always recognizable thanks to the "tignon," the seven-knotted handkerchief, that she wears around her neck.

Laveau's ghost has been seen in numerous other New Orleans locales, but to my knowledge never at the museum itself.

Perhaps the cramped quarters are even less hospitable for an individual considered to have been a queen of her domain.

————

New Orleans Historic Voodoo Museum
724 Dumaine Street
New Orleans, LA 70116

————

Though it might be true that diamonds are a girl's best friends, other beauteous baubles might have some very unhealthy baggage attached.

Cursed Jewels and Macabre Minerals

Museums around the world contain collections of precious jewels and minerals that dazzle visitors with their brilliance, price, or history. However, there are some gems that have transcended their physical beauty to become jewels of legend. But the reason these particular rocks are prized, speculated about, and fire the imaginations of the hundreds of thousands of visitors is not for their intrinsic beauty or value, but because they are associated either with a curse that plagues their owners, or with strange, unexplained powers.

The Hope Diamond

The most famous cursed gem currently resides in the United States, in the Smithsonian Institution National Museum of Natural History in Washington, D.C. At first glance, the 45.52-carat deep-blue Hope Diamond, in its setting of sixteen smaller white diamonds, is a beautiful if small gem compared to other famous jewels. However, the myths and legends surrounding this stone have made it one of the most famous—or perhaps notorious—jewels in the world.

Of course, whether there is a curse on this stone or any others is subject to speculation, since many times, including in the case of the Hope, the legend of a curse was invented to increase the allure of the stone. There is no doubt, however, that a number of owners of this diamond have met with either untimely deaths or other misfortunes.

The origins of the Hope Diamond span more than four hundred years of world history, and go back to India during the mid-seventeenth century. The first legend says that the original owner, Jean-Baptiste Tavernier, stole it from a Hindu idol of Sita, the wife of Rama, the seventh avatar of Vishnu, which led to the curse placed on him and successive owners. (Supposedly the priests of the temple the stone was taken from cursed it with the following words: "Bad luck and death not only for the owner of the diamond, but for all who touched it.") The reality of the gem's beginnings is actually much less sinister.

The Hope Diamond was originally part of a larger stone, the 112-carat Tavernier Blue, which was most likely mined at the Kollur Mine in Guntur, in the Andhra Pradesh state of India. Tavernier acquired the roughly cut triangular stone during one of his trips to India—the exact date is unclear—and sold it to Louis XIV in 1668. (One of the rumors surrounding the Hope's original owner was that he was torn to pieces by wild dogs or wolves while traveling in either Russia, India, or Constantinople, but again the myth is more gruesome than reality. Tavernier was made a French noble and passed away in Russia at age eighty-four, although the exact cause of his death is unknown.)

Louis's court jeweler, Sieur Pitau, cut it into a triangular, pear-shaped 67.5-carat stone that became known as the French Blue, or the Blue Diamond of the Crown. The jewel was kept by his successor, Louis XV, who had the stone reset in 1749 by his jeweler, André Jacquemin, into the *Toison d'Or*, or the Royal Order of the Golden Fleece. Next, Louis XVI, the next of the

diamond's owners, and his lover, Marie Antoinette, met truly
unfortunate ends (although one could make a case that his complete disdain for the starving and oppressed French citizens,
rather than possession of the French Blue, was what did him in).

During the French Revolution, the French Blue and other
jewels were stolen in 1792 by six men. One of them, Cadet
Guillot, took it and other gems to London to sell. Four years
later Guillot was deeply in debt, and he surrendered the diamond to a man named Lancry de la Loyelle, who repaid Guillot
by having him arrested and imprisoned.

The French Blue then disappeared for almost twenty years,
until it appeared in London in the hands of diamond merchant
Daniel Eliason (conveniently, it reappeared approximately one
week after the statute of limitations on its theft expired), and
was cut to its present shape. There is evidence that King George
IV acquired the diamond, notably a portrait painted in 1822 showing him wearing a large, dark-blue gem identical to the Hope
Diamond in the Royal Order of the Golden Fleece. Although
there is no official record of his owning the piece, George did
descend into madness over the next several years, making the
potential link between him and the stone too tantalizing to ignore. After his death in 1830, the king's estate was so impoverished that the stone, if it was part of his holdings, was most
likely sold.

The next confirmed purchaser was the man who gave the diamond its name, a British banker named William Henry Hope
(unfortunately, his business records do not state how or from
whom he acquired the gem). It continued to bring strife to its
owners. When William died in 1839, a court battle ensured among
his heirs for the estate, with one of his nephews, Henry Thomas
Hope, acquiring the diamond, along with other gems, ten years
later. After Henry's unremarkable death in 1862, the gem passed
to his wife, Adele, and after her death in 1884, it passed to their
daughter, Henrietta. She married into nobility with her wed-
ding to Henry Pelham-Clinton. When both of them passed

away, the diamond was bequeathed to their son, Henry Francis Pelham-Clinton Hope, who was broke and supported by his wife, American actress May Yohe. Before he could sell the diamond, May ran off with another man in 1902. Compared to some of the other owners, Hope got off relatively lightly, although he did die impoverished, mostly due to a terrible gambling habit.

The stone changed hands several times over the next few years. The next purchaser of the diamond, an English jewel merchant named Adolf Weil, sold it to an American diamond merchant named Simon Frankel, who sold it to Salomon Habib, who tried to auction it off in 1909, but was unsuccessful. Soon after, however, he sold the stone to another jewel merchant named C. H. Rosenau, who in turn sold it to Pierre Cartier, who sold it to heiress Evalyn Walsh McLean. It is speculated that Cartier spun much of the stone's wilder tales of its provenance, including that it was owned by Abdul Hamid II, a former sultan of Turkey, out of thin air to increase McLean's interest. His stories must have worked, because in 1911, she bought the stone for $180,000. Although Cartier warned her of the curse, McLean bought it anyway, since, she said, what was unlucky for other people was often lucky for her. In this case, however, she might have been incorrect.

Besides William Hope, Mrs. McLean is one of the people who is most associated with the Hope Diamond, primarily because she wore it practically all of the time (one apocryphal story says that her doctor had to plead with her to remove it for a goiter operation), but also because of the series of tragedies that befell her while she owned it. Soon after acquiring it, her mother died of pneumonia. Then her son, Vinson, was killed at the age of nine in an automobile accident. Her husband, Ned, heir to the *Cincinnati Enquirer* and *Washington Post* newspaper empire and an alcoholic, ran off with another woman and eventually ended up in a sanitarium, dying there in 1941. The family business went bankrupt, and Evalyn was forced to sell much of

her family holdings. Finally, her daughter died of a drug over-
dose at age twenty. Also not the thriftiest of women, McLean's
entertaining and socializing among Washington's elite society
depleted her family's fortune to the point that she had to sell her
jewelry to survive, although she always kept the Hope Diamond. (Ironically, she received warnings of the diamond's dark
curse throughout her life, including one letter from May Yohe
herself.) Of its possible influence on her life, she said matter-of-
factly: "What tragedies have befallen me might have occurred
had I never seen or touched the Hope Diamond. My observations have persuaded me that tragedies, for anyone who lives,
are not escapable."

According to *Oval Office Occult* by Brian M. Thomsen, Evalyn would often allow her friends to try on her favorite piece of
jewelry and, as luck would have it, the Hardings were indeed
among the McLean circle of friends, and Florence Harding did
indeed take advantage of the opportunity to try out her friend's
favorite bauble.

So what did this have to do with President Harding's downward spiral?

Well, given the social whirl of the White House and the influence of the McLeans in the Washington, D.C., political circle, it
is easy to conclude that once ensconced at 1600 Pennsylvania
Avenue, the Hardings made their first acquaintance with the
cursed gem early in Warren's presidential tenure.

And what was the result?

Scandals galore, including the legendary Teapot Dome affair,
which involved the secretary of the Interior accepting bribes in
exchange for the leasing of public oil fields to private interests.

Other scandals included:

- Harding appointee Thomas Miller being convicted of accepting bribes;
- the head of the Veteran's Bureau embezzling funds while en-
  gaging in other illegal activities;

• and the suicides of no less than two aides who were under investigation.

Though Harding himself was never directly implicated in any of the scandals, his presidential aura was quickly tarnished, and his administration was forever stained by its cronyism and corruption.

Harding himself failed to outlive his administration's scandals. From his official White House biography:

Looking wan and depressed, Harding journeyed westward in the summer of 1923, taking with him his upright Secretary of Commerce, Herbert Hoover. "If you knew of a great scandal in our administration," he asked Hoover, "would you for the good of the country and the party expose it publicly or would you bury it?" Hoover urged publishing it, but Harding feared the political repercussions.

He did not live to find out how the public would react to the scandals of his administration. In August of 1923, he died in San Francisco of a heart attack.

Evalyn McLean passed away in 1947, and two years later—and against her dying wishes—the Hope Diamond was sold to pay off some of the debts of her estate. It was purchased by the jeweler Harry Winston, the last private owner of the gem. While he owned it, nothing unusual happened to him, and he died peacefully in 1978. He offered the jewel on several occasions to be worn at parties to raise money for charity. In 1958, he sold it to the Smithsonian Institution for $1 million, where it resides on permanent display, and it is one of the most popular exhibits today. However, the stone might have claimed one more victim before arriving at its final resting place. Jason Todd, the postman who delivered the Hope Diamond to the Smithsonian, suffered an uncanny series of tragedies: His wife died of a heart attack; his house burned down; and his dog died.

One final note: In 2005 the Smithsonian published a report based on its yearlong examination and geometric measurement of the Hope Diamond, and confirmed that it is a part of the French Blue gemstone, establishing at least one part of the gem's long history. Although much of the rest of the diamond's storied past is fact, there is just as much fiction surrounding the deep-blue diamond, including the idea that the fabulous gem is cursed. Still, given the fates of some of those who have owned, or even handled, it, who can really say what influence it might have on those who would seek to own it?

The Delhi Purple Sapphire

One of the lesser-known cursed gems, the Delhi Purple Sapphire, recently made a reappearance in the public eye when it was placed on permanent display in 2007 in the mineral gallery known as the Vault in the Natural History Museum in London, England. It had been kept out of public sight for the previous fifty-five years, and might have remained so for many more if a curator named Peter Tandy hadn't discovered the stone while working in the mineral cabinets thirty-four years ago.

The stone itself, actually a beautiful, medium purple oval amethyst, isn't all that unusual, although its setting is: The sapphire is bound in silver decorated with astrological symbols, with two gems carved into scarabs attached to it. What is more intriguing is the typewritten note that was found with it, which read: "This stone is trebly accursed and is stained with the blood, and the dishonour of everyone who has ever owned it." The note was written by Edward Heron-Allen, a scientist, benefactor of the Natural History Museum, friend of Oscar Wilde, and the last owner of the gem.

Heron-Allen supposedly had been so disturbed by the stone that he surrounded it with charms that were supposed to protect against its baneful influence, and he placed it inside seven boxes before giving it to the museum. Even then he was not sanguine about anyone keeping it for long. His letter concludes: "Whoever shall then open it, shall first read out this warning, and then do as he pleases with the jewel. My advice to him or her is to cast it out into the sea."

Whether there is a curse on the sapphire or not, there is no doubt that some people believe it is a baneful one. Ivor Jones, Heron-Allen's grandson, refuses to handle it, and said that his mother never touched it either. Although Heron-Allen is one of the Natural History Museum's greatest benefactors, it is apparent that even he was caught up in the legend of the sapphire.

The only known history of the gem comes from him, and he ascribes its origin to India, where supposedly it was looted by a British cavalry officer, one Colonel W. Ferris, from the Temple of India in Cawnpore during the Indian Mutiny in 1857. The officer was purported to have immediately lost his money and his health (although apparently not the stone itself), and he passed the gem on to his son, who also suffered a reversal of fortune. A friend of the Ferris family who owned the sapphire for a short while committed suicide while it was in his possession.

After Heron-Allen acquired it, the stone remained in his life for almost fifteen years, during which time he was beset by financial and personal misfortune. He tried giving it away more than once, first to a friend who was, in his own words, "thereupon overwhelmed by every possible disaster," and next to a singer friend of his who had asked for it, who then suffered the loss of her voice and reportedly never sang afterward. Heron-Allen even went so far as to throw the stone into the Regent's Canal in London, but it came back to him three months later from a dealer who had bought it from a dredger who found it while cleaning the canal. Finally, fearing the jewel's potential harmful influence over his newborn daughter, he sent the sapphire to his bankers with instructions that it be locked away until after his death. Afterward, it ended up in the Museum of Natural History in London, where it remained until its rediscovery decades later.

Although scientists at the museum dismiss the idea of a cursed sapphire, at the same time even they aren't wholly immune to the idea that the gem might have a malevolent aspect to it. In 2001, Dr. John Whittaker, former head of micropaleontology at the museum, took the sapphire with him to the first annual meeting of the Heron-Allen Society, which had been founded to discuss the man and his life. On the way home from the meeting, Whittaker and his wife encountered the most violent thunderstorm they had ever seen, so strong that they considered abandoning their car. According to the scientist, his wife knew what the cause of the weather was, shouting, "Why did you bring that accursed stone?" Misfortune plagued Dr. Whittaker in the years following as well: He became violently ill with a stomach ailment the night before the second meeting, and he missed the third completely when he developed a kidney stone. Subsequent meetings seem to have occurred without incident, although he did admit to feeling a bit of trepidation before the 2004 meeting—which was held in the museum itself, under the very roof where the Delhi Purple Sapphire was residing. No unusual occurrences were reported, however, and it remains to be seen whether the supposed curse of the Delhi Purple Sapphire will prove to be a bane to the National History Museum—or a boon, as intrigued tourists from around the world come to see one of the few cursed gems currently on display.

The Kohinoor Diamond

In the Jewel House at the Tower of London is one of Great Britain's most prized displays—the Crown Jewels of England. And one of those jewels—a magnificent, 108.93-carat diamond— rests in the crown of the queen of England, currently Elizabeth II. It is the Kohinoor Diamond, one of the oldest and most trouble-plagued gemstones in the world.

Its curse is legendary not only for its breadth, but for its specificity. Written in 1306, it reads: "He who owns this diamond will own the world, but will also know all of its misfortunes. Only God, or a woman, can wear it with impunity." Given its bloody history, this particular description of the fate of its owners may be most apt.

Although its first recorded appearance in history was in 1306, Indian history traces ownership of the Kohinoor back more than one hundred years earlier, to several dynasties, including the Slave, Khiliji, Tughlaq, and Lodi, all possessing the gem at one time or another from the thirteenth through the sixteenth centuries. Given the continual state of unrest on the Indian subcontinent at this time, it is hard to determine whether ownership of the diamond, then a 186-carat monster the size of a hen's egg, was prerequisite to meeting a grisly end, or whether the natural state of affairs was simply turbulent enough to ensure that anyone powerful enough to own it would die a violent death. Nevertheless, many owners of the Kohinoor have met untimely ends.

- The Mughal emperor Shah Jahan, famous builder of the Taj Mahal, had the Kohinoor set into his ornate peacock throne. When he became ill his four sons fought over who would succeed him, plunging the empire into civil war in 1657. The two surviving sons were Dara Shikoh, the heir apparent, and Aurangzeb, who defeated Dara Shikoh and executed him and his family in 1659, and confined his father to house arrest until his death in 1666. (Ironically, Jean-Baptiste Tavernier, the same man who purchased the French Blue, now the Hope Diamond, wrote about a gigantic diamond he saw in 1665, calling it the "Great Mogul.")
- The Mughal Empire then entered a period of long decline, beginning with Aurangzeb's forty-eight-year rule of war, revolutions, and bloodshed. In 1739, the Persian king Nadir Shah invaded the shrinking empire, defeated the current emperor, and stole the Kohinoor Diamond. However, Nadir Shah was assassinated in 1747, and his empire crumbled soon after. The great gem passed to his successors, each of whom was blinded when he was deposed, as a burden on his community.
- In 1800, Ranjit Singh took over the Sikh empire and the Kohinoor, and ruled for thirty-nine years, creating a land of unparalleled harmony and prosperity. Unfortunately, after his

death in 1839, the empire fell apart, and it was annexed by the British less than ten years later. All of Singh's sons but one also died within five years of his death, with the last, Duleep Singh, put under protection of the British Crown after his empire was taken from him. One of his last official acts was to bring the Kohinoor to the British court to present to Queen Victoria. Singh died in poverty in Paris in 1893.

In 1851, the Great Exhibition was held in Hyde Park, where the Kohinoor was placed on public display. The next year, Prince Albert ordered the gem cut from 186 carats to its current size, in order to increase its brilliance. Although the steam-powered cutting tool worked on the diamond for more than four weeks, the end result had cut the gem almost in half while hardly improving its refractive properties. In 1936, the diamond was set in the crown of the wife of King George VI, Queen Elizabeth, who is also known as the Queen Mother.

The British royal family, although perhaps not publicly acknowledging the curse, has always made sure that the crown is passed down to the wife of the male heir of the throne, technically insuring that the tenets of the curse have been met. Of course, given the state of the British empire since it acquired the Kohinoor, with the loss of India, Hong Kong, and the ravages of World Wars I and II, a case could be made that the entire empire has suffered due to its possession of the fabled, cursed diamond.

The Crystal Skulls

Sitting silently in some of the great museums in the world, including the British Museum, the Smithsonian Institution, and the Museum of Man in Paris, are some of the most fascinating worked gems ever created—the crystal skulls.

The "works," each made of a single piece of solid crystal and ranging from 1 to 15 centimeters high, have all been fashioned into crude human skulls, complete with eye sockets, nose holes, and two rows of teeth fixed in a permanent, macabre grin. Although proponents of these skulls claim that they were made thousands of years ago by ancient Central American civilizations, alien visitors, or members of lost cultures such as Lemuria or Atlantis, and ascribe such powers to them as precognition, (the ability to foretell the future), healing, or "the will of death," the truth about the crystal skulls is much more mundane.

The crystal skull in room 24: Living and Dying, in the Wellcome Trust gallery in the British Museum, does indeed have a long history, if one counts that it is more than a century old. Its provenance before 1897 is murky, but it supposedly came from Mexico, where it was acquired by a Spanish officer, who brought it back to Europe and then sold it to an English collector. Upon his death, it was sold to a French antiquities dealer named Eugène Boban, who in turn sold it to the famous jewelers at Tiffany. Boban apparently made a living dealing in these supposed "artifacts," as he brokered the sale of at least three other crystal skulls during his career, including two smaller ones to the Museum of Man in Paris. In 1897, the British Museum purchased the skull, and it has been on permanent display ever since.

The rose quartz skull at the Smithsonian (which, unfortunately, is currently not on display) is one of the largest of its kind. Donated anonymously in 1992, the thirty-two-pound skull was purchased in 1960 in Mexico City, and came with a warning not to look into its eyes, supposedly because of a curse on the gemstone. Jane Walsh, an anthropologist with the Smithsonian's National Museum of Natural History, has been researching and studying the origins of the crystal skulls for the past sixteen years, and has done much to determine their true provenance.

There have been many attempts to determine when and how the crystal skulls were created, but it has only been in the past decade that it was conclusively proved that the various skulls at museums are fakes. Although the skulls contained no carbon, the essential element for carbon dating, there were other ways to learn about how they had been fabricated. Using electron microscope technology, scientists at the British Museum examined both their skull and the one at the Smithsonian and found uniform polishing marks that showed each one had been made with rotary, disk-shaped tools, which were used in jewelry making during the nine-teenth century, and were wholly unknown to Central American civilizations; they didn't even know the concept of the wheel un-til the Spanish arrived in the mid-seventeenth century. The scien-tists also found evidence of Carborundum on the skull, an artificial polishing agent that was invented in the twentieth century. Also, analysis of its mineral composition revealed that it had been most likely quarried in Brazil, far from the Central American empires' trading routes. There is also the fact that no crystal skull has ever conclusively been unearthed in an archaeological expedition: The lone claim that one was found at an archaeological site, the pri-vately owned Mitchell-Hedges skull that was supposedly un-earthed in a Mayan temple in Belize, was actually purchased by the owner at a Sotheby's auction in 1943.

The Mitchell-Hedges skull, a realistic, transparent sculpture with a hinged, removable jawbone about ten centimeters high and weighing twenty-three kilograms, is the most famous crystal skull in private hands. It was purportedly found by seventeen-year-old Anna Mitchell-Hedges while on an archaeological expedition with her father, adventurer and investigator of the supernatural F. A. "Mike" Mitchell-Hedges, at the ancient Mayan city of Lubaantun in Belize, South America. Mr. Mitchell-Hedges was looking for the ruins of Atlantis, but his daughter supposedly un-covered an artifact there whose origins are still hotly debated to-day. Although there are pictures of both father and daughter at the dig site in Belize, there are no photos of them with the skull, nor was it written about in any inventory or personal journals kept at that time. Friends who accompanied them on the trip state that there was no mention of finding such an artifact at the site either.

Regardless, Mitchell-Hedges soon began displaying the skull to friends and acquaintances, embellishing its history by saying it was more than 3,600 years old and had taken more than 150 years to create, with generations of natives working on it their entire lives. He even went so far as to describe it as "the embodiment of all evil."

After her father's death, Anna continued displaying the skull, claiming it came from outer space and was kept in Atlantis before being "found" in Belize. She also had it examined by a crystal carver, Frank Doland, who claimed that the skull itself was excellent for scrying, and that it emits sound and light, depending on how the planets are aligned. However, he claimed that the skull originated in Atlantis, and had been owned by the Knights Templar during the Crusades. Not one of these claims has ever been proven.

The true origins of the crystal skulls most likely date to sometime between 1860 and 1880, when large amounts of Brazilian crystal was being shipped to Europe, to Germany in particular, to be fashioned into these eerie facsimiles that soon made their way into the public view and have enthralled people ever since. People have hypothesized that the skulls are connected with everything from the Mayan calendar and its purported forecast of planetary doom in 2012 to the idea that there are thirteen skulls altogether, and that when they come together their grouping will unlock some kind of ancient, mystical power source. The use of modern science in unlocking the skulls' true history would seem to eliminate any of these theories, by revealing the skulls to be exactly what they are—a set of unusual, fake artifacts carved to satisfy the public's insatiable curiosity about the unusual and the bizarre.

And to now, of course, provide fertile entertainment fodder for Hollywood franchises featuring the Phantom and, most recently, Indiana Jones.

The Hope Diamond, the Delhi Purple Sapphire, the Kohinoor Diamond, and the crystal skulls all have the same thing in common. They are all items that, while certainly unusual in their own right, have attained a status in the eye of the public of near legendary proportions because of their supposed history. Even when that history is proven to be embellished, or altogether false, the mystery and fascination remains, sometimes because of the people associated with them, as in the case of the Hope Diamond, or because of strange qualities associated with them, such as for the Delhi Purple Sapphire and the crystal skulls that have taken on a life of their own. Whatever the reason, they will hold a fascination for people for many more years to come. And perhaps someday a future generation of scientists will be able to determine whether any of them *really* have any curses or supernatural powers. But until then, we'll just have to look at them and wonder . . .

National Museum of Natural History
Smithsonian Institution
On the National Mall
At the intersection of 10th Street and
Constitution Avenue NW
Washington, DC 20560

John Helfers

It seemed like a match made in Hollywood. Everyone's favorite doomed ship meets the cursed Egyptian in the Ace bandage suit.

The Mummy on the *Titanic* and Its Curse

Some stories get told and retold and told again, so details get embellished or misstated, and the errors creep into the retellings and become part of the "facts." Couple that with a legendary disaster that had myths of its own, and suddenly two ghost stories become intertwined.

An entire generation probably believes that Jack and Rose really had their doomed romance aboard the RMS *Titanic*.

Generations earlier, people believed that the cruise liner sank because it had been caught up in a mummy's curse.

The legend has it that Amen-Ra, who lived fifteen centuries before Jesus Christ, died and was laid to rest in a wooden coffin and buried at Luxor. She lay undisturbed until archaeologists discovered her in the late 1890s. Rather than bring her to a museum, four wealthy British men bought the coffin and its mummified contents.

As the story goes, after drawing lots, the winner paid for the prize and had it taken to his hotel room. For whatever reason, he later went for a walk in the desert and was never seen again.

Then, to embellish the story, it is said that one of the others was accidentally shot the following day, surviving but losing an arm in the process. Another returned to England, only to learn that his bank had failed and his savings were wiped out. The final member of the quartet took ill and lost his job, and ended up selling matches to survive.

The princess's coffin somehow made its way to England, where a London businessman bought it. Soon after, three members of his family were hurt in a car accident and his home was damaged in a fire. Deciding the coffin was cursed, he donated it to the British Museum.

But wait, there's more.

(All these legends tend to snowball.)

At the museum the truck mysteriously went into reverse and trapped a pedestrian. One of the men carrying the coffin fell and broke his leg. Two days later the other men unexpectedly died. The princess, now in the Egyptian Room, rested uneasily in place. The night watchman reported sobbing sounds coming from the closed coffin in addition to pounding on the wood. Another watchman died on duty, causing the others to quit.

Other tales included a visitor who snapped a cloth at the coffin's head, and then his child died from measles. Enough was enough, it seemed, and the coffin was to be taken into the basement, but one of the men assigned to move it came down with an illness and the supervisor died at his desk.

Finally, the media caught wind of the problems, and an enterprising photographer took a picture of the coffin. Rather than develop the picture, he went home and shot himself.

The museum inexplicably sold the prized coffin to a private collector. Misfortune followed, so the new owner had the coffin placed in his attic. He was soon after visited by the renowned Madame Helena Blavatsky.

A visit from the Russian-born woman is significant, given her standing in the occult world of the day. Born Helena von Hahn, she was raised in a family steeped in the occult and mythology. Her sister, Vera Zhelikhovsky, wrote fantasy fiction. She broke free from her family's expectations and arranged marriage and escaped to New York in 1873. She impressed those around her with her faith in the supernatural, and they accepted her as having psychic powers. By this time the notion of Spiritualism had arrived in America and was said to have been founded by the Fox sisters in upstate New York. Blavatsky embraced this new belief and became a celebrity medium. During her career she was said to have demonstrated the powers of levitation, clairvoyance, projection, and telepathy, although she always claimed to be more interested in the theory behind the beliefs. She founded the Theosophical Society in September 1875, and her writings are credited by some as the beginnings of New Age belief.

Arriving at the collector's home, she suffered a seizure and knew evil was present. The new owner asked about an exorcism, only to be told that such evil cannot be extinguished. Desperate, the man attempted to sell or even donate the coffin, but by now the stories had spread and no one would touch it.

That is, until an American archaeologist actually paid to take the dangerous artifact away from England in April 1912. He and his prize booked passage back to New York on the maiden voyage of the RMS *Titanic*.

The White Star liner, of course, crashed into the icebergs and sank. Most died in the spectacular disaster, and the coffin went to the bottom of the Atlantic Ocean.

Unless . . .

It was actually the sarcophagus of an ancient Egyptian king, not a princess. Rather than an American buying it, the mummy was being smuggled by a criminal art dealer. He had hoped to sell it to a Manhattan museum for $500,000.

Word had it that Anubis, one of the Egyptian gods, was displeased. He vented his wrath by sinking the vessel attempting to ferry the stolen coffin. This, too, was said to be the *Titanic*.

Unless . . .

Rather than a brash American, it was Lord Canterville who was trying to take the cursed coffin away from the United Kingdom. Oh, and the coffin had been found in the small temple whose name translated as "Temple of the Eyes." Anyone said to look directly at the mummy's eyes would meet a horrible fate.

Unless . . .

Maybe the coffin was rescued in a rowboat and brought to New York aboard the *Carpathia*. The curse followed the coffin to the New World, and chaos continued until its new, unnamed owner took it to Canada to prepare to return it to Europe. The cargo was aboard the *Empress of Ireland* that was departing Quebec City en route to Liverpool on May 29, 1914. A Norwegian coal ship struck the *Ireland*, sinking it quickly, with only seven out of forty lifeboats launched successfully. The mummy survived, and a second attempt was tried aboard the *Lusitania*.

Unless . . .

The curse came from Queen Hatshepsut. It all began in 1910, when British Egyptologist Douglas Murray was approached by an American, who was offering him pieces of Hatshepsut's coffin. Before he could cash the man's check, the American died; then Murray's gun exploded, taking off his right hand. Soon after, the injury turned gangrenous, and the forearm had to be amputated. Not only that, two of Murray's friends and their servants died. Finally, in England with the coffin, Murray left it with a female compatriot. She then came down with a wasting illness, and her mother died. Her solicitor delivered the coffin to Murray, who quickly turned it over to the British Museum. They chose to sell it to the American Museum of Natural History in New York, in exchange for North American dinosaur bones. Prior to shipping, the British Museum's director of Egyptology and his photographer died. Finally loaded aboard a vessel, the *Titanic* took it toward America.

But here are the real facts about this cursed coffin.

The MacGuffin of the piece, the mummy of Amen-Ra, is

questionable. Amen-Ra is the name of a god, not a prince or princess. The coffin or sarcophagus was actually a coffin lid with no mummy associated with it. The mummy of Amun, a priestess of Amen-Ra, *was* at the British Museum—and has never left the premises, and remains in place today. The lid is said to be from Thebes, dating to either the end of the Twenty-first or the beginning of the Twenty-second Dynasty. It was donated to the British Museum by Mrs. Warwick Hunt of Holland Park, London (on behalf of Mr. Arthur F. Wheeler), in July 1889, and went on display the following year. The Amen-Ra name appeared in early museum publications and was subsequently corrected. During the two world wars it was packed up for safekeeping, and it visited Australia in 1990 but otherwise has remained in the Second Egyptian Room.

Note how few real names and dates were used. The occultist Helena Blavatsky, for example, died in 1891, some twenty years prior to her supposed arrival in the man's home according to the legend. And it was certain she was dead, since her body had been cremated, the ashes divided into thirds and sent to Europe and India.

The *Titanic* may be one of the most studied artifacts in existence and Charles Haas, president of the national Titanic Historical Society, said in 1985 that their study of the ship's manifest gave no indication that a sarcophagus had been loaded onboard. Haas said at the time, "The cargo manifest throws those myths right out the window."

So how did the story spread?

Blame William Thomas Stead, a journalist, and Douglas Murray, the aforementioned Egyptologist. The two started to spread the story of a mummy brought to the drawing room of an acquaintance, and the following morning the homeowner found the room destroyed. Each room it was moved to suffered the same fate, they told eager listeners.

Soon after, they happened to notice the coffin lid and the pained expression painted on it at the British Museum, and they spun a new yarn, that of the anguished spirit that roamed the earth. They told the story to reporters, who took the stories as true facts and published them to an excited audience. As a result, their stories were intertwined, and the legend endured for decades.

The *Titanic* angle was added when Stead went down with the vessel after telling passengers his fanciful tales. Of course, even the truth has its variations, with some telling that he began his stories on Friday, April 12, but continued telling them after midnight on the thirteenth, bringing the curse on himself.

Sadly, Stead was coming to America at the request of President William Howard Taft to speak at a peace conference.

One of the survivors recounted Stead's stories to *The New York World,* and the legend lived anew, with the mummy now aboard the doomed ship, though its curses did not necessarily go down with the ship.

A decade later America was gripped with the news of a true curse killing people.

Howard Carter, the noted archaeologist, found the tomb of the boy king Tutankhamun in November 1922. The tomb's entrance had been obscured by the rubble created by the digging for a tomb for a later king, so it had sat undisturbed until Carter found it in the legendary Valley of the Kings.

Such a discovery caused a worldwide sensation, and the footage of the dig and the vast treasures brought huge audiences into the movie theaters. It also inspired novelist Marie Corelli, also known as Mary Mackay, to issue a warning, saying that those who entered the sacred resting place would be sorry. Why she did this remains unclear, although she may have seen a warning when Carter's canary was swallowed by a cobra the day he found Tut's entrance.

Soon after, there was one tragic occurrence after another, and a susceptible public came to believe that Corelli's warning referred to an actual curse. As a result, each incident added to the legend. Unlike the *Titanic*'s mummy, these stories had names and real facts to support the notion.

First, there was Lord Carnarvon, who had financed Carter. In poor health for over twenty years, he died of pneumonia in Cairo on April 5, 1923, just weeks after the warning saw print. That's all it took to convince the media and the public that Corelli knew of what she spoke.

Sir Arthur Conan Doyle, a believer in the supernatural, added fuel to the fire by telling Fleet Street that Carnarvon's death could have been the result of a "Pharaoh's curse." That's all it took for that phrase to stick, and to fuel countless novels and movies ever since (there's a reason *Frankenstein* and *Dracula* were followed by *The Mummy*).

One newspaper even went so far as to reprint a curse said to have been found in the tomb (a falsehood): "They who enter this sacred tomb shall swift be visited by wings of death."

One list went so far as to credit the curse of Tut with twenty-six deaths within a decade. The fact is that just six people died during those years. Most who were there when the tomb was opened, and who were exposed to the "curse," actually died years later, often from old age.

You would think the first to die would have been Carter, since he found and opened the tomb. The canary would not be price enough, you would think. Carter went on to live another seventeen years, and died at age sixty-four. For ten of those years he worked within Tut's tomb, providing plenty of opportunity for the curse to take hold.

When the treasures from Tut's tomb went on tour for the first time, in the 1970s, the curse was revisited. A San Francisco museum guard blamed his mild stroke on the curse, which rejuvenated the old stories and gave new life to the legend.

Given how unique the Egyptian culture once was, it has fascinated much of the world since research began in earnest. The notion of curses associated with these sacred tombs and temples began nearly a century before the *Titanic*.

It was in the 1820s that the idea of a curse first entered the public consciousness. After a mummy was publicly unwrapped in a bizarre spectacle, Jane Webb Loudon wrote a novel, *The Mummy*. Set three centuries in the future, the book told of a mummy brought back to life that threatened the lives of humans.

The Fruits of Enterprise, a children's book, was written in 1828 and saw mummies used as torches to light the way within an Egyptian pyramid.

The stories, the whispered legends, and the whiff of the mysterious led people to believe there might be a real curse. This was solidified for all when Louisa May Alcott wrote, in 1869, "Lost in a Pyramid: The Mummy's Curse." The idea of the curse lingered and appeared in other literary works for the next three decades.

————

**British Museum
Great Russell Street
London
WC1B 3DG**

————

Robert Greenberger

You don't get any more American than Henry Ford and Thomas Edison—and you don't get any creepier than the idea that one of them took custody of the other's last breath.

Edison's Last Gasp at the Henry Ford Museum

Some say Thomas Edison's spirit floats through the halls of the Henry Ford Museum in Dearborn, Michigan, a diaphanous haunt that comes close, but never touches, the tourists. Some claim also to have seen his ghost in the adjacent Greenfield Village—including one woman who ran in terror from his approaching apparition.

Is Edison's ghost tied to the village because pieces of his life have been reconstructed and put on display? Is he forever trapped in the museum because the parting sigh of the genius inventor is held there?

What's on Exhibit

The famed inventor's last breath is on view in the museum, nestled amid exhibits of vintage cars and planes, early appliances and kitchen inventions, and the chair in which Lincoln was shot and the car in which Kennedy was assassinated.

Edison's breath is encased in a simple stoppered glass tube

that is ogled by the hundreds of visitors who walk the museum's hallways each day, some not even taking note of it because the tube is so small.

Edison was undeniably one of the greatest American inventors. He was born February 11, 1847, in Milan, Ohio. Eight years later he and his family moved to Port Huron, Michigan. And forty years later Edison became known for having the world's largest testing laboratory, in West Orange, New Jersey. By 1892, the Edison General Electric Company had merged with another firm to become the General Electric Corporation, which is still in operation today. His patents included the incandescent lightbulb, the phonograph, the Dictaphone, the mimeograph, the storage battery, and the motion picture projector.

Henry Ford counted Thomas Edison as a hero and friend, and some believe Ford asked that Edison's dying breath be captured and given to him. Edison died on October 18, 1931, reportedly waking from a coma to tell his wife, Mina: "It is very beautiful over there." Ford supposedly was interested in reincarnation and believed that the soul left a body through its final breath. Perhaps he thought Edison could be brought back by scientists in the future via the tube housed in his museum.

In any event, the sealed vial was offered to Ford—and was discovered nearly twenty years after Edison's death. When Ford's wife, Clara, died, hundreds of historical items were transferred from the Ford residence to the museum. One of those items was labeled "glass case containing Mr. Thomas Edison's hat, shoes, and sealed test tube containing (?)." It was put in storage and forgotten.

In 1978 the vial was rediscovered in a cardboard mailing tube—along with the hat and shoes. Some museum staff members remembered that there was a note attached to the tube, stating something along the lines of: "This is the test tube you requested from my father's bedroom."

While the note could not later be accounted for, the vial was put on display with this label: "Edison's Last Breath? It is alleged that Henry Ford asked Thomas A. Edison's son, Charles, to collect an exhaled breath from the lungs of Ford's dying hero and friend. The test tube was found at Ford's Fair Lane mansion, along with Edison's hat and shoes after Clara Ford's death in 1950."

Further, the museum obtained a photocopy of a letter from Edison's son. It is dated June 27, 1953:

> During Mr. Edison's last illness there was a rack of eight empty test tubes close to his bedside. They were from his work bench in the Chemical Room at the Laboratory in West Orange. Though he is mainly remembered for his work in electrical fields, his real love was chemistry. It is not strange, but symbolic, that those test tubes were close to him in the end. Immediately after his passing I asked Dr. Hubert S. Howe, his attending physician, to seal them with paraffin. He did. Later I gave one of them to Mr. Ford.

Neither Ford nor Edison's son referred to the test tubes as filled with the inventor's "last breath."

Expiration Date . . .

Edison's last breath stirs the action in Tim Powers's *Expiration Date,* which was published in 1996. In it, an eleven-year-old inadvertently breaks the vessel holding Edison's last breath, which he inhales. It takes the boy a while to realize he's absorbed a ghost, and longer to realize just whom the ghost belongs to. Edison's memories wash over him at times—lighting firecrackers for his children, driving a Ford, and more. The famed inventor talks to the boy—and through the boy, and takes control on occasion. Powers wrote of the boy, Kootie: "He had inhaled some kind of ghost, the ghost of an old man who had lived a long time ago, and Kootie had briefly lost his own consciousness in the sudden onslaught of all the piled up memories as the old man's whole life flashed before Kootie's eyes."

Some of the characters in Powers's book trap ghosts to be inhaled like a junkie would snort cocaine—held in tightly corked bottles, not unlike the vial at Ford's museum. One man boasts of inhaling hundreds of ghosts—and he seeks Edison's ghost in particular, angry that the Menlo Park exhibit at Ford's Greenfield Village splintered the spirit, and thereby made his quest for the spirit more difficult. Each inhaled ghost adds an extra one three-thousandth of an ounce to his weight. Powers wrote: "He caught the flat muskiness of ectoplasm, the protean junk that squirted out of mediums to lend substance to ghosts."

Last Breaths

It is generally accepted that the last breath signals the end of life. Some people—both spiritualists and followers of Christian and Hindu religions—believe that the soul departs the body with the last breath. Because the body no longer functions, the soul has left it, they claim. They call it "expiration," from the Latin *ex,* meaning out of or from, and *spiritus,* meaning breath, or, out of breath. Conversely, the soul enters the body with the first breath, that startling inhalation of air when a child is born and cries out.

Christians support this by citing the Bible, Genesis 2:7: "And the Lord God created man from the dust and breathed into his nostrils the breath of life; and man became a living soul."

In some cultures a spouse or relative tries to catch a dying person's final breath in a kiss, in an attempt to keep a part of that person's spirit with them.

In the Hindu religion the place of that last breath is crucial. For example, death in a hospital, or in any other building for that matter, is frowned upon. Some Hindus believe that a person should try to breathe his last while praying at the bank of a river. In addition, they encourage the newly departed soul to hurry along on its journey. Often a body is cremated as soon as possible, so that the soul does not linger around the corpse.

About the Henry Ford Museum

Ford was a noted philanthropist. He donated $7.5 million for Detroit's Henry Ford Hospital, and $5 million for a history museum in Dearborn.

Historians say that the museum sprung from a $1 million libel suit that Ford brought against *The Chicago Tribune* in 1919. In June 1916, the publisher of the *Tribune* directed his reporters to contact prestigious businesses to find out if employees called to duty in the National Guard would still be paid their regular wages. The treasurer of the Ford Motor Company responded that men called to the Guard would forfeit their jobs and salary. However, the treasurer, Frank Klinginsmith, was incorrect; the nearly one hundred Ford Motor Company employees deployed in the Guard at the Mexican border had been assured their jobs would be waiting for them when they came back home. The *Tribune*, which did not verify Klinginsmith's original statement, printed an editorial questioning Ford's patriotism and calling him an anarchist and an "enemy of the nation." The newspaper also charged that articles Ford published were ghostwritten, and that he was an "ignorant idealist" and knew little about history. The jury found in favor of Ford, but required the *Tribune* to pay only six cents in damages.

After the trial Ford reportedly informed his secretary that he was going to start an American history museum—certainly something no ignorant idealist would bother to do. He opened the museum a decade later, in 1929, and filled it with tokens from everyday rural life, focusing on items that were innovative and important to American culture, including an array of automobiles. Today the museum's one-story complex of buildings with forty-foot-high ceilings covers nine acres.

What's Not on Exhibit in Any Museum

In the 1920s Edison supposedly built a device he believed would communicate with the dead. Although Edison did not have strong religious beliefs, he had faith in the spirit world. His parents considered themselves spiritualists and members of a religion founded in New York in the late 1840s by Katie, Margaret, and Leah Fox.

Edison was quoted as saying of his invention and spirits: "If our personality survives, then it is strictly logical or scientific to assume it retains memory, intellect, other faculties and knowledge we acquire on Earth. Therefore . . . if we can evolve an instrument so delicate as to be affected by our personality as it survives in the next life, such an instrument, when made available, ought to record something."

Edison tinkered with his device, called a spirit phone, up until his death in 1931. After his death the machine was expected to find its way into a museum—like so many of Edison's inventions. However, the machine itself, blueprints, and notes disappeared.

Some questioned if the spirit phone or "psycho-phone," ever really existed. The Edison National Historic Site has more than five million pages of documents, none of which mention the device or anything similar to it. In Edison's lab museum in Menlo Park, New Jersey, there is no mention of the spirit or psycho-phone.

However, people who claimed to be invited by Edison to be witnesses to the device's testing reported that the machine resembled a phonograph, and that it operated with potassium permanganate—an oxidizing agent that can be used as a disinfectant, a propellant, or an antidote for some poisons. Skeptics said that perhaps the so-called witnesses watched Edison inscribing a cylinder for a phonograph, and that there was an anomaly, which made them believe spirits were speaking through the apparatus.

The device was said to include a photoelectric cell. A thin

beam of light, emitted from a powerful lamp, supposedly struck the cell, whereupon it became an electric current. Edison had maintained that even a transparent or tiny object would register on the cell if said object passed through the beam. The spiritualists among the witnesses were asked to summon a ghost and ask it to walk through the beam to verify its presence. The experiment was said to last hours, and supposedly the night was stormy and windy and set the right atmosphere for the event, but no spirits manifested. Some witnesses said Edison did not want news of the failed experiment released, which is why no proof of the device has been found.

A noted magician, Joseph Dunniger, claimed that he saw one of the prototypes—but he made the claim after Edison's death.

Edison was known to have corresponded about the psychophone with Sir William Crookes, the inventor of the vacuum tube. Crookes was known for his fascination with the paranormal and ghost photography. Crookes's otherworldly photograph collection supposedly gave Edison the notion that if ghosts could be captured on film, his spirit phone might be able to capture their voices.

Edison also mentioned his device in scientific journals. He wrote in an essay in 1920:

Now what I propose to do is furnish psychic investigators with an apparatus which will give a scientific aspect to their work. This apparatus, let me explain, is in the nature of a valve, so to speak. That is to say, the slightest conceivable effort is made to exert many times its initial power for indicative purposes. It is similar to a modern power house, where man, with his relatively puny one-eighth horse-power, turns a valve which starts a 50,000-horse-power steam turbine. My apparatus is along those lines, in that the slightest effort which it intercepts will be magnified many times so as to give us whatever form of record we desire for the purpose of investigation. Beyond that I don't care to say anything further regarding its nature. I have been working out the details for some time; indeed, a collaborator in this work died only the other day. In that he knew exactly what I am after in this work, I believe he ought to be the first to use it if he is able to do so.

In an interview in *Scientific American,* Edison said it could be possible to construct a device "so delicate that if there are personalities in another existence or sphere who wish to get in touch with us in this existence or sphere, this apparatus will at least give them a better opportunity to express themselves than the tilting tables and raps and Ouija boards and mediums and the other crude methods now purported to be the only means of communication."

In the October 1920 issue of *American Magazine* an article appeared headlined EDISON WORKING TO COMMUNICATE WITH THE NEXT WORLD. Newspapers and magazines around the world covered the topic. *The New York Times* carried a story about Edison working on a device that could measure "one hundred trillion life units" in a person's body that "may scatter after death." The reporter, A. D. Rothman, wrote that Edison denied any link between his experiment and the spiritual world. Rothman said that Edison refused to discuss the details of the device.

One tale says that a decade after Edison's death the inventor made contact with participants at a séance in New York. Edison's ghost reportedly claimed that his blueprints for the spirit phone were with three of his former assistants. Also according to the story, a machine was built from the blueprints, but it did not function.

At a later séance Edison supposedly suggested some changes to the device. One of the séance participants, J. Gilbert Wright, was said to have made those changes and then was able to make contact with the ghost of inventor Charles Steinmetz. That ghost made more suggestions for improvements, and Wright was said to have tinkered with the spirit phone until his death in 1959. Wright's device was never found.

The San Diego Paranormal Research Project, which maintains a Web site, reports that in an April 2003 channeling with the spirit of someone named Jesse Shepard, the existence of the psycho-phone was verified. Shepard, also known as Francis Grierson, was a musician and spiritualist who lived in Chicago in the 1880s. Shepard's spirit said that Edison had patents on all of the components of the device, and that he had made a few prototypes. The spirit claimed that Edison had some limited successful results.

Other Haunts at the Ford Estate and Museum

At Henry Ford's estate, tourists have reported windows and doors opening and closing on their own in the various buildings, and said they spotted a man wandering the hallways dressed in an out-of-date uniform. One witness identified the wandering spirit as Ford's butler—after having seen the man in a photograph. While the Michigan Ghost Watchers did not confirm this sighting as official, the group itself reported seeing mists forming at the estate, and members took pictures of mysterious orbs and a ghostly figure perched inside one of Ford's cars. Another photograph shows a man in the car, and a second apparition behind the car.

Several years ago the Ford Museum offered tours that featured stops at exhibits where visitors had claimed to see ghosts. Among the most famous spirits is President John F. Kennedy. The museum displays the convertible in which Kennedy was shot while riding in a motorcade in Texas. On the anniversary of Kennedy's death a museum guard claimed that he spotted the president's ghostly form next to the car. Kennedy reportedly waved at the guard and left a red rose on the hood. Some museum patrons claimed to feel a cold wind blowing near it. Others said

Kennedy's spirit had appeared to them, and he said that Oswald did not kill him, that there was another man outside the building where Oswald was apprehended, and that there was still another man on the lawn hidden by trees—this being the man who shot him.

A Dearborn man has said that his wife used to manage the IMAX theater at the Ford Museum and would feel uneasy some evenings when she was closing. One such incident was on a night the museum had offered one of its famed haunted tours around Halloween, when visitors were taken behind the scenes to shipping rooms and other places the public was not normally allowed to venture. He said that his wife felt a presence, even though no one was around, and that she got out of the building quickly. He also said that he would feel "creeped out" just sitting in the parking lot waiting for her.

Spirits at the Greenfield Village

Helen Mamalakis, an employee of the Dearborn Historical Museum, has gathered some of the Ford- and Edison-related ghost sighting stories in a series of "eerie tales" books. Mamalakis has also reported on sightings of Henry and Clara Ford at their estate, and at the Greenfield Village. In 1933 the Greenfield Village, a reproduction of an early American town, was opened adjacent to the museum—with buildings purchased from various locations, dismantled, and reassembled at the village.

There are many reports of hauntings in Greenfield Village, most of them concerning ghosts spotted at the Firestone Farm, where a man had committed suicide in the barn; at the Webster House, where the spirit is just said to be sorrowful; and at the Wright bicycle shop, once owned by Orville and Wilbur Wright and taken down and reassembled in the village.

"People tell me stories," Mamalakis said, "about things they have seen. Like at the Eagle Tavern in the village. Furniture is always moved around there, with no explanation. The Wright House is supposedly haunted, and the Cogswell Cottage, too."

She's received reports from tourists at the Henry Ford estate about people appearing and disappearing.

"A friend of mine who works in the Ford Museum told me that he once saw an old man who approached him and said, 'It looks like you're lost.' My friend said, 'Yes, I am.' They talked back and forth for a while, and then my friend's boss arrived. My friend said his boss acted rude and ignored the nice old man. The boss told my friend later that there was no old man there," Mamalakis said.

Although Mamalakis has not seen any of the spirits herself, she said a close friend had a too close encounter that has stayed with them for three decades.

"Many years ago one of my girlfriends was working at one of the restaurants in the Greenfield Village. She was seventeen. They'd left a seventeen-year-old girl to clean up and close at 11:00 P.M. She called security to walk her to the front gate, but no one came. Then she saw a light in the building at Menlo Park and started walking toward it."

Edison's Menlo Park Laboratory is the building where the inventor created the electric lightbulb, the phonograph, and many other devices. The building was reconstructed in 1929 in Greenfield Village using Edison's dismantled original building from Menlo Park, New Jersey. Even some of the soil around the original building was brought along.

Mamalakis said: "The light was going on and off, and my girlfriend thought it odd, because the light wasn't supposed to work at all. She looked closer and noticed a man, who started heading toward her. And then she noticed that he doesn't have feet. She ran, of course."

Mamalakis's girlfriend called her at midnight and asked to come over, too frightened to stay alone. Still, the girl went back to work the next day. "She was seventeen," Mamalakis repeated, "too young to know better."

That footless spirit could have belonged to Edison, Mamalakis said, as others have reported seeing a similar apparition in the Menlo Park building and made the connection to the inventor. "Edison has been seen from here to the East Coast," she said.

———

The Henry Ford Museum
20900 Oakwood Boulevard
Dearborn, MI 48124

———

Jean Rabe

Someone once said that "pictures don't lie" (probably someone working for Kodak), but sometimes it's "what lies beneath" that is creepiest, especially when it is captured on film.

Spirit Photography

In the early days of photography, the photographic plate had to be left exposed for a period of time. During that lengthy exposure, it was said that ghostly images could be captured. It was two decades later, in 1860, when the first official "spirit" photograph was identified.

The cameraman was W. Campbell of Jersey City. He was taking a test photo of a chair in his studio, but when he developed the plate later, the printed image showed the chair plus a small boy. When he attempted to re-create the image, he failed, and a mystery began.

Since then, people have often believed that film can capture spirits. When photographers arrived in Africa and south of the American border, some cultures believed the camera was stealing a person's soul, and that the images possessed power over the subject.

Once people learned of film and turned photography into an art form, people also began using it to create hoaxes. Many, though, fully believed that spirits and other supernatural life were being captured on film.

The original method of photography began with the preparation of a glass plate by coating it with a film of collodion, a cotton-based solution containing iodide of potassium. The treated plate was then dipped in a bath of silver nitrate and was ready for use. When the wet plate was inserted into the camera and exposed to the light, the image was captured.

With the long exposure time, any movement would blur the finished image. It wasn't long before photographers learned how to use double exposures to create unique images. Records indicate that the trick photo was written about as early as 1856, just scant years before Campbell had his singular experience in 1860.

A year after Campbell, Bostonian William Mumler, an amateur photographer, was working in his Washington Street studio. He was standing for a self-portrait when he felt a trembling in his right arm, and once it passed, he felt exhausted. Upon development, the picture showed him standing beside a young woman, and a closer examination startled him. The face was that of his cousin, who had died in 1849. He declared to colleagues, "This photograph was taken by myself of myself and there was not a living person in the room besides myself."

Since this moment, many unexplained images have been recorded on film, giving birth to an entire field of spirit photography. Others are counterfeits, and even worse, there are charlatans who are out for the quick buck and have spoiled it for those who find comfort in the belief that the spirits can be photographed.

All the arguments played out almost immediately as word of Mumler's picture spread. Newspapers covered the story, and Mumler's work sped around the globe. When he repeated the feat, he was as amazed as anyone. Others began asking him to photograph them in the hopes of seeing their dearly departed. The demand grew so much that he wound up taking two hours a day away from his day job—as an engraver for Bigelow Bros. and Kennard, among Boston's finest jewelers—to satisfy the people.

Soon after he opened up a new business, now claiming to be a medium who used his camera to commune with the beyond. For someone who professed to not being very spiritual before his first picture, he now declared he could speak with friends, family, celebrities, you name it. He was in such demand that he began to charge $10 ($131.31 in 2007) per photo.

The *American Journal of Photography* scoffed.

How wonderful is the recent progress of our art! We now in the usual way go through the process of having our picture taken, but when the finished photograph is presented, lo! Beside our lovely image is the attendant spirit, a babe, or a grandfather, or an unknown! ... spirit photographs show, that the spirits dress in cloths of earthly fashion, that they sit in chairs, and that in sitting for their pictures they put on the smirks which some have supposed peculiar to mortals.

To silence some of the questioning, William Black, the man who invented the acid nitrate bath that helped improve photography, came to the studio and watched Mumler at work. He studied the setting, the camera, and other equipment before being photographed. Black took the plate and developed it himself, unable to explain how a previously unseen person wound up leaning over his shoulder, an image captured on film.

Similarly, in 1863, a Dr. Child was invited to come north from Philadelphia to observe Mumler at work. From cleaning the plates to developing the exposed plates, he and others watched carefully. Each plate that day had been marked with a diamond, and they were the ones used, and in every case a spirit image appeared on the plate. Child returned home baffled as to how the images were made, not yet ready to concede the supernatural explanation.

Mumler's best known photo occurred when a veiled woman in a heavy black dress arrived and introduced herself as Mrs. Tydall. He later wrote, "I requested her to be seated, went into my darkroom and coated a plate. When I came out I found her seated with a veil still over her face. The crepe veil was so thick that it was impossible to distinguish a single feature of her face. I asked if she intended having her picture taken with her veil. She replied, 'When you are ready, I will remove it.' I said I was ready, upon which she removed the veil and the picture was taken." The finished print is one in which Abraham Lincoln, shot just years before, appears. Most who have studied the print think it is a sophisticated fake. For some others, it proves their belief that love does not end when a spouse dies.

Black and Child were not the only ones to question Mumler and his followers. Other professionals insisted on an investigation into Mumler and his methods. They were spurred into action when some of the spirits captured on film were recognized as residents living in Boston. He was more or less run out of town in 1869 by people who felt deceived. He headed south to New York City, where he set up shop, only to be arrested and charged with public fraud, larceny, and obtaining money under false pretenses. The mayor of New York had prosecutors issue a warrant for Mumler's arrest on charges of "swindling credulous persons by what he called spirit photographs."

While he tried to fight the charges, his work sparked a keen interest in the Old World. The *Photographic Journal of London* sang Mumler's praises: "No single phenomenon could possibly awaken deeper interest than will follow this new revelation." They were clearly delighted by the new field of study. Supportive letters were published in subsequent issues.

Mumler's trial lasted seven days, as a former judge and Jeremiah Gurney, a noted Broadway photographer, took the photographer's side. No less a showman than P. T. Barnum testified that he had bought Mumler's work to display as examples of humbug. The nation followed the trial avidly, through coverage included in the prestigious *Harper's Weekly*.

He was acquitted of the charges after professional photographers testified that they could not find any evidence of the images being faked. The judge said, according to *The New York Daily*

Tribune, "However he might believe that trick and deception had been practiced [by Mumler], yet, as he sat there in his capacity as magistrate, he was compelled to decide . . . the prosecution had failed to prove the case."

Mumler went right back to work, publishing a pamphlet in 1875 to boast about his work. However, he only eked out a living, never managing to recover the three thousand dollars he had spent on his defense. Despondent, he destroyed all his negatives and died soon after, in 1884.

How did Mumler do it? Did he do it?

No one ever knew for certain. Researchers today feel that mixed in with the genuinely mysterious images are fakes he manufactured to satisfy the customers.

In 1866, Sir David Brewster, an optical scientist, was the first to suspect "trick photography" was used to create the spirit photos that had become vogue. He wrote in his book *The Stereoscope*:

> The value and application of this fact did not at first present itself to me, but after I had contrived the lenticular stereoscope I saw that such transparent pictures might be used for the various purposes of entertainment.
>
> For the purpose of amusement, the photographer may carry us even into the realms of the supernatural. His art enables him to give a spiritual appearance to one or more of his figures, and to exhibit them as "thin air" amid the solid realities of the stereoscopic picture.

Mumler may have been second, but he was not last. Other photographers began to claim they, too, could capture the spirits on film. All used the term "medium," like the faith healers in traveling carnivals. In addition to the professionals, countless amateurs also tried their hand at photography. William Hope, for example, made the claim of possessing in excess of twenty-five hundred spirit photographs. Modern day study has shown them to be entirely inauthentic.

While Mumler sat on trial, London's Frederick Hudson gained notoriety as well. His spirit photography caught the attention of Mrs. Samuel Guppy, a medium popular at the time. As he gained celebrity status, he began charging a steep rate for his photos, with the understanding that there was no guarantee that a spirit could be captured, covering him whenever his ploy failed. His fame lasted until 1873, when professional photographer John Beattie experimented with Hudson's work. The results were published in the *British Journal of Photography*. Beattie and a friend had examined Hudson's operation: the garden-based glass room where the work was done, the operating room with its yellow light and porcelain baths, the 10-inch by 8-inch camera with its 6-inch lens.

As described in the article, the photographic exposure took one minute, with Beattie as the subject and Hudson's daughter next to him.

"All was the same except that the medium sat behind the background," he wrote about the second picture.

On the picture being developed, a sitting figure beside myself came out in front of me and between the background and myself. I am sitting in profile in the picture—the figure is in a three-quarter position—in front of me, but altogether between me and the background. The figure is draped in black, with a white colored plaid over the head, and is like both a brother and a nephew of mine. This last point I do not press because the face is like that of a dead person and under lighted.

In my last trial—all, if possible, more strictly attended to than before, and in the same place relative to me—there came out a standing female figure, clothed in black skirt, and having a white-colored, thin linen drapery something like a shawl pattern, upon her shoulders, over which a mass of black hair loosely hung. The figure is in front of me and, as it were, partially between me and the camera.

Beattie was stunned that he could not determine how the images appeared, given his examination and methodical approach. What he missed at the time was that the plates themselves had been swapped for prepared ones that had an image in place, a standard trick of the day.

Nor was the pastime limited to America. Frenchman Édouard Isidore Buguet started making spirit photographs in London in 1874. Soon after, he was allied with fellow photographers in France, who by then had been linked with the study of mesmerism. Buguet was the first to fully integrate spirit photography with mesmerism, a quasi-science that was part self-healing and part self-hypnosis.

Like Mumler, though, Buguet was arrested in 1875 and charged with fraud. He made a complete confession though his "victims" had said they recognized departed loved ones in many of his prints. This despite one identified "spirit" proving to be alive and well and completely unaware of being included in a photograph. Buguet confessed that he used double exposures, with assistants outfitted to resemble a ghost. The props were among the items seized by police and used as evidence during the trial. He was fined and given a one-year prison sentence. Buguet recanted his confession once the trial concluded, but he never managed to restore his reputation.

Spiritualism had sprouted up in Europe during the eighteenth century but didn't arrive in America until 1848, when two young women, Kate and Margaret Fox, claimed to be able to speak with the spirits. It began the night of March 31, in the small upstate New York town of Hydesville, when the young girls seemed possessed by the supernatural. Coupled with the growing interest in spirit photography, they rode out a wave of popularity until one of the girls confessed their duplicitous actions, causing them both to be ostracized and leading them to die destitute.

As a result, the issues of the paranormal remain up for debate with as many believers as skeptics.

The debate continued through the years, flaring up in the media every now and then. The *British Journal of Photography* published an article by its editor, J. Traille Taylor, reviewing the history and outlining methods that had been used to dupe the paying public. He attempted to re-create the false images, and did indeed create some pictures with ghostly people captured in manners even he could not explain.

A year later spirit photography gained credibility when Alfred Russel Wallace, who did landmark work with Charles Darwin, advocated that spirit photography be studied as a science.

James Coates wrote *Photographing the Invisible* in 1911, which proved immensely popular. It was a survey of the field, and was successful enough that he released an expanded edition in 1921.

Charles Cook conducted experiments in 1916, working with photographers Edward Wyllie of Los Angeles and Alex Martin of Denver. To control the process and avoid being hoodwinked, he provided the plates used and had a commercial outfit handle the developing. In both cases, spirit images appeared, and Cook was led to conclude that the men both used psychic means to make the spirits appear.

Still, for every report from a Cook, there were reports by others who challenged the very notion of spirit photography. While some skeptics changed their tune, such as Sir William Crookes, most remained adamant that the spirits, if they existed at all, could not be caught on film.

Crookes is notable since he spent six months researching the phenomenon in the early twentieth century. A three-decade member of the Royal Society, his turnaround was newsworthy. He wrote a book on the topic but failed to convince other members of the society.

With increasingly sophisticated computer and digital technology, the old photos and negatives have withstood rigorous examination and, in many cases, a plausible explanation has failed to emerge. Among those examined were two remarkable photographs. The first, known as the Brown Lady, was taken by a professional, Captain Provand in Norfolk, England. While shooting Raynham Hall for *Country Life* magazine, his assistant, Indre Shira, saw the Brown Lady walk down the staircase. She urged Provand to take the picture even though the photographer couldn't see the apparition.

The other picture was of a figure called the Greenwich Ghost. Snapped at Queen's House, Greenwich, London, in 1966 by Reverend R. W. Hardy, the resulting image included a shrouded figure. Kodak, among other experts, examined both negative and prints and could not explain how the spirit was caught on film.

One of the most legendary examples of false spirit photography involved Sir Arthur Conan Doyle, creator of Sherlock Holmes. It all began innocently enough with two young girls, Frances Griffith and Elsie Wright, in Cottingley, England.

In July 1917, the girls decided to show people that they were serious about their purported fairy sightings. Following Claude A. Shepperson's depiction of fairies in the 1914 book, *Princess Mary's Gift Book,* Elsie drew up her own creations. She was then instructed on how to use her father's Midg quarter-plate camera, and set up a shot of Frances with two fairies. That night Elsie developed the photographic plate alongside her father, Arthur, a noted electrical engineer. He questioned the fairies seen in the picture.

A month later the girls created a gnome, and this time Frances photographed Elsie. As an annoyed Arthur stuck the prints in a drawer, he was dismayed to learn that his wife, Polly, thought the fantasy creatures real.

It wasn't until 1920, when Polly attended a lecture on folklore, that things began to stir. Mrs. Wright spoke with the lecturer afterward, mentioning the photo she had seen. Another attendee, Edward Gardner, heard this, and asked to see the prints. He, too, thought they were real.

Gardner showed the photographs to Fred Barlow, who was recognized in his day as an authority on psychic photography.

In June 1920, he believed the photos to be fake, but he said in December, "I am returning herewith the three fairy photographs you very kindly loaned to me, and have no hesitation in announcing them as the most wonderful and interesting results I have ever seen."

Still, Gardner sought further verification, and he showed them to Harold Snelling, who was an expert at discovering faked photography. He declared on July 31, 1920, "These two negatives are entirely genuine unfaked photographs of single exposure, open-air work, show movement in all the fairy figures, and there is no trace whatever of studio work involving card or paper models, dark backgrounds, painted figures, etc. In my opinion, they are both straight untouched pictures."

Convinced, Gardner made more paper prints as well as two lantern slides, which he used during a lecture at London's Mortimer Halls. In the audience was Doyle. He was given to spiritual beliefs and had developed a reputation as an easy mark.

Doyle was already commissioned to write about fairies for *The Strand*'s Christmas issue, so he was fascinated, but he wanted the negatives verified as authentic by another expert, such as those at Kodak. Four employees studied the negatives and concluded that there was but one exposure; the negatives had not been tampered with. They did refuse to fully certify that the pictures were real, since increasingly sophisticated processes were being developed to manipulate images.

Satisfied, Doyle wrote about the pictures for *The Strand*. He wrote AN EPOCH MAKING EVENT—FAIRIES PHOTOGRAPHED, which appeared in the November 1920 issue.

Still seeking verification, Doyle asked the medium Geoffrey Hodson to come see for himself. On an August 1921 night, Hodson claimed to have seen wood elves and dancing fairies, which were reported in his *Fairies at Work and Play*. A year later Doyle followed up with *The Coming of the Fairies,* reporting on the girls, the pictures, and the importance of the discovery.

On February 17, 1983, Elsie finally admitted to the hoax. In a letter she admitted to illustrating the fairies and using hat pins to make them appear to float. Undaunted, Frances continued to claim publicly the fairies' existence right up until her final television interview in 1986, before her death later that year.

The entire notion of spirits caught on film has remained a part of world culture, and has been used as a plot point in movies including the 2008 release *Shutter*, based on a Japanese film, showing its universal appeal. In Japan, *Shinrei Shashin* is almost as popular as in the United States.

Whatever the truth, the images cannot be disputed, nor can the entire field be debunked, leaving one to wonder where the truth lies.

———

American Photography Museum
photographymuseum.com

———

Robert Greenberger

There is always a problem with prison overcrowding,
sometimes even after the prison has been shut down.

Doing Life . . . and Beyond

The Burlington County Prison Museum is a National Historic Landmark located in historic Mount Holly, New Jersey. Designed by Robert Mills, one of America's first native-born and -trained architects, the Burlington County Prison was completed in 1811. One of Robert Mills's first designs as an independent architect, the interior vaulted ceilings of poured concrete and brick-and-stone construction made the building virtually fireproof. In fact, it was so well constructed that it remained in constant use until 1965.

Among its alumni was a man named Albert DeSalvo, who was passing through New Jersey and was arrested on lewd and indecent exposure charges. He later graduated to notoriety as the Boston Strangler.

Now no longer an active penal institution, this stately old fortification is an authentic model of prison history complete with perusable volumes of arrest records that are filled with a colorful lot of prisoners, crimes, and punishments to fill your appetite for reading pleasure.

But not all of the remnants of the past exist solely in the records and displays/exhibits that have been arranged for public education as part of the establishment's role as a landmark and attraction.

Apparently some of those who served time here may have not yet completed their sentences or moved on to some further punishment or halfway house to heaven. According to *Weird New Jersey Stories,* some of those who met their final punishment never left the grounds of the prison: Museum workers have reported seeing apparitions on the first floor, ghosts "with no legs" floating from the massive front entrance toward the small back door that leads out to the prison yard. Visitors have heard voices and seen shadowy figures out of the corners of their eyes in the basement. Some have even reported witnessing a tall man wearing a uniform or work clothes hanging around the basement area.

The dungeon, or maximum-security cell, was in the center of the top floor. That location was carefully chosen to prevent escape by digging, to minimize communication with criminals in the cell blocks, and to ensure constant surveillance by guards making rounds. This was the only cell without a fireplace. It is flanked by niches for guards or visitors and has one very high, very small window and an iron ring in the center of the floor to which the prisoner could be chained. As one might expect, tradition states that this cell is haunted. Policy of the time was to chain the condemned to a ring on the floor, naked. Accordingly, Joel's spirit has been heard moaning and languishing there, and electro-magnetic indicators (used in ghost hunting) routinely register a "hit." The Death Cell, complete with its metal ring, and all the "accommodations" at the prison, welcome inspection, and in many cases prisoner graffiti has been preserved on the walls.

Other visitors have reported feelings of being watched or of physically feeling other presences in the cells that they visited.

Such feelings are common when visiting such a stern and history-laden locale as a prison that had seen more than its share of condemned men.

Sometimes the mind reacts and our senses play tricks with us.

Which is not to say that there isn't the possibility that there is something else going on, and that perhaps the sentences of the condemned were far longer in practice than anyone could ever imagine.

———

**Historic Prison Museum
128 High Street
Mount Holly, NJ 08060**

———

*Perhaps otherworldly neighbors are just competing for
media coverage.*

Haunting Utah's
History Museums

Utah is home to numerous exemplary museums with a special affinity for the heritage of western expansion, and for the very specific legacy of the state of Utah.

The Pioneer Memorial Museum located in Salt Lake City is noted as the world's largest collection of artifacts on one particular subject, and it features displays and collections of memorabilia from the time the earliest settlers entered the Valley of the Great Salt Lake until the joining of the railroads at a location known as Promontory Point, on May 10, 1869. Here are the belongings of a hardy pioneer people who migrated two thousand miles west across the plains from Nauvoo, Illinois, and from all parts of the world to seek religious freedom and to build a great city of Zion in the Salt Lake Basin.

Lehi's John Hutchings Museum of Natural History has its origins in its inquisitive founder, Mr. Hutchings. His collections soon overflowed his home. In 1955, Mr. Hutchings, his wife, Eunice, and the Hutchings family donated the collections to the nonprofit museum corporation to be held in trust for the people of Lehi, Utah. There are two sides to the museum. First, the natural history side allows you to visit the rocks and minerals, fossils and marine life, and fauna of the area. Second, the cultural history side includes the Native American Room, the Wild West Room, and the Pioneer Room, which represents pioneers through the Depression era.

Both are noteworthy tourist destinations, and if recent studies are to be believed, both of these forums for the commemoration of the past may have attracted some of the pertinent spirits as well, since paranormal investigators have determined that both sites may actually be haunted, or at least places of spectral activity.

According to *The Deseret Morning News*, "A ghostly image seen on a surveillance camera has some wondering if Utah's Pioneer Memorial Museum is haunted. The Utah Department of Public Safety has even been asked to investigate, but museum officials are staying quiet—only adding to the mystery. . . .

"The DUP said in a statement that the image lingered in front of the surveillance camera for about five minutes, but as soon as an officer arrived to investigate, the image vanished. The trooper found no sign of life in the museum." Since then the ghostly face has reappeared several times.

Security cleaned the camera's lens and checked to make sure it was functioning properly, but no cause for the spectral appearance was evident.

The image only comes at night, when the room is dark.

(Some speculated that it's only a reflection, because there's a lot of glass in the gift shop.)

At the Hutchings Museum no less than three paranormal investigative groups were called in: key2rip.com, Wasatch Paranormal Investigators, and Paranormal Utah. *The Utah Daily Herald* reported, "The teams fanned out, poking into the museum's nooks and crannies with thousands of dollars of high-tech equipment, hoping to catch the voice of a ghost on tape or an image on film, or even just the electromagnetic signature of the disembodied. . . . Not only is the museum haunted, the ghosts can be rather, er, physical, said Michelle Lowe of Key2rip.com. . . . Investigators several times heard what sounded to be 'additional footsteps, like people were being followed through the basement,' she said. One of the investigators was grabbed on the leg by a ghost, she said."

Though both hauntings have attracted the attention of local media (and not only during the ever popular Halloween haunting season), it is worth noting that neither paranormal occurrence seems to be linked to any specific exhibit or artifact from the past.

Perhaps these nocturnal visitors are merely past visitors keeping up on new additions to the collections even after they have passed on.

———

The Pioneer Memorial Museum
300 N. Main Street
Salt Lake City, UT 84103

John Hutchings Museum of Natural History
55 N. Center Street
Lehi, UT 84043

———

Having seen their fair share of action, some spirits apparently rebel against being put into dry dock.

Who Haunts the *Hornet*?

Ghosts do not exist.

People who feel a creepy presence on the USS *Hornet* beg to differ.

The old aircraft carrier, a sturdy warhorse of World War II, is now a floating museum moored at port in Alameda, California. The *Hornet*'s service in World War II was certainly commendable and commands respect, but the carrier never suffered a single hit from the enemy.

So where did all the ghosts come from?

During the ship's renovation, and, later, after its opening almost a decade ago, several hundred incidents allegedly occurred, in which young men in uniform or work clothes were spotted in different parts of the ship, just passing through.

Or things that don't move by themselves did move, like a wrench or a hammer.

Or a locked hatch was found open.

Or a lone person got that creepy feeling of not being alone.

Some theorize that the ghosts belong to people who served on the ship, or died on the ship, attached to a place where they spent their best years and had their peak experiences—or where their worst fears came true.

If so, then why are *Hornet*'s sister ships *not* haunted?

Intrepid (CV-11) is docked at a Hudson River pier in Manhattan. The ship suffered two kamikaze hits during the war that killed over a hundred sailors. The *Intrepid* has plenty of visitors, but no ghosts. *Yorktown* (CV-10) is in Charleston, South Carolina, but is not haunted. *Lexington* is tied up at Corpus Christi, Texas, and even had a bit part as a Japanese aircraft carrier in the movie *Tora! Tora! Tora!* That is an interesting story, but no ghost tells it.

Hornet (CV-12) and its three sisters are the only surviving examples of the Essex-class aircraft carrier, the standard U.S. flattop that carried the war to Japan in the latter half of World War II.

Twenty-four of them were built.

None were sunk.

So why should the *Hornet,* of all of these ships, be ghost-ridden?

Just remember that the *Hornet* you stand on is not the same ship by that name.

Back During the War

The United States started World War II with just seven carriers. *Lexington* and *Saratoga* were built on the hulls of battle cruisers that could not be completed due to naval treaty limitations in the 1920s. *Ranger, Wasp, Yorktown, Enterprise,* and *Hornet* (CV-8) rounded out the lineup.

It was not the Navy we wanted to go to war with, but it was the Navy we had.

Yorktown, Enterprise, and *Hornet* were all sister ships, with the smaller *Wasp* a half sister. Only *Enterprise* survived the war, having taken part in just about every major battle. *Yorktown* took a hit at the Battle of Coral Sea in May 1942, the first carrier battle in naval history. Refitted quickly at Pearl Harbor, *Yorktown* fought again at the decisive Battle of Midway in June 1942, alongside *Enterprise* and *Hornet*. Sadly, *Yorktown* did not survive the battle.

Hornet was already famous by the time of the Battle of Midway. Earlier in the year the ship was loaded with sixteen B-25 medium bombers belonging to the U.S. Army. Steaming across the North Pacific, *Hornet* launched the planes to bomb Tokyo and several other Japanese cities. The Doolittle Raid was a major morale booster for the United States, as the first six months of the war in the Pacific had been nothing more than a string of defeats.

Late summer 1942 saw the United States contest Japan for control of the Solomon Islands, starting with the Marines landing at Guadalcanal.

Mission kills mounted.

Enterprise took a bomb hit and had to retire for repairs.

Saratoga then had to leave after a torpedo slammed into its hull.

Wasp was smashed by several torpedo hits from a Japanese sub, sinking quickly.

For two months *Hornet* was the only American carrier fighting in the Pacific. Finally, in late October, *Enterprise* rejoined *Hornet*. Fighting the Japanese Navy near Santa Cruz, *Hornet*'s luck finally ran out. Repeated Japanese air attacks inflicted seven bomb and torpedo hits.

A stricken ship becomes its own battlefield as the crew fights to control fires, restore power, and get underway. Cobbling together a working system from wreckage is victory. Sailing home under your own steam is glory.

Hornet didn't have time for that. The task force commander signaled to the cruiser *Northampton* to rig a towline. Just as repair crews were getting ready to restore power to just one of *Hornet*'s propellers, Japanese planes struck again, putting one more torpedo hit near a previous hole.

The order was given to abandon ship.

But the burning *Hornet* would not sink.

Another Japanese air strike scored a single bomb hit on the carrier, killing another 118 crew members as the ship was being evacuated.

By the end of the day escorting destroyers received orders to scuttle the burning *Hornet*.

Two destroyers fired sixteen torpedoes at an easy target. Nine hit. None sank the ship. They opened fire with their five-inch guns, pumping *Hornet* full of holes. Still nothing.

Now the Americans had to get out of Dodge quickly, as a Japanese task force was approaching. The destroyers *Akigumo* and *Makikumo* arrived. Each fired two torpedoes. All four hit. *Hornet* finally sank, taking with it any ghosts to Davy Jones's locker.

Obviously this is not the *Hornet* visitors step on in Alameda today.

Ships may die.

Their names live on.

Hornet Reborn

U.S. naval tradition is very good at preserving the names of previous ships that fought well or first. *Hornet* (CV-8) was the seventh ship to have that name. The first was a ten-gun sloop that fought in the American Revolution. When the first nine Essex-class carriers were under construction, the Navy used these ships to preserve the names of carriers already lost in the war.

The USS *Kearsarge* (CV-12) was under construction when the *Hornet* (CV-8) was lost. The right memo going to the right place in the naval bureaucracy magically changed CV-12's name to *Hornet*, though according to legend the name *Kearsarge* is still stamped on her keel plate.

This same bureaucratic magic trick worked to bring other ship names back from the dead. *Lexington*, which fought alongside *Yorktown* and was lost at Coral Sea, became the new name for CV-16. The same resurrection took place for CV-10, now *Yorktown*. The USS *Wasp*, lost in one of many naval battles around Guadalcanal, was reborn under the pennant of number CV-18.

The Essex-class carriers marked an important step up from the previous Yorktown class, of which the old *Hornet* was one. The older *Hornet* had three elevators spaced along the flight decks to bring planes up from the hangar deck. Hard-earned experience had shown the shortcomings of this arrangement, as the pace of plane takeoffs or landings was compromised by the need to shuffle aircraft above or below. The reborn *Hornet* would retain two elevators on the flight deck, but a third elevator was moved to the deck edge amidships. Thus, flight operations never had to work around an elevator in the down position during launch or recovery.

The flight deck was strengthened and enlarged to handle bigger and heavier aircraft. Catapults were installed to help get the larger planes airborne. (Catapults were rarely used on the Yorktown class.) The hangar deck was also heavily modified and expanded to give air crews lots of working space, after enough storage space was provided for spare parts equal to half of each aircraft onboard.

Radar, communications, and antiaircraft guns were finally integrated. A quartet of five-inch guns, with a range of ten miles, provided the first layer of antiaircraft protection. They could put out ten to fifteen rounds per minute, which doesn't sound like much. But they were firing shells with radar-proximity fuses, which made them deadly if they exploded too near enemy aircraft. Another array of seventeen twin 40mm guns provided an intermediate-range punch. The guns were much better than the old 1.1-inch AA guns, and had proven effective on the older *Hornet*, despite the ship's demise. Another sixty-five 20mm rapid-fire cannon rounded out the AA array, providing close-in protection. Over the course of the war shipwrights would pack still more AA guns on anything that floated, since too much was never enough. While an aircraft carrier's main defense would always be its fighter planes, carriers and escorts steaming in formation could put up huge clouds of exploding shells and lead that could chop up all but the luckiest attack pilots in the Japanese Navy.

Essex-class carriers would take hits over the course of the war, some of them catastrophic. But none were ever sunk.

Hornet Stings Again

March 1944 marked *Hornet*'s resurrection as a fighting ship, when she rejoined the fleet at Majuro Atoll in the Marshalls. She was nicknamed the "Gray Ghost" for bearing the name of her predecessor. This was the big year for the United States in the Pacific, as the Essex-class carriers began showing up in great numbers. In less than eighteen months, this unstoppable force would grind its way through half of the Pacific, taking the war to the Japanese home islands.

Hornet's battle honors read like a tour sheet for a lethal rock band. Support one amphibious invasion in New Guinea. Raid the Carolines. Raid Saipan and Tinian. Bomb Guam and Rota. Raid airfields on Iwo Jima and Chichi Jima. Then came the Battle of the Philippines Sea, also known as the Marianas Turkey Shoot. Over four hundred Japanese naval aircraft were splashed, with few American aircraft lost. The Navy had pilots that made ace in one day—or even in one mission.

Still, there was more to be done. *Hornet* saw action raiding Palau, Formosa, and Okinawa. Late 1944 saw *Hornet* providing air support at Leyte in the Philippines. In February 1945, *Hornet* raided mainland Japan, then supported the invasion of Iwo Jima, raided Japan again in the spring, then supported the invasion of Okinawa. *Hornet*'s aircraft even dished out punishment to the Japanese battleship *Yamato*, helping sink the largest battleship ever built.

In all that action, Japanese aircraft attacked *Hornet* fifty-nine times, failing to score a single hit. *Intrepid* was hit twice by kamikazes. *Bunker Hill* also suffered two kamikaze hits. *Franklin* suffered one really bad bomb hit off the Japanese home islands and was nearly lost. The *Hornet* was lucky indeed.

After World War II ended, *Hornet* sailed on. She went through several modifications, the most important being the conversion from a straight to an angled flight deck, thus easing flight operations significantly. Planes landing on the aft flight deck that failed to catch arrestor cables posed no risk of crashing into planes marked for takeoff. They simply shot off the edge of the angled deck amidships and came around for a second try.

Starting in the 1950s with the Forrestal class, larger aircraft carriers came into service, relegating many of the surviving Essex-class carriers to the second-string team. Naval aircraft kept getting bigger, especially when the transition was made to jet aircraft. Several Essex-class carriers, including *Hornet,* saw conversion to antisubmarine duty, fielding a squadron of ASW helicopters.

Like her sister ships *Intrepid* and *Ticonderoga, Hornet* could be spared for spacecraft recovery. *Hornet's* finest hour came in 1969, when it was the recovery ship for Apollo 11, the mission that put the first men on the moon. Astronauts Neil Armstrong, Buzz Aldrin, and Michael Collins strolled from the space capsule into a quarantine chamber that looked like a modified Airstream trailer. Their path is marked by a series of painted footprints on the floor of the hangar deck. (Tourists can retrace those steps if they wish without having to spend three weeks in lunar quarantine.)

Hornet did the mission again for Apollo 12. Then it was on to decommissioning in 1970, where she joined the older ships in the mothball fleet. She was finally struck from the Navy's registry in 1989, no longer needed for anything. She left the service with seven battle stars and a presidential unit citation.

Hornet became a National Historic Landmark in 1991, but that designation was going to prove meaningless if the ship remained homeless. *Hornet* was sold for scrap in 1995 for $188,000. Being broken up for scrap had been the fate of nineteen Essex-class carriers, so things looked bleak for *Hornet*.

(*Oriskany* [CV-34] proved the exception. It was scuttled in 2006 about twenty-four miles south of Pensacola, Florida, to become an artificial reef. A young naval officer named John McCain took off from the *Oriskany* during the Vietnam War, was shot down, and spent five years in a POW camp, but that story belongs in another essay.)

Hornet escaped the scrapper when former crew members raised the money to purchase her, with the intention of turning her into a museum. She was reopened as a museum in 2000, and languishes today tied up to a pier at the former Alameda Naval Air Station, located just west of Oakland and across the bay from San Francisco.

Now about those ghosts . . .

Haunted *Hornet*

Today *Hornet*'s mission is to commemorate the sacrifice and service of the sailors and Marines who served aboard her, from World War II through the cold war. The ship was never meant to be a haunted house.

So how did the Gray Ghost get all these ghosts?

The *Hornet* was a lucky warship that never took a hit. True, some sailors died in battle during wartime, but an aircraft carrier is not the safest place to work. Sailors fall overboard. Planes crash. Some of the flight deck crew get hit by whirling propellers or get clipped by taxiing jets. Below decks, sailors sometimes have bloody encounters with working machinery or falling tools. Close to three hundred died on *Hornet* over the course of its service, from 1943 to 1970.

Marketing director Bob Rogers, also a former *Hornet* crewman, is not keen about telling ghost stories. "I'm a little uneasy about it sometimes," he once told a reporter for *The San Francisco*

Chronicle. "I realize it could be perceived by some people as a publicity stunt."

Noting that angle with an asterisk of caution, Rogers still invited local clairvoyant Aann Golemac of Oakland, to visit in the ship in 2000 to give a little talk about ghost sightings. About two hundred people attended the event.

"Every time I go to *Hornet*, I am just blown away," Golemac told *The San Jose Mercury News*. "The spirits are a very cohesive bunch, and there are a lot of them. The fact that it is on a warship is an ironic location." The ghosts want their stories to be told, Golemac added, and want restoration work on *Hornet* to continue.

Many tourists and volunteers have had run-ins with the *Hornet*'s permanent crew. Typical of many ghost stories was one told by volunteer Alan McKean to a reporter for *The San Jose Mercury News*: "One day I saw an officer in khakis descending the ladder to the next deck. I followed him, and he was gone. I have no explanation for it." McKean added skeptically that he is "not a true believer in all that stuff," but he sticks to his story. "I saw what I saw."

Volunteer Ron Todd added to the story: "The spirits are real pranksters . . . I've felt them five or six times. Whenever I come on board, I say 'Hi' to them." Among the pranks were strong winds *inside* the ship and a urinal that flushed itself in the men's room.

One account was recorded by Owen Gault, writing for *Sea Classic* magazine in 2008. Norma Harrelson, a Girl Scout on a sleepover aboard *Hornet,* recounted how she and two friends met a sailor in his dress whites in one of the passageways. His uniform was smeared with blood. Burnt flesh hung from his bones. His bare eyes bulged. "No, it wasn't our imaginations at work," Harrelson told Gault. "He was really there staring at us, pleading for help. We froze as if ice had suddenly filled our veins. We screamed and . . . poof . . . he just vanished. All of a sudden the air felt oddly humid. The foul tinge of burned flesh still clung to our nostrils. Frightened out of our wits, we scrambled topside, rushing to gulp down fresh air." This ghost may have once been a crewman who died when a steam line ruptured, enveloping the hapless young man in a cloud of 1,500-degree superheated steam. He boiled to death.

Gault cataloged many ghost stories in his piece. Another ghost is dressed like a pilot and walks down the middle of the flight deck only on cloudy, full-moon nights. Was he the pilot of the F6F Hellcat who disappeared after taking off into a heavy fog? Then there was another overnight camper who wandered below decks to the *Hornet's* brig and lay down on a cot in one of the cells, only to be awakened when something unseen was trying to strangle him. Was it the ghost of a Japanese pilot who committed suicide there?

Like many museums, the *Hornet* does allow sleepovers and conducts flashlight tours. However, ghost sightings tend to increase after ghost stories are told, *Hornet* staffers have noted, according to Gault. Like the Navy's policy of neither confirming nor denying the existence of nuclear weapons aboard its vessels, some *Hornet* volunteers will neither confirm nor deny the existence of ghosts aboard ship.

Volunteer Roy Nash, a former chief aviation machinist mate, had once stood "cold iron watches" on *Hornet,* when it was laid up in dry dock in the 1950s. For three months he walked the passageways—at night. Usually, nothing happened. "Of course, there was the odd situation of that unexplained bright blue light coming from a place where there were no lights . . . but I suppose an explanation was to be found somewhere," he told Gault. Today Nash would rather let visitors find their own answers to their ghost questions. "All we ask is that visitors not be too hard on *Hornet's* ghost crew, or try to drive them away. They've never hurt a living soul and we kind of like having them around. Besides, they are good for business."

Golemac offered a different perspective to *The San Jose Mercury News*. "Everyone thinks that California is full of a bunch of wackos. . . . But we've just become more aware of spiritual activity. It's around us all the time."

What Really Haunts *Hornet*

Ghost stories are not enough to keep a museum afloat. Ships are very expensive to maintain and operate, especially without a crew. *Hornet* has been haunted by money woes in recent years, as it struggles to pay its rent and utilities, just to stay open.

In 2005, *Hornet* received a shutoff notice from Alameda Power and Telecom for $26,000 in unpaid electric bills. The ship also owed $500,000 in rent to the Alameda Reuse and Redevelopment Authority—about four years' rent on its pier. Another dustup emerged when the U.S. Maritime Administration wanted *Hornet* to move to a new pier because it was located too close to docked ships of the ready-reserve fleet. Moving to a new pier would have cost the nonprofit *Hornet* about $1 million it did not have.

Fortunately, *Hornet* was not shut down.

Starting in December 2005, *Hornet* was able to make its monthly rent payments on time. But the museum is still afflicted by $700,000 of debt. Revenues have not kept up with expectations, due to many reasons: lack of development in the surrounding area; a decline in tourism; and lackluster pursuit of new revenues, be they from event rentals, philanthropic grants, or outreach programs, according to an August 2007 article in the *Oakland Tribune*. The *Hornet*'s debt was kept on the books while new lease terms were supposed to be negotiated between the museum and the Alameda Reuse and Redevelopment Authority.

Meanwhile, the tourists still trickle in.

The ghosts can only watch and occasionally lend a hand with some fortuitous media coverage, especially around Halloween.

———

USS Hornet Museum
Pier 3, Alameda Point
Alameda, CA 94501

———

William Terdoslavich

He was just an odd fellow with a menial job whom nobody ever noticed—which seems to have been fine by him, as he had created a world all of his own.

An Unassuming
Artist of the Unreal

Henry Darger was born on April 17, 1892, at home, at 350 24th Street in Cook County, Illinois.

In 1930, Darger settled into a second-floor room on Chicago's North Side.

Except for a brief stint in the U.S. Army, and some institutionalization during his childhood, his life was a model of monotony: Mass daily; menial but steady work at a Catholic hospital, with occasional leisure-time ventures in the neighborhood in search of usable trash; and for the rest—solitary living in his small apartment.

Henry kept to himself, shabby but clean, an unexceptional member of the lower-class urban proletariat of the big city.

His one known friend moved away in the mid-1930s, and with the exception of his landlord, with whom he conversed only about the weather, Henry Darger lived a solitary existence. There is no evidence that he ever sought female companionship, and it has been conjectured that because he was aware that he had a biological sister whom he had never met, he feared the commission of that most grievous of sins: incest.

The last entry of his diary reads as follows: "January 1, 1971. I had a very poor nothing like Christmas. Never had a good Christmas all my life, nor a good new year, and now. . . . I am very bitter but fortunately not revengeful, though I feel should be how I am. . . ."

Henry Darger died in 1973 in a Catholic mission operated by the Little Sisters of the Poor. He was buried in a paupers' cemetery. He had no family or friends. The neighbors in his north Chicago apartment building remembered him as an odd, unkempt man who scavenged through garbage cans and talked to himself in numerous voices.

Yet this sad and lonely individual is also the subject of major art exhibitions in both New York and Chicago.

According to its Web site, the American Folk Art Museum is home to the single largest repository of works by one of the most significant artists of the twentieth century, Henry Darger (1892–1973), who created nearly three hundred watercolor and collage paintings to illustrate his epic masterpiece, *The Story of the Vivian Girls, in What Is Known as the Realms of the Unreal, of the Glandeco-Angelinnian War Storm, Caused by the Child Slave Rebellion,* which encompasses more than fifteen thousand pages.

The Center for Intuitive and Outsider Art in Chicago took possession of the contents of artist Henry Darger's living and working space, which was located at 851 Webster Street in Chicago. Intuit's Henry Darger Room Collection includes tracings, clippings from newspapers, magazines, comic books, cartoons, children's books, coloring books, personal documents, and architectural elements, fixtures, and furnishings from Darger's original room. The archive and material represents a vital resource, and the installation will enhance the understanding and appreciation of the art of Henry Darger by providing artists, scholars, and the public access to a unique and innovative archive of study materials.

The chasm between the perceptions of this individual during his life and the esteem that his work is now held in is indeed extreme.

It is not just the quality of his work, or the volume of his output, or indeed the effect that it has had on subsequent artists that has attracted so much attention to this previously unheralded recluse, but rather the circumstances of how he worked and how he evidently never intended on sharing it with another human being.

Indeed, the art of Henry Darger was an intricately fashioned fantasy world, a cavalcade of borrowed and married images illustrating an epic storyline to rival both Tolkien and Tolstoy for the artistic fulfillment and amusement of its creator alone.

Through art and text Darger tells the two-volume story (*In the Realms of the Unreal* and *Crazy House: Further Adventures in Chicago*) of a large heavenly body around which Earth orbits as a moon, and where most people are Christian. The hero's plot line concerns the adventures of the daughters of Robert Vivian, seven sisters who are princesses of the Christian nation of Abbieannia, who assist a daring rebellion against the evil John Manley's regime of child slavery imposed by the Glandelinians. (The full title of this work is *The Story of the Vivian Girls, in What Is Known as the Realms of the Unreal, of the Glandeco-Angelinnian War Storm, Caused by the Child Slave Rebellion,* comprising over fifteen thousand single-spaced, typewritten pages in twelve binders for the first volume and eight thousand pages for the incomplete second volume.)

However, it is not the Joycean surreal stream-of-consciousness storytelling for which Darger has attracted the most attention.

Indeed, it is the accompanying artwork for this epic tale—several hundred epic landscapes of battles, maelstroms, and heroic deeds on large sheets of paper, some attached by Scotch tape to allow for even longer murals, some illustrated on both sides, suggesting a miserly/pragmatic rationing of materials based on the supplies at hand.

These works of art are part the product of tracings of maga-

zine and book illustrations, part reimagining of the art composition of movie posters and murals that were used as illustrations
in history texts, and part childlike original construction of a
fairy-tale world valiantly rebelling against the technological
forces of darkness and modernity.

When the characters and images are examined closely and
cross-referenced with the books and magazines that were in his
apartment they reveal inspirational lifts from sources as varied as
the illustrations of the works of L. Frank Baum, to the movie ads
for John Wayne's film *The Alamo*, to simple advertising for Cop-
pertone and Campbell soups. (The Folk Art Museum was given
the more than 3,500 individual items that were found in Darger's
rented room on Chicago's North Side. Amassed by the artist from
the 1910s to the 1970s, this motley collection includes seventy volumes from Darger's personal library—*The Wizard of Oz* and the
Bible are among the most well-worn tomes—Catholic prayer
cards; paper dolls; thousands of pages ripped from comic books,
magazines, newspapers, and coloring books.) In many cases
Darger would repeat a tracing numerous times in a given mural
to allow for maximum consistency of look for his centrally fo-
cused heroines, the Vivian girls, and indeed many of the isolated
images look like nothing less than the sort of image one might
find in a Whitman coloring book, composed of simplified images
from some popular film or TV license.

And whether it was intentional or not, Darger's own style re-
sulted in an execution of color and precision not unlike that of a
capricious child more concerned with colors than reality and
staying within the lines.

The entire Darger collection, his works of literature and art as
well as his inspirational texts, were discovered and preserved by
fortuitous accident. According to an article in *Slate* magazine by
Gavin McNett,

Darger's landlord, Nathan Lerner, was an art-world figure with
Bauhaus ties who tolerated Darger with a certain bohemian

noblesse—forgiving lapses in rent, ignoring strange behavior
and strange noises, and even (if perhaps a bit ironically) throw-
ing all-tenant birthday parties for him. But failing health finally forced the old man to move out in late 1972 . . . and when
they opened up his close-smelling rooms and walked the narrow footpaths that wound from door to bed to bathroom
through a ceiling-high mountain of clutter, they found . . .
hundreds of paintings and collages that are now scattered
among the world's museums, and the longest single piece of
writing ever known.

If Lerner and his wife had not taken the care and time to sort
through what could easily have been considered the detritus of
one of society's less fortunate stepchildren, and recognized its
quality and potential/worthiness, then the legacy of this artist
who at the time was on his deathbed in a mission would all have
been lost. His carefully and personally crafted imaginary world
would have winked out before another human being ever acknowledged its existence.

Numerous phrases can be used to describe Darger's work,
ranging from "refreshingly naïve and fauve" to "pop culturally
savvy" to "downright surreal and disturbingly perverse." The
juxtaposition of happy little Kewpie-doll girls performing com-
mando raids against cowboys and Civil War soldiers is only half as
unsettling as the images of children morphed with beasts and indeed prepubescent girls running naked, and in doing so revealing
their very surprisingly rendered penises for all to see. (One theory
suggests that Darger was unaware of the anatomical differences in
the sexes, given his sheltered, apparently asexual existence.)

Darger also narrates his landscapes with bits of dialogue reminiscent of the type of narration used by the Yellow Kid in the
comic strip Down Hogan's Alley, which is credited with being
the first modern comic strip involving in-frame captioning. The
Yellow Kid's dialogue was written on his nightshirt in a stylized
dialect. These bits of Darger dialogue have been used as the titles

for the pieces currently on display, though it is unknown if that was the artist's intent.

Recently the term "Dargerism" has sprung up to define a branch of outsider art by self-taught artists, and Darger himself was the subject of an acclaimed 2004 documentary by Jessica Yu entitled "In the Realms of the Unreal."

The great mystery of all of Darger's work is indeed his intent, because despite the voluminous pages written and illustrated in secret during his lifetime, the lack of any expression of the author/artist's own intent is quite puzzling.

Was Darger a Chicago-based Tolkien constructing his own Middle-earth, a Hieronymus Bosch artistically dealing with questions of soul and salvation, or an Emperor Norton chronicling his own reality that was far different from that perceived by everyone else in his Chicago neighborhood?

This simple question remains the mystery . . . and most of the clues are on display in either New York or Chicago, with innovative presentations to allow maximum observation. (Several two-sided pieces are displayed in mounted panels that allow easy viewing of both sides, while other pieces are displayed side by side with the original images that were borrowed and traced by the artist.)

One thing is certain: The dark and disturbing world that exists within the works of Henry Darger is definitely worthy of display, even if its meanings have yet to be discerned.

American Folk Art Museum
45 W. 53rd Street
New York, NY 10019

The Center for Intuitive and Outsider Art
756 N. Milwaukee Avenue
Chicago, IL 60622

Acknowledgments

Grateful acknowledgment is made for the following contributions: Jeff Grubb, "The Carnegie Sauropods, or Bring Me the Head of *Apatosaurus Louisae*"; Kerrie Hughes, "Bog Bodies"; Paul Thomsen, "An Illinois Revelation: The Mormon Sunstone Capital"; Robert Greenberger, "The Cardiff Giant," "The 1897 Living Eskimo Exhibit," "The Mummy on the *Titanic* and Its Curse," and "Spirit Photography"; Gerardette Hearne, "Man-Eaters at the Museum: The Lions That Stopped a Railroad"; William Terdoslavich, "Lindbergh's Swastika," "So Where Is Amelia Earhart?" and "Who Haunts the *Hornet*?"; Jean Rabe, "Shrunken Display: Three Heads Are Better than None" and "Edison's Last Gasp at the Henry Ford Museum"; Allen C. Kupfer, "The Mysterious Dr. John Dee"; Peter J. Heck, "The Enigmatic Voynich Manuscript"; and John Helfers, "Cursed Jewels and Macabre Minerals."

Special thanks also to editor Brian M. Thomsen and agent Frank Weimann, the best tag team in publishing when it comes to cracking the whip and getting things done on a short deadline.

Special thanks also to the preternaturally beautiful Elyse Tanzillo and Jaimee Garbacik of the Literary Group International, who spurn my advances ever so nicely when I come by the East Coast office.